Volume 22. **Sage** Criminal Justice System Annuals

COMMUNITY CRIME PREVENTION
Does It Work?

Dennis P. Rosenbaum
Editor

SAGE PUBLICATIONS
The Publishers of Professional Social Science
Beverly Hills   Newbury Park   London   New Delhi

To Jim and Lucille

Copyright © 1986 by Sage Publications, Inc.

For information address:

SAGE Publications, Inc.
275 South Beverly Drive
Beverly Hills, California 90212

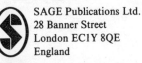

SAGE Publications Inc.
2111 West Hillcrest Drive
Newbury Park
California 91320

SAGE Publications Ltd.
28 Banner Street
London EC1Y 8QE
England

SAGE PUBLICATIONS India Pvt. Ltd.
M-32 Market
Greater Kailash I
New Delhi 110 048 India

Printed in the United States of America

Library of Congress Cataloging-in-Publication Data

Main entry under title:

Community crime prevention.

(Sage criminal justice system annuals; v. 22)
Includes index.

1. Crime prevention—United States.   2. Crime
prevention—United States—Citizen participation.
I. Rosenbaum, Dennis P.   II. Series
HV7431.C66   1986   364.4   85-26057
ISBN 0-8039-2607-3
ISBN 0-8039-2608-1 (pbk.)

FIRST PRINTING

CONTENTS

FOREWORD

This volume contains some of the best evaluations of community crime prevention programs that have been implemented to date. Many of these evaluation efforts were supported by the National Institute of Justice, the research arm of the U.S. Department of Justice, in order to develop more effective means of dealing with crime and fear in both residential and commercial areas. In general, the results of these evaluations are favorable, indicating that community crime prevention programs can serve to reduce crime and fear, and at the same time improve the quality of life and the economic viability of urban neighborhoods and commercial settings.

The evaluations that are presented in this volume have focused on a number of program strategies, including various citizen and community efforts, police activities, and other forms of intervention directed at enhancing community safety and security. Overall, the results indicate that crime prevention programs need to be comprehensive in focus, mobilizing both citizen and police resources and promoting the effective collaboration of these efforts. In addition, program planners need to take the physical and social environment into consideration, a well as the most effective means of promoting citizen involvement through the use of appropriate channels of communication and social support.

The evaluation studies discussed in this volume have also been useful in highlighting the range of factors that influence fear of crime, including not only direct and indirect experiences with crime, but also those signs of social and physical disorder that may influence the public's sense of safety and security. In addition, these studies have addressed a number of important program issues relating to the process of organizing and encouraging citizen involvement, the setting of program goals, and useful forms of program assessment. The National Institute has devoted special attention to these issues in order to identify program elements that relate most directly to the effective organization and development of community crime prevention efforts. Consequently, these evaluations have served to produce a wealth of information that has been useful to practitioners and criminal justice scholars alike.

The evaluation studies that are discussed in this volume are very helpful in outlining some of the lessons learned concerning crime prevention activities and the factors that influence the success of these efforts. However, there is still much to be learned about what communities can do to develop and maintain crime prevention activities, and to reduce the barriers that limit the effectiveness of particular neighborhood strategies for dealing with crime and fear. In addition, there is a need to develop a better understanding of the relationship between crime prevention activities and other neighborhood problem-solving efforts in order to develop an increased sense of community and public safety. In any event, this collection of evaluation studies reflects our progress to date and should be of particular interest to practitioners, policymakers, and criminal justice scholars.

—Fred Heinzelmann, Ph.D.
National Institute of Justice

I

THE EVALUATION PROBLEM

Chapter 1

THE PROBLEM OF CRIME CONTROL

DENNIS P. ROSENBAUM

Crime, incivility, and fear of crime continue to plague American cities at unacceptably high levels relative to other countries. Since the "war on crime" began in the 1960s we have witnessed extensive research on the crime problem and billions of dollars spent to develop anticrime policies and programs at the local, state, and federal levels. Although the nature of this war on crime periodically changes with the winds of politics, there has been a steady and growing recognition that the police and the citizenry are on the front line of this battle and must do more than just react to the problem after the fact.

Within the public policy arena, the initial groundwork for community crime prevention was laid in a 1967 Presidential Crime Commission report that explicitly stated the need for an active and involved citizenry, both in enhancing the performance of the criminal justice system and in rectifying the social and environmental conditions that give rise to criminal behavior. In response, Congress passed the Omnibus Crime Control and Safe Streets Act of 1968, which established the Law Enforcement Assistance Administration (LEAA) and officially heralded the nationalization of the war on crime.

The bulk of LEAA funds were expended on efforts to improve the efficiency of law enforcement agencies in *reacting to crime* (with new technologies and management strategies), not in *preventing crime* by stimulating community involvement (Rosenbaum, 1981). In the early 1970s, a few federally funded demonstration projects were implemented to explore the potential effectiveness of citizen participation in individual and collective crime prevention activities. In the mid-1970s, LEAA funded and published a series of national evaluations of specific crime prevention strategies (e.g., citizen patrols, citizen crime reporting projects, Operation Identification, and security surveys). These assessments contributed to the national visibility of citizen crime prevention efforts and highlighted the paucity of rigorous evaluation data in these areas. Since then, citizen involvement in such programs as

Neighborhood Watch, Operation Identification (marking property), and Home Security Surveys has become a national phenomenon.

Federal funding for a consolidated effort in community crime prevention appeared in 1977 with the inauguration of LEAA's Community Anti-Crime Program, which was authorized by Congress to dispense $30 million to "assist community organizations and neighborhood groups to become actively involved in activities designed to prevent crime, reduce fear of crime, and contribute to neighborhood revitalization" (U.S. Department of Justice, 1978, p. 1). For the first time, the federal government was asserting that organized groups of residents are perhaps the best vehicle for responding to local crime. Indeed, a key assumption driving the program was that "the formal criminal justice system by itself cannot control crime without help from neighborhood residents in fostering neighborhood-level social controls" (U.S. Department of Justice, 1978, p. 3).

Meanwhile, there is recent evidence of change in law enforcement that signals a recognition of the joint police-citizen responsibilities for crime prevention. More and more police departments are looking beyond their crime prevention units to explore additional crime control strategies that might complement and further enhance the efforts of community organizations and individual residents. After experimenting unsuccessfully with various preventive patrol strategies in the 1970s, many police departments are now exploring alternative strategies that allow police officers more opportunities for interaction with neighborhood residents. Foot patrols, door-to-door contacts, storefront offices (ministations), and security surveys are among the latest innovations in policing. The most popular of these "new" approaches—foot patrol—is really an old strategy used by law enforcement before motorized patrols isolated the police officers from the community. Indeed, many of these innovations signify the return of police officers to the streets, where they can become familiar, once again, with the people and the unique problems of the neighborhood.

THE UNANSWERED QUESTION

The fundamental question that must be asked of both citizen and police initiatives is, Do they make a difference? Do these strategies have any impact on crime, incivility, fear of crime, and other important indicators of the quality of life in residential and commercial areas? Every year, I personally receive dozens of calls and letters from individuals across the nation (and in other countries) who usually want answers to two questions: (a) Is there any evidence that crime prevention programs work? and (b) What is the best way to go about implementing these programs? After struggling with these questions for many years (and realizing that my colleagues must be doing the same), I decided that one way to satisfy this information need would be to collect the best "evidence" from existing evaluation research and to see that it is published in a single book. After digging through piles of evaluation reports, I have concluded that the research you will find in this volume represents the best evaluations in the field of community crime prevention. If I have overlooked an important piece of work, I apologize in advance to the authors and trust that I will hear from my colleagues.

In this book we have attempted something that is rarely attempted in other scholarly publications. The contributors have made a serious attempt to address more than one audience. By presenting detailed descriptions of the intervention, the evaluation of the intervention, and the issues surrounding both, the authors have provided considerable substance for practitioners, policymakers, and scholars interested in community crime prevention and/or evaluation research. The reader not only gains an understanding of how the programs were designed and implemented, but also becomes familiar with the evaluation techniques that currently represent the state of the art in this field.

The public policy issues are very important and directly addressed by the evaluation research. Community crime prevention is not so widely practiced or accepted that it is inappropriate to ask (a) does it represent an effective group of strategies for controlling crime, and (b) what factors are operating to limit or enhance the observed effects of such interventions? We must remember that while a growing number of law enforcement agencies, community organizations, and individual citizens are adopting preventive strategies, the fact remains that today these individuals and agencies are only a small minority. The vast majority of Americans today are *not* involved in any collective crime prevention activities, and most police departments continue "business as usual," with traditional motorized patrols and follow-up investigations serving as the standard response to crime. Therefore, given the potential for much greater support for and utilization of crime prevention programs, policymakers at all levels should be interested in whether these programs actually produce the public and private benefits that the mass media and other parties so often claim they do.

FOCUS OF THE BOOK

Before covering the major evaluations in Chapters 3 through 12, this volume begins with Lurigio and Rosenbaum's critical assessment of evaluation research as practiced in the field of community crime prevention. After examining the historical and theoretical roots of citizen anticrime projects, the authors provide a critical overview of "research" that has been accepted by the media and the general public as evidence of program success. They systematically review the major threats to validity that make such evaluation findings questionable, at best. The low quality of research that characterizes this field stands in contrast to the few studies reported in this volume.

The evaluations in this book are presented in four groups: (a) citizen initiatives to prevent residential crime; (b) police initiatives to prevent residential crime; (c) programs to prevent commercial crime; and (d) media strategies for influencing citizens' crime prevention attitudes and behaviors. The evaluations do not always fit neatly into these categories, but the distinctions are meaningful and meant to be helpful to the reader.

Part II of this book focuses on citizen initiatives to prevent residential crime. In Chapter 3, Lindsay and McGillis describe the pioneering Seattle Community Crime Prevention Program initiated in the early 1970s. This program, staffed by civilians in the city government, vigorously attacked the problem of residential burglary with door-to-door organizing of Seattle neighborhoods. The authors provide a rich description of how the program worked and the evaluation data that earned it the title of "Exemplary Project" from LEAA.

In Chapter 4, Ann Schneider describes her evaluation of the Portland (Oregon) Anti-Burglary Program, implemented in 1973 as part of the LEAA-funded Impact Cities Program. Schneider also atriculates the logic underlying the opportunity reduction model (which serves as the basis for many community crime prevention programs) and grapples with some of the tough issues facing evaluators in this field, including displacement effects and reported versus total crime as measures of program success. As a political scientist, she raises an important public policy issue regarding the extent to which community crime prevention programs produce "private" rather than "public" benefits, or, stated differently, the extent to which these interventions can result in a redistribution of protection across various socioeconomic groups.

In Chapter 5, Fowler and Mangione report on an innovative and highly publicized program to reduce crime and fear of crime in Hartford, Connecticut. While the Portland and Seattle programs focused on citizen efforts to protect themselves and their neighbors from victimization, the Hartford program (beginning in 1973) was a three-pronged approach involving changes in the physical environment, changes in police service, and efforts to organize neighborhood residents. Fowler and Mangione describe their initial and follow-up evaluation of the Hartford project—evaluations that take us beyond the crime-reduction focus of earlier studies to examine fear of crime and other quality-of-life indicators. The authors argue that the proper combination of design and use of the built environment is the key to reductions in crime and fear of crime. The physical environment, offenders, residents, and the police are all interdependent elements that produce the "synergism" needed for crime reduction.

In Chapter 6, Rosenbaum, Lewis, and Grant describe their recently completed evaluation of neighborhood-based crime prevention programs in four Chicago neighborhoods. This project, funded by the Ford Foundation, is the first major evaluation of community crime prevention programs carried out entirely by voluntary citizen organizations. Funding for these neighborhood organizations was provided on the premise that community groups are the most appropriate and effective vehicles for implementing crime prevention programs. Drawing on the cumulative knowledge of the previous decade, the authors were able to test a variety of hypotheses about the effects of the interventions on crime, fear of crime, perceived efficacy, social cohesion, and various crime prevention behaviors. Faced with unexpected findings, Rosenbaum and his colleagues explore possible deficits in theory, measurement, and program implementation. Arguing that the theoretical basis for making predictions in this field is rather shaky, they call for a rethinking of the current models that promise such glowing outcomes.

Part III contains some key evaluations of police interventions designed to close the gap between police officers and citizens that was created over the years by motorized patrols. In Chapter 7, Pate describes the most rigorous assessment of foot patrol conducted to date—the Newark Foot Patrol Experiment. Unusual care was taken to check that the experimental manipulation (that is, adding, dropping, or retaining foot patrols) was effectively implemented and accurately perceived by local residents. Pate also places the Newark Experiment in the context of previous research on foot patrol.

In Chapter 8, Trojanowicz reports on his three-year study of foot patrol in Flint, Michigan, funded by the Charles Stewart Mott Foundation. Unlike in the Newark Experiment, the police officers in Flint were assigned as *full-time* foot patrol officers and were expected to take on a number of nontraditional functions, including identifying neighborhood problems or needs, organizing citizen action, and making referrals to appropriate service agencies. Trojanowicz does a fine job of specifying the critical ingredients needed to implement and manage a foot patrol program successfully—everything from funding to supervision. He discusses how foot patrol can be an important tool for "neutralizing" and "redistributing" political power in the community.

The most recent large-scale effort to bring police closer to the communities they serve and help maintain order was the NIJ-funded Fear Reduction Project in Houston and Newark, evaluated by the Police Foundation. In Chapter 9, Wycoff and Skogan describe one of the fear reduction strategies employed in Houston called the "Storefront," in which Houston police officers set up a small office in the community to help remove the "physical, social, and psychological distance" that existed between citizens and police officers. Wycoff and Skogan describe the intervention and the well-controlled field experiment used to test the hypothesized effects on citizens' fear of crime, perceptions of crime in the neighborhood, attitudes toward the police, and other key variables.

Part IV of this volume contains two important evaluations of programs directed at commercial crime. In Chapter 10, Lavrakas and Kushmuk team up to report on two consecutive evaluations of the Crime Prevention Through Environmental Design (CPTED) Commercial Demonstration Project in Portland, Oregon. This multimillion dollar NIJ funded CPTED demonstration was based on the earlier work of Jane Jacobs, Oscar Newman, and others that suggested a connection between the design of the physical environment and the behavior of its users. As part of the demonstration, parks were renovated, streets and sidewalks were redesigned to change both vehicular and pedestrian traffic patterns, high-intensity street lighting was installed, clean-up campaigns were mounted, and security surveys of businesses were conducted. Lavrakas and Kushmuk describe the operationalization of CPTED theory in terms of hypotheses about access control, surveillance, activity support, and motivation reinforcement. Their research illustrates the use of theory-based evaluation in lieu of tight controls over the implementation process. The reader is able to gain a clear picture of the difficulties associated with the implementation and evaluation of a large-scale multicomponent crime prevention program.

In Chapter 11, Tien and Cahn offer a totally different approach to crime prevention evaluation in the commercial sector. While the CPTED evaluations examined a multifaceted, uncontrolled intervention, Tien and Cahn report on their assessment of the Commercial Security Field Test Program in Denver, Long Beach (California), and

St. Louis. This evaluation involved a controlled quasi-experimental design to determine whether this particular crime prevention strategy (security surveys) was effective in reducing commercial burglary and fear of crime. Having developed a risk model to predict the likelihood that a particular commercial establishment will be victimized, the authors apply this knowledge to suggest the development of security surveys that produce "rational" recommendations to minimize the risk of future victimization.

Part V focuses on media strategies for preventing crime through public awareness, education, and persuasion. In Chapter 12, O'Keefe summarizes the evaluation results from a very prominent national media campaign called "Take a Bite Out of Crime," featuring "McGruff" the trench-coated crime dog who educates the American public about ways to prevent crime. This public information campaign is a rare example of attempts to encourage crime prevention behavior at the national level. Given how little we currently know about the effects of such media campaigns—especially in the area of crime prevention—this evaluation takes on added importance. Moreover, O'Keefe offers extensive advice for anyone interested in planning future crime prevention media campaigns.

Moving from Chapter 12 to Chapter 13 takes the reader from electronic media to the print media as a tool for crime prevention. One of the latest strategies for increasing public knowledge about crime and motivating citizens to engage in crime prevention behaviors is the dissemination of police-community anticrime newsletters. In Chapter 13, Lavrakas reviews the findings from three separate evaluations of this strategy in Houston, Newark, and Evanston, Illinois. Consistent with the crime prevention philosophy that police and citizens must "co-produce" public safety, the newsletter is viewed as a mechanism for police and knowledgeable citizens to share crime statistics and crime prevention tips with community residents. Lavrakas and his colleagues have carefully examined the impact of newsletters on recipients' fear of crime, concern about local crime problems, and crime prevention behaviors. Lavrakas points out that providing citizens with local crime information is a controversial issue because of concern that these statistics will heighten fear of crime. Because these experiments directly tested this hypothesis, the chapter should be of great value to anyone concerned about the adverse effects of community newsletters.

In sum, this book is a collection of highly related and complementary works. Many of the evaluations share substantive content, and, in some cases, intentionally build upon one another, thus amassing a cumulative knowledge base after more than a decade of research. These projects were well funded, and this better-than-average support was translated into stronger research designs, larger sample sizes, better sampling techniques, more sophisticated measurement, and more extensive analysis. Above all, this volume offers an unprecedented discussion of key issues in the field by nationally respected criminal justice scholars. These contributors are now in a position to reflect upon the research they are reporting and identify key theoretical questions, practical lessons, and major obstacles to good evaluation in the area of community crime prevention.

The final question addressed in the book—and perhaps the most important—is, What have we learned from this collection of eleven major evaluations? In the closing chapter, Yin provides a synthesis and critique of these studies. He assesses whether the results are generally favorable or unfavorable and what set of conditions is most likely to engender a positive impact. Yin also examines the internal and external validity of these evaluations in general terms, covering such issues as the uniqueness of the treatment and the types of neighborhoods selected for the interventions. Finally, he asks, "Where do we go from here?" and proceeds to assess whether we now know more about how to prevent residential and commercial crime.

This collection of "classic" and recent evaluations is designed to stimulate more discussion, research, and policy analysis in the field. There is still a paucity of solid evaluation research addressing the basic questions of whether police-citizen efforts to prevent crime and to enhance the quality of neighborhood life can make a difference, and under what conditions such programs can be most effective. Nevertheless, the research reported herein should be viewed as a good starting point. Let's hope that our second decade of evaluation research will be as fruitful as the first.

REFERENCES

Rosenbaum, D. P. (1981, June). *Controlling crime: Some fundamental limits of traditional police practice and some promising approaches for the future.* Luncheon address at the First National Conference of Police Planners, Kansas City, MO.

U.S. Department of Justice, Law Enforcement Assistance of Administration. (1978). *Got a minute? You could stop a crime.* Washington, DC: Ad Council, Inc.

Chapter 2

EVALUATION RESEARCH IN COMMUNITY CRIME PREVENTION
A Critical Look at the Field

A R T H U R J. L U R I G I O
D E N N I S P. R O S E N B A U M

Since the mid-1970s, community crime prevention programs have appeared in growing numbers throughout the United States. These programs, which operate under aegis of local police departments and community organizations, are designed to mobilize citizens in a concerted effort with law enforcement for the purposes of preventing, detecting, and reporting criminal offenses (Greenberg, Rohe, & Williams, 1983). The fundamental philosophy of community crime prevention is embodied in the notion that the most effective means of combating crime must involve residents in proactive interventions and participatory projects aimed at reducing or precluding the opportunity for crime to occur in their neighborhoods (Lockhard, Duncan, & Brenner 1978; Podolefsky & DuBow, 1981). In practice, this involvement translates into a wide range of activities, including resident patrols (Yin, Vogel, & Chaiken, 1977), citizen crime reporting systems (Bickman, Lavrakas, & Green, 1977), block-watch programs (Rosenbaum, Lewis, & Grant, 1985), home security surveys (International Training, Research and Evaluation Council [ITREC], 1977) property-marking projects (Heller, Stenzel, & Gill, 1975), police-community councils (Yin, 1979), and a variety of plans for changing the physical environment (for example, see Fowler & Mangione, this volume; Lavrakas & Kushmuk, this volume).

Despite all the impressive statistics and laudatory accomplishments attributed to community crime prevention programs, the standard evaluations in this field, which structure the foundation of public opinion about the success of these programs, are seriously wanting. Findings relating to the impact of crime prevention efforts comprise a large set of data generated by an assortment of evaluation approaches that vary in their quality and usefulness. Although a number of methodologically sophisticated investigations have been conducted to assess anticrime projects (including those presented in this volume), our review of the literature suggests that they are outweighed by a much larger collection of studies characterized by weak designs, an underuse of statistical significance tests, a poor conceptualization and definition of treatments, the absence of a valid and reliable measurement of program implementation and outcomes, and a consistent failure to address competing explanations for observed effects. Thus, any claims regarding the successfulness of citizen crime prevention activities must not be categorically accepted apart from a studious examination of the integrity of the research designs and data-analyses strategies predicating these assertions.

The purpose of the present chapter is to provide a critical overview of studies that have been accepted by the media and general public as "evaluations" in the field of community crime prevention. Our presentation will center on an analysis of this work as it stands up to the crucible of research validity. However, before we embark on this exposition, the chapter begins with a discussion of the historical, political, and theoretical roots of citizen anticrime projects. We also present the general conclusions of the National Evaluation Program assessments of community crime prevention projects, which identified knowledge gaps and investigative deficiencies spanning several citizen-based efforts. After our research analysis, we close the chapter by acknowledging some of the major obstacles that impede the conduct of sound evaluations of anticrime programs.

THE ROOTS OF COMMUNITY CRIME PREVENTION

Early Conceptualization of Community Anticrime Strategies

The sentiments underlying community crime prevention arose partly out of a growing realization that the institutions represented by the police and the court system were failing in their mission to reduce the crime problem and to restore and maintain the existing social order (Silberman, 1978). For example, the popular truism that more police lead to less crime was simply not substantiated by empirical evidence (Jacob & Lineberry, 1982; Wilson, 1975; Levine, 1975). The increasing recognition of the inherent limitations of policing is encapsulated in a 1977 U.S. National Advisory Commission report that notes, "Criminal justice professionals readily and repeatedly admit that, in the absence of citizen assistance, neither more manpower, nor improved technology, nor additional money will enable law enforcement to shoulder the monumental burden of combating crime" (Cirel, Evans, McGillis, & Whitcomb, 1977, p. 2).

In short, this extended conception of citizen involvement through community crime prevention programs acknowledged that the success of law enforcement was highly dependent upon the participation and cooperation of the populace in anticrime efforts, and that some crime prevention activities were better conducted by residents themselves—notwithstanding the fact that the content and thrust of most programs were, and are, shaped predominantly by law enforcement agencies (DuBow & Emmons, 1981). Although a fair number of community relations and crime prevention officials had long espoused a kindred view, it was not until the mid-1970s that community crime prevention fully crystallized as an integral component of widely held criminal justice doctrine.

Theoretical Models of Community Crime Prevention

In principle, community crime prevention is grounded in several basic theoretical models. The general framework of informal social control posits that reductions in crime and the fear of crime are by-products of various overlapping and interactive processes, including the following: (a) the vigorous enforcement of societal norms (Jacobs, 1961; Greenberg et al., 1983); (b) a clearer delineation of neighborhood boundaries and identities (Suttles, 1972); and (c) the establishment of a stronger sense of community and increased social interaction (Conklin, 1975; DuBow & Emmons, 1981). These models reflect what Podolefsky and DuBow (1981) describe as a *social problem approach* to community crime prevention that seeks to reduce crime via the amelioration of the broad social conditions that breed criminal activity.

Additionally, community crime prevention projects are rooted in an *opportunity reduction model* of crime prevention that emphasizes the deterrence value of designing or modifying the physical environment to enhance the safety and security of commercial and residential settings (Heinzelmann, 1981, 1983), and of promoting and maintaining a vigilant and informed citizenry that actively adopts precautionary measures to minimize its vulnerability to criminal predation (Lavrakas, 1981; Lavrakas & Lewis, 1980). The latter is often achieved through formal educational campaigns sponsored by the media, law enforcement officials, and citizen groups to increase public awareness of crime and crime prevention strategies. Opportunity reduction may also involve fostering a closer working relationship between local police and citizens by restructuring the deployment of patrol officers in a manner that furthers their contact with community residents.

The Endorsement of
Community Crime Prevention

The endorsement of community crime prevention programs extends from many quarters, including federal, state, and local government agencies, as well as community organizations. The enthusiastic embracing of community crime prevention is perhaps most apparent at the grass-roots level, where practitioners acclaim the utility of their efforts through popular press articles and numerous homespun program publications, newsletters, and guidebooks that also serve to assist interested communities in the planning and implementation of programs (for example, see Cook County Criminal Justice Commission, 1979). The following published declarations of success are typical:

(1) A 1982 study by the Northwest Neighborhood Federation in Chicago found that in 10 months, a neighborhood-watch program there had reduced crime 12%.
(2) The Figgie Report on crime reduction indicated that the neighborhood-watch program in Detroit reduced burglary by 60% in a target community, and that serious crime fell 58% overall.
(3) An investigation in Sangamon County, Illinois, which has formed 253 neighborhood-watch groups, found that some have achieved as much as an 85% reduction in crime rates.
(4) A multifaceted crime prevention project in San Diego, California, claimed a 21% reduction in burglary, a 50% drop in petty thefts, a 73% decline in vandalism, and a 50% reduction in auto thefts.
(5) Crime prevention efforts in a public housing development in Charlotte, North Carolina, reportedly led to more calls for police service, improved police-community relations, a diminution in residents' fear of crime, and a 32% decrease in all non-assaultive offenses.

The above represent only a few of the many "success stories" that appear in the media on a regular basis. We mention these endorsements and claims of success to emphasize a few points of caution. Evidence of apparent success is easy to find during a period of declining crime rates, especially if one is not well versed in evaluation methods. Also, not everyone has the same level of interest in presenting the "hard facts." To obtain program funding from public or private sources, grant applicants often have a strong motivation to convince the funding agency that it will be investing in a proven, highly effective program for preventing crime in their community. Likewise, the granting agencies, although wanting to remain neutral in the absence of hard data, also want to believe that they were supporting a good "product." Moreover, the media are very interested in success stories inasmuch as our losses in the seventeen-year "war against crime" have greatly outnumbered our victories. Consequently, we have witnessed literally hundreds of media stories about the proven successes of community crime prevention over the past decade. Given this state of affairs, the primary "checks and balances" must come from the academic community, armed with evaluation research skills and disinterested in the direction of the outcome.

NATIONAL EVALUATION PROGRAM SUMMARIES

Amid serious government sponsorship and funding to develop and implement crime prevention projects, a National Evaluation Program (NEP), comprising a series of meta-evaluations, was launched in 1974 by the research/evaluation arm of LEAA, which is currently known as the National Institute of Justice. The program was not designed to yield meta-evaluations in the sense of pooling the results of experiments to test for treatment effects, nor was it designed to yield meta-evaluations in the sense of carefully scrutinizing the methodologies of a collection of studies to issue judgments about the quality of research in an area. Rather, the purpose of the NEPs was to offer a national descriptive and analytic summary of projects in the field, as well as a comprehensic state-of-the-art review of the existing research and knowledge in a particular area. In addition, they were designed to identify knowledge gaps, to make suggestions for future studies to fill those gaps, and to offer policy recommendations regarding any subsequent support for investigative and programmatic pursuits.

There are five NEP meta-evaluations in the domain of community crime prevention. These national assessments focused on (a) property-marking projects referred to as "Operation I.D." (Heller et al., 1975); (b) security survey projects (ITREC, 1977); (c) citizen patrol projects (Yin et al., 1977); (d) crime reporting projects (Bickman et al., 1977); and (e) street lighting projects (Tien, O'Donnell, & Barnett, 1979). The NEP assessments were essentially based upon the results of previous evaluations and upon project performance data amassed during the course of the reviews. An extensive elaboration of the contents of these studies is well beyond the scope of the present chapter. Interested readers should consult the summary and final reports, which are available through NCJRS.

Operation Identification Projects

Description. "Operation Identification" (O-I) is a collective term denoting crime prevention projects that are devised to urge and instruct citizens to mark their personal property permanently as a means to diminish their risk of being burglarized. There were more than 100 known O-I projects operating in cities across the country 10 years ago. The prototypical O-I program model consists of three processes: (a) recruitment, enrollment, and material distribution; (b) burglary deterrence; and (c) property recovery and return. The putative working ingredients of the project lie in its value to prevent burglaries (burglars are presumably dissuaded when they learn that valuables are inscribed with a traceable serial number), and in its potential to assist law enforcement officials in tracking the source of stolen goods and in expediting the return of those goods to their rightful owners (the existence of a unique, personal identifier provides a crucial link between stolen property and burglary victims).

Conclusions and Recommendations. The sponsors of O-I have been largely unable to achieve a satisfactory level of citizen participation in the program (on the average, only 10% of the targeted households were enrolled). Moreover, the costs and efforts of fostering enrollment are much greater than anticipated. In addition, although results reveal that O-I recruits are burglarized at a significantly lower rate when compared to periods prior to their enrollment in the project, this relationship does not hold at the citywide level, where no appreciable reductions in burglary rates are shown. Further, there is no substantive evidence demonstrating any differences in the number of apprehended or convicted burglars found in O-I and non-O-I communities. Individual reductions in the incidence of burglary are attributed to the propensity of O-I participants to employ other crime prevention strategies in conjunction with property engraving. In short, it is plausible that O-I's apparent burglarly reduction benefit may actually be due to one or more alternative security measures in lieu of (or supplementary to) the deterrent effects of marked property. Finally, contrary to expectations, O-I does not appear to facilitate the recovery and return of stolen property.

Crime Prevention Security Surveys

Description. Security surveys are crime prevention efforts that are generally under the direction of specially trained law enforcement personnel (including nonpaid, sworn personnel and civilians), who enter the premises of homeowners, tenants, and businesspersons to conduct an in-depth, on-site inspection of a residence or workplace and its surroundings (such as doors and windows, locks, lighting, concealing shrubbery or entry ways). The purposes of the security survey are to ascertain a site's security status and deficiencies, to formulate a set of measures to protect the setting (for instance, techniques that upgrade the safety of the area and lower the liklihood of a break-in), and to issue recommendations for maintaining the setting in a manner that minimizes the potential for criminal opportunities.

Conclusions and Recommendations. In the main, security survey projects seem to exert a measurable efect on reducing victimizations among survey recipients and on improving police-community relations. Nonetheless, the technique has not been exploited to its fullest advantage. Although program success is predicted upon the responsiveness of individuals to security recommendations, little information is available regarding compliance rates, which are often inconsistently defined within and across the agencies administering the surveys. Hence, it is not clear whether compliance rates are a useful index of program success. The limited compliance data that do exist, however, indicate that when survey recommendations are enacted, a recipient is less likely to be victimized. Low compliance with security recommendations is frequently a function of the inadequate follow-up and monitoring of suggested improvements by survey units, which cannot realistically perform such inspections because of personnel shortages. Hence, to ensure that a security survey program will be successful, it is imperative to design and implement the project in parts of local jurisdictions that can be satisfactorily served by available human resources.

Prescribed courses of future research include studies of (a) the impact of security codes and ordinances on survey administration; (b) the effectiveness of different public education and direct solicitation approaches to garner project enrollment; (c) the relative merit and utilization of various incentives to further participant compliance; (d) the characteristics and motivations of persons who request the surveys; and (e) the usefulness of media campaigns in increasing the community's awareness of and enrollment in security survey projects.

Citizen Patrol Projects

Description. Citizen patrol projects encompass specific patrol or surveillance routines that are executed by private citizens, and are under the auspices of a community organization or a public housing authority. Contemporary citizen patrols share a supraordinate interest in neighborhood crime prevention, as opposed to a prior orientation that focused on the alleviation of civil disorders. At the time of the report, approximately 800 identified patrol projects with an average life expectancy of four years were found throughout the United States, and were predominantly situated in urban areas. The projects were not restricted to locations of any particular racial composition or socioeconomic status, and often arose in communities that expressed an abiding interest in preserving a previously crime-free environment.

There are four basic types of citizen patrol projects: (a) *neighborhood*—residents survey their streets and other public areas in automobiles or on foot for the purpose of reporting or directly responding to observed behaviors that are deemed undesirable or suspicious; (b) *building*—specific buildings, compounds, and housing projects are monitored by tenants or paid guards who are stationed at entrances to mark the passage of strangers; (c) *community protection*—citizens' patrol efforts are extended to include the overseeing and review of police activities; and (d) *social service*—patrols service the community by organizing around an amalgam of citizen needs (such as ambulance transport, escort services, civil defense, youth placement, and food co-ops).

Conclusions and Recommendations. Although citizen patrol projects are difficult to document and have not undergone formal evaluation, available evidence suggests that they might be a potentially effective deterrent to residential crime under the right conditions. Further, programs can be efficiently operated with minimal financing and, on balance, they apparently enjoy resounding support from local police and community residents. The most successful patrols are affiliated with a larger community or neighborhood organization, are conscientious in sustaining a working relationship with law enforcement, and are flexible enough to engage in non-crime prevention activities when patrolling is patently unnecessary. One of the few drawbacks of citizen patrols is the potential of such efforts to evolve into vigilantism. While this occurs with relative infrequency, neighborhood-type patrols appear to be most susceptible to assuming vigilante-like postures. Future evaluative and nonevaluative research is necessary for a broader understanding of the emergence, operations, and effects of citizen patrols as well as the legal status and legal liabilities of patrol members.

Citizen Crime Reporting Projects

Description. Citizen crime reporting projects (CCRPs) are grouped under two major headings, each subsuming three distinct types of programs. The first group consists of programs that facilitate the avenues through which citizens can report suspicious/criminal activities. It includes Whistlestop, Radiowatch, and Special Telephone Line projects. Whistlestop projects represent a modern-day "hue and cry" in which citizens carry whistles that are blown to alert the populace that a crime is in progress. Those hearing the whistle respond by telephoning the police and by "sounding the alarm" (that is, blowing their whistles) in a concerted attempt to interrupt the commission of a crime. Radiowatch projects are administered by citizens who own radio transmission equipment, which they use to report observed illegalities through dispatchers or directly to police departments that monitor emergency frequencies. Special Telephone Line projects offer monetary rewards and guarantee the anonymity of callers who volunteer information about criminal acts.

The second category of citizen crime reporting projects comprises educational efforts to encourage crime reporting, such as Group Presentation, Membership, and Home Presentation projects. Group Presentation projects are instructive crime prevention sessions that are held for the benefit of civic and service groups, schools, parent-teacher associations, and church organizations. Membership projects closely resemble Group Presentation projects in their objectives and activities; however, they demand greater allegiance from participating individuals (for example, carrying a membership card and publicly committing themselves to continued involvement in the program).

Finally, Home Presentation projects or Block Watch programs educate residents to be aware of any signs of criminal behavior in their neighborhoods and to call an emergency telephone number immediately to report the episode. They may also include a membership component and regular group activities that focus on the prevention of crime in the community. (For a detailed description of the now popular Block Watch program, see Lindsay & McGillis, 1986.)

Conclusions and Recommendations. The absence of systematic planning to designate the target areas of citizen crime reporting projects has made the valid assessment of the impact of these programs highly problematic. Generally, citizens show a sufficient awareness of CCRPs where efforts are exerted to publicize the programs via media outlets, billboards, and bumper stickers. However, there is a dearth of hard evidence demonstrating that crime reporting projects increase the level of surveillance in an area or the frequency and quality of citizens' reports regarding suspicious or illegal activities. In addition, at the time of this national assessment, there were no quantifiable outcome data suggesting that the presence of CCRPs results in an improvement of police-community relations, an increase in community cohesiveness, or a reduction in crime. The assessment suggested that future evaluations of Citizen Crime Reporting projects include measures of (a) descriptive information about target area residents; (b) program publicity efforts; (c) the short- and long-term impact of projects on a variety of variables (such as, citizen awareness, the number of crime-related calls); and (d) the potential constructive and adverse "side effects" of programs.

Street Lighting Projects

Description. Street lighting projects arise out of the Crime Prevention Through Environmental Design (CPTED) approach to combating crime, which posits that the proper design and effective use of the built environment can lead to a reduction in crime and the fear of crime, and a concomitant improvement in the quality of urban life. Basically, the thrust of the effort is to increase the illumination of neighborhood streets to promote pedestrian safety and to diminish criminal opportunities.

Conclusions and Recommendations. Although inadequate evaluation studies have yielded a paucity of reliable and uniform data to render definitive statements about the impact of street lighting, available research indicates that it *does not* decrease the incidence of crime in participating target areas. Nonetheless, findings suggest that street lighting projects may be useful in reducing residents' fear of crime and in enhancing their feelings of security. It is not likely, however, that improved street lighting, by itself, will be effective against crime in the absence of the conscious and active support of both citizens (in reporting what they observe) and police (in responding and conducting patrols). Similar to the advice offered in other NEPs, the impact of street lighting projects can be determined more reliably if researchers would develop valid and precise measures of *input* (performance specifications, system design, target area), *process* (program implementation), and *impact* (attitude, behavior, and crime) variables. Moreover, carefully controlled studies are needed to assess the effect of varying light intensities on both individual perceptions of safety (micro-level analysis) and on areawide crime statistics (macro-level analysis).

NEP Synthesis

Overall, the results of the NEPs demonstrate that a significant number of individuals and communities are participating in various crime prevention activities and are touting their efforts as novel and effective approaches to combat crime. However, the meta-evaluations also make it quite clear that we have failed to build a solid empirical base from which policymakers and practitioners can render scientifically informed judgments regarding the relative merit of citizen anticrime programs. Indeed, most research endeavors did not generate reliable and uniform data. To date, we are left with little understanding of the emergence, development, operations, and effects of community crime prevention interventions or the reasons for their success or failure.

Notwithstanding a host of exhortations from the authors of the NEPs calling for researchers in the area to produce methodologically sound evaluations and to generate useful studies for planning purposes, nearly a decade later there has been little progress toward generating a solid knowledge base in this field. Because an inordinate share of the "studies" are conducted by persons without research expertise, the results of the investigations are generally unreliable. Hence, it is not known with any degree of confidence whether these interventions actually result in their purported outcomes (such as reduced crime, enhanced police-community relations, diminished fear among residents), nor is it apparent what future courses of action should be pursued with reference to their continued support and propagation.

In the next section, we will address the major shortcomings typifying the bulk of studies in community crime prevention. The concept of validity is presented as a point of departure for examining the research. Our discussion draws on a number of sources, including the NEPs, seminal papers and presentations in the field, and a review of the methodology and findings of 111 citizen-based crime prevention programs conducted in cooperation with Leonard Sipes at the National Criminal Justice Reference Service. The 111 programs reviewed represent two types of community crime prevention projects that have become prevalent in recent years: neighborhood watch and citizen patrols. All of the projects provided published evidence of reduced crime and many were conducted *after* the NEPs described above.

A CRITICAL ANALYSIS OF
COMMUNITY CRIME PREVENTION EVALUATIONS

To develop a framework in which to assess evaluations in the field of community crime prevention, we will invoke four types of research validity: construct, internal, external, and statistical conclusion. We have adapted definitions and elucidations of these concepts from Cook and Campbell (1979) and Judd and Kenny (1981). In some instances, the application of a particular aspect of research validity is "looser" than in others, and incorporates our own interpretations.

We recognize that "good" researchers will be familiar with our discussion of validity, but we feel a compelling need to bring this type of rigorous thinking to the area of community crime prevention evaluation. In our view, a lack of concern for (or knowledge of) validity issues characterizes the evaluation shortcomings in this field.

Construct Validity

Construct validity is concerned with the extent to which a program has been fully conceptualized and explicated. A "construct valid" characterization of an intervention is one that is patently differentiable from others, and allows reliable measurement of the intervention and all its functional components. Further, construct validity refers to whether or not the intervention is closely linked to its theoretical formulation (that is, whether the treatment in practice corresponds to the fundamental elements of the treatment in theory). This is ultimately a question of how precisely and concretely a treatment has been operationalized.

The problem of poor construct validity in the context of community crime prevention has been discussed incisively by Yin (1977, 1979), who notes that sketchy or obscure descriptions of projects seriously hamper effective implementation and the diffusion of efforts to new sites. This definitional deficiency assumes two basic forms: (a) the absence of an explicit theoretical identification and documentation of the contents and active ingredients of programs; and (b) the failure to operationalize program components properly.

Community crime prevention is frequently undertaken without the guidance of specific formulae for establishing or continuing operations. Furthermore, any given project is likely to consist of a complex package of responses, rather than a single or unidimensional set of activities. This creates substantial, and often insurmountable, difficulties for any attempts at rigorous evaluation, or at gaining a thorough comprehension of the exact nature of a program. For example, citizen crime reporting projects may comprise several interventions, including the dissemination of literature to residents, the enactment of media campaigns to promote involvement, the organization of group meetings in homes to educate the public about crime prevention, and the participation of individuals in reporting crime through alternative avenues (Bickman et al., 1977). Because there are virtually no accepted standards of operation, there generally exists a low level of uniformity and systematization in the delivery of these various strategies. Consequently, there are often marked internal variations in activity from day to day and from participant to participant (that is, interventions are rarely "fixed" or structured). In addition, different crime reporting programs incorporate a range of philosophies, styles, personnel, and methods. This inseparable mixture of approaches is endemic to virtually every category of community crime prevention projects.

Without a clear articulation of program procedures, a researcher is left in a vacuum with little or no opportunity to measure if, when, and how implementation efforts were successfully executed. The researcher will be unable to formulate empirical questions that are grounded in structured observations and that translate into measures that are amenable to pertinent analytic techniques. Hence, a specification of the factors underlying any program effects becomes highly problematic. In other words, it cannot be confidently known whether outcomes are a product of an entire program and all its activities or a circumscribed subset of those activities. Unless there is some reasonably accurate and coherent definition of a project or treatment to drive an evaluation, an investigator cannot speak definitively to the intervening mechanisms or processes that mediate program inputs and impacts, nor can he or she make a meaningful interpretation of research findings (Sechrest & Redner, 1979). As stated by Yin (1979, p. 37), "If we don't know what happened at the site, little can be said about the causes for its success or failure." This problem becomes greater as the scope of a program broadens.

Low construct validity also impedes the diffusion of projects across different locations. Any attempts to replicate a community crime prevention activity cannot be achieved effectively unless the key operations of the original program are carefully documented in reproducible terms. A case in point is revealed in the review of street lighting projects, which showed that none of the 41 programs studied adequately described the system characteristics of street lighting efforts (Tien et al., 1979). For example, the principal mechanism of the treatment (that is, the amount of illumination produced by newly installed systems) was never ascertained due to a lack of knowledge and equipment for recording sufficient light measurements. Neglecting to specify this kind of primary information sorely limits the degree to which practitioners can consistently transfer their endeavors from one community to another.

Another aspect of construct validity is reflected in the correspondence between the conceptualizations of the program (the project in theory) and the translation of those conceptions into measurable interventions (the project as implemented). Construct validity encompasses the notion of "treatment integrity," which refers to the fidelity with which a program plan is enacted (Sechrest & Redner, 1979), and the strength with which an intervention is delivered. Such validity is minimized as the gap separating theory and practice begins to widen. Low treatment strength is often the cause of type II errors, or false negatives, in which potentially useful programs are abandoned because of less than optimal administration.

The evaluation literature abounds with examples of large gaps between theory and practice in the realm of social interventions, and community crime prevention is no exception. Also, there are instances in which it is difficult to attribute project ineffectiveness to either misguided theory or a miscarriage of implementation, which essentially is the classic distinction between theory failure and program failure (Weiss, 1972). An apt illustration of these problems in the area of community crime prevention is provided by the Operation ID project (Heller et al., 1975). First, program designers were negligent in developing a standard set of property engraving procedures. Hence, there were no adequate means for ascertaining the thoroughness with which property had been marked. Second, police officers affiliated with the programs expended little more than a "token amount of effort" in inspecting stolen goods for identification numbers, and in monitoring the continued participation of residents in the project. Generally, those evaluating the programs did not conduct a detailed process analysis of procedures, and therefore could not definitively locate the sources of conceptual or operational breakdown. Due to the lack of measurement, it was not possible to determine whether the theory underlying Operation ID was ill conceived, or whether program ineffectiveness arose entirely from the faulty implementation of well-designed concepts. If this situation exists with Operation ID research, it is easy to envision the intricacies confronting evaluators of other crime prevention activities that involve more complex implementation processes.

Internal Validity

Internal validity refers to the tenability of causal inferences that are drawn about the impact of treatments on outcome variables. Internal validity, which is the sine qua non for interpreting the results of an evaluation, connotes the confidence with which a researcher can assert that the findings of an investigation are primarily attributable to the intervention being studied and not other factors apart from the intervention. Internal validity focuses on the question, Can the investigator conclude that a treatment made a difference in this specific instance (Campbell & Stanley, 1966)? An evaluation is deemed internally valid if it permits a researcher to establish an explicit causal linkage between the implementation of a program and changes in dependent measures (that is, if the researcher can determine that the treatment was the causal agent via an exhaustive refutation of alternative explanations for observed findings).

The internal validity of evaluation research lies on a continuum ranging from true experimental to preexperimental designs. The true experiment, involving random assignments of units (for example, persons, classrooms, neighborhoods) to treatment and nontreatment conditions, provides the greatest degree of internal validity by controlling for all the extraneous sources of variance that could potentially account for any effects, or could operate to dampen any real differences between treated and untreated groups. In sum, an experimental design is an elegant means for making inferences of superior dependability about cause and effect (Riecken & Boruch, 1974).

In situations where random assignment is not practicable, the evaluator may employ a variety of quasi-experimental designs. As an evaluation approach, quasi-experiments—although frequently the best possible design one can employ under the circumstances—are not as rigorous as true experiments inasmuch as they fail to account for many of the uncontrolled variables that interfere with definitive statements of causality. Consequently, quasi-experiments are subject to a range of so-called threats to internal validity (Cook & Campbell, 1979), which can be viewed as plausible rival hypotheses to explain the causes of observed effects.

Although quasi-experiments cannot attain the precision of true experiments or warrant an unambiguous interpretation of results, they do yield considerably more dependable information than is ordinarily obtained from a preexperimental design—the least sophisticated approach to evaluation. Preexperimental designs (for instance, designs without control groups) are seriously jeopardized by numerous threats to internal validity, and therefore do not readily permit causal inferences about program effects. The application of quasi-experimental and preexperimental designs—both of which lack sufficient controls—oblige an evaluator to identify the major threats to internal validity and to eliminate systematically those threats before he or she proceeds to asseverate the potency of a treatment. The fewer such threats that remain, the greater the degree of internal validity and the higher the confidence that can be placed in the integrity of results.

Our examination (with Leonard Sipes) of 111 neighborhood watch and citizen patrol projects that have claimed program success indicated that the most common research design employed by local evaluators was the one-group pretest-posttest design. Indeed, an overwhelming 92% (or 102) of the projects collected their data through this methodology. Although other types of evaluative schemes were uncovered, we will restrict our discussion to the pretest-posttest design because of the apparent marked prevelance in the field.

THE MOST COMMONLY USED RESEARCH DESIGN

The pretest-posttest design is one in which an area or group is selected and measures are taken both before and after the introduction of a program or intervention. The cardinal feature of this mode of research is that a group is compared against itself. The design is typically utilized when evaluators wish to ascertain that a target improved or at least did not deteriorate while being exposed to a treatment. Also, it is often chosen when researchers are unable to identify or obtain a comparision or control group for study. By analyzing the before and after scores, the investigator may determine whether any changes occurred between the periods of observation. It is generally problematic, however, to demonstrate that such changes were solely the effect of the treatment. In essence, it is not possible for the researcher to infer that differences between pretest observations and posttest observations were primarily a function of the program or of one or more of the confounding variables that threaten the internal validity of the study. The one-group pretest-posttest design is vulnerable to six threats to internal validity, which are briefly described below and are applied to the evaluation of community crime prevention projects.

(1) History. The first uncontrolled source of variance that may obscure the effects of a community crime prevention program in a one-group design is history. History comprises any change-producing event or sequence of events that transpire between the pretest and posttest, and present themselves as alternative explanations for outcomes. To illustrate, suppose the initiation of a crime prevention activity coincides with the installment of a new police administration that institutes blanket "innovations" in the department's practices (for example, patrolling, record keeping, discretionary arrests). These modifications presumably affect some of the same variables that evaluators typically measure in assessing citizen anticrime strategies (such as crime statistics, police-community relations, residents' perceptions about crime). More specifically, "crackdown" and other special enforcement efforts may shift the proportion of reported events that surface as official reports and often serve as the primary source of information for community crime prevention evaluations. The greater the time lapse between pre- and postmeasurement, the more likely outside events will rival the program as plausible causes of change. In addition, an event could affect the posttest observations but not the pretest, or could affect both but in varying directions.

(2) Testing. The second threat to internal validity in the one-group pretest-posttest design is testing. Questionnaires and interviews that survey the attitudes, perceptions, and behaviors of respondents are reactive measurements that can alter the nature of what is being studied (that is, the surveys themselves act as an impetus for change rather than an inert measure of variables). The "demand characteristics" of a survey often elicit responses that are high in social desirability. For ex-

ample, a participant may report knowledge of or compliance with a program as a means to satisfy the imputed expectations of an interviewer, and to present him- or herself in a manner that occasions a favorable impression. Further, merely sensitizing an individual to certain factors (such as program objectives) through the pretest may color his or her responses during the second wave of measurement. Testing is a special problem for the one-group pretest-posttest design because the evaluator does not have a control group to separate testing effects from program effects.

(3) Instrumentation. A third source of invalidity is instrumentation —the effect of any inaccuracies or changes in measurement procedures or devices that may account for pretest-posttest differences. For example, evaluators in community crime prevention rely heavily on official police data as the basis for assessing program impact. Approximately 52% of the studies we examined employed "offenses known to the police" as the *sole* indicator of project effectiveness. The unreliability of police records has been widely documented (see Inciardi, 1978). Two principle problems impugn the accuracy of official estimates of crime rates. First, because police statistics depend entirely on citizens' crime reporting behavior, they tend to grossly underestimate the prevalence of offenses. For example, according to the National Crime Survey, two-thirds (67%) of all criminal victimizations are never brought to the attention of law enforcement(U.S. Department of Justice 1983). Hence, police data do not represent a true reflection of the total occurrence of crime. Also, crime prevention projects that enhance the propensity of victims to report crimes to the police may produce an artificial increase in the crime rate independent of any changes in the actual incidence. Second, the procedures adopted by the police to "generate" crime statistics are subject to numerous sources of bias. At various times, departments have been alleged to under or overreport offenses purposely to advance a particular objective. These orchestrated fluctuations in offenses are achieved through policy decisions regarding how reported incidents are counted and classified. Various other alterations in police and investigative practices may also affect the recording and reporting of crime (Skogan, 1979).

(4) Statistical Regression. Regression to the mean, which is the fourth threat to internal validity, is a potential confound when the treatment of interest is administered with persons or areas that are particularly "high" or "low" on the phenomenon being studied. If a community adopts a crime prevention project during a period of extraordinarily high (low) crime, which is elevated (depressed) due to random variation, there is a great likelihood that subsequent crime

totals will drift closer to their "true" mean or average levels despite the absence of any program effects. In other words, if crime rates are fluctuating over time and a target area was selected in the midst of a high (low) point in the fluctuation, it is expected that the area will evidence a lower (higher) crime rate during subsequent periods of time even if the exposure to the treatment had not transpired.

(5) Mortality. The fifth threat to internal validity is mortality, that is, the differential attrition of participants during the pretest-posttest interval. Those who "drop out" of a project evaluation may be systematically different from pretest participants who are available at the second wave of measurement. Thus, the groups are, to some extent, incomparable. Evaluators in the community crime prevention field have recently shown a strong preference for panel designs that offer repeated measurement on the *same* respondents. However, as Lavrakas (1985) has documented, the bias in panel samples due to attrition may be rather sizable, and basically limits the external validity of the results. For example, in Chicago residential samples (typical of samples found in many community crime prevention evaluations), Lavrakas found that a panel design overrepresented such groups as homeowners, older residents, less fearful residents, and those who engage in crime prevention activities.

(6) Selection. Selection, the final threat to internal validity in the one-group pretest-posttest design, becomes apparent when participants in an evaluation are not randomly sampled or representative of the target area or population exposed to the intervention. The evaluation sample may possess traits or characteristics that existed before the program, and could produce responses that are unrelated to the treatment or do not typify the community at large.

Selection is a big problem in the area of crime prevention evaluation. Evaluators almost never have control over the selection of neighborhoods to receive the crime prevention program or the selection of residents to participate in the program. Self-selection usually operates at both levels and can produce confounding effects. When a group of citizens decide to form their own block watch or start a community organization to address crime-related issues, these citizens are not typical of the majority of residents who elect not to get involved. Changes in the behavior of participants may be due to their own motivation or predisposition rather than to the program itself.

External Validity

External validity revolves around the issue of whether the outcomes of an evaluation generalize across various times, targets, settings, and projects. The lack of external validity indicates that the results of a study are inordinately confined to a particular period, place, or sample. Essentially, any test of external validity is a test of the robustness of findings. Examples of basic external validity questions germane to citizen crime prevention include the following: Can a successful project in a stable community be transplanted to a neighborhood characterized by instability? Can a program that documents crime reduction in a high-income area demonstrate similar effects in a location where the majority of residents occupy lower-income strata?

Threats to external validity may be conceptualized as statistical interaction effects. Two major threats are applicable to community crime prevention evaluations. The first is the interaction of setting and treatment. Collective anticrime activities may be more viable in target areas that are predictably different from those in which such programs are never spawned. For example, Greenberg et al. (1983), having reviewed the literature, maintain that crime prevention efforts (which are generally predicated upon self-initiated resident involvement and the presence of formal organizations) achieve little success in poor and heterogeneous neighborhoods that are characterized by diminished social solidarity, loose community integration, and weak informal social control mechanisms. In contrast, crime prevention projects are more likely to thrive in middle-class neighborhoods where informal social control is firmly established and residents share a common set of norms and a commitment to community. These conclusions are confirmed by the results to Roehl and Cook's (1984) evaluation of Urban Crime Prevention Programs. Hence, the social character of a neighborhood can set a limiting condition on the degree to which program results may be replicated.

The second threat to external validity is the interaction of history and treatment. This refers to the existence of special circumstances or events in a community that either favor or hinder the development and maintenance of local crime prevention activities. These contingencies often stand in the way of generalizing the findings from current to future situations.

Establishing external validity presents a sizable task for evaluators. Although one may conceivably array the settings in which crime prevention programs are implemented according to gradient of similarity, determining whether results are widely applicable is hardly possible without attempting the actual replication or reviewing the literature for highly similar evaluations under different conditions. Further, as discussed in a previous section, the problem of low construct validity is a major obstacle to the assessment of external validity. Because program components in community crime prevention are frequently ill defined and therefore difficult to replicate precisely, the external validity of the results is largely undetermined. Indeed, it is virtually impossible to gauge the applicability of findings without a clear delineation of program procedures, target characteristics, and outcome measures. This underscores the intextricably intertwined relationship between construct and external validity.

Statistical Conclusion Validity

The final aspect of validity that we will present is statistical conclusion validity. It generally refers to limitations or errors in the *analysis* of data and in the *measurement* of variables that can lower the sensitivity of an evaluation to real program effects or can mislead an investigator to falsely infer the existence of program effects. The following are two major categories of problems that are common to the study of community crime prevention programs and constitute basic threats to statistical conclusion validity.

CONVENTIONAL STATISTICAL TECHNIQUES

The use of conventional statistical techniques to examine pretest-posttest changes or treatment-nontreatment group differences is surprisingly rare in assessments of anticrime projects. Evaluation results are often proffered in the absence of any consideration or reporting of standard levels of statistical significance. For example, Tien et al. (1979) found a dearth of statistical significance testing in evaluations of street lighting programs. Their review demonstrated that appropriate methods of data analyses were typically not applied to determine the reliability of survey results or to test whether recorded crime reductions were greater than expected by random error or seasonal variation. Moreover, it was revealed that many analyses were performed without regard to the fundamental assumptions of techniques or a recognition of how a violation of those assumptions could possibly vitiate the findings of an evaluation (for example, researchers ignored the serial dependency of successive observations when analyzing time-series data).

Even the more sophisticated evaluations often contain inappropriate analyses that can lead to false conclusions. One of the more common errors we have observed is the *independent* analysis of experimental and control group data to look for pretest-posttest differences. To show that the experimental area experienced a significant reduction in crime, and then to show that the control area did not change significantly, is inappropriate. Given possible pretest differences between the two groups, only analyses that demonstrate significant *differential* changes over time between the experiment and control areas should be accepted as evidence of a program effect.

MEASUREMENT OF OUTCOME VARIABLES

In studies of citizen-based crime prevention projects, the measurement of outcome variables is fraught with numerous deficiencies. First, investigators who have adopted a survey approach to assess the impact of crime prevention programs on local residents have generally employed a limited set of measures. Most have not exploited the pool of validated scales with known reliabilities that have been developed to evaluate community crime prevention programs. Dimensions of interest include fear of crime, direct and indirect victimization experience, attributions of responsibility for crime prevention, perceived efficacy of individual and collective crime prevention behaviors, and social cohesion and various crime prevention behaviors (see Rosenbaum et al., 1985). Researchers are frequently remiss in tapping a broad enough range of factors when assessing the effects of a project. Our review of crime prevention evaluations with Leonard Sipes showed that only half of the studies incorporated one or more measures of program impact beyond crime statistics. These measures included fear of crime, police-community relations, increased calls to police, and a cost-benefit analysis of the activity.

The displacement of crime is an important issue in community crime prevention evaluations, but one that is infrequently examined, even in the best evaluations. Displacement occurs when a project causes crime to shift to contiguous geographic locations or neighborhoods, to different times of the day (for example, more crime occurs during the daytime in communities participating in a street lighting project), to other offense types (for example, there is a higher incidence of thefts in a neighborhood implementing an antiburglary program), or to nonparticipating residents. Basically, displacement signifies a redistribution rather than a reduction in crime. Evaluations that focus attention only in the experimental target area may conclude that crime was reduced, when in fact it was only displaced. Hence, the collective or ultimate benefits of an anticrime strategy remain dubious unless displacement effects can be dismissed. We found that a scant 3% of programs had tested for displacement.

Finally, the time frame used in most evaluations is rather limited (due to a variety of constraints), which raises the question of whether sufficient time has elapsed to conduct a fair assessment of long-term program effects. Of the projects that reported their comparison years, 60% collected posttest data after a measurement period of only one year or less.

OBSTACLES TO SOUND EVALUATIONS

Although the primary objective of this chapter is to provide a synopsis of the limitations of community crime prevention evaluations, we are fully cognizant of the exigencies, obstacles, and constraints (temporal, financial, and political) that force investigators in this field to conduct studies that are less than optimal vis-à-vis the accepted standards of social science research. The following represents a sample of these difficulties (see Yin, 1977):

(1) The desire to include identifiable and measureable objectives in an evaluation usually means that investigators will rely on crime data as a central outcome measure.
(2) Target communities are generally characterized by a complex of diffuse geographic, political, and social factors. This complexity creates a formidable barrier to the selection of equivalent comparison or control areas.
(3) Planned interventions and activities are always subject to unavoidable complications and vagaries that inevitably arise during the mundane day-to-day administration of programs.
(4) The pressure to demonstrate reductions in crime to justify the continued support and funding of projects hampers attempts to measure long-term effects.
(5) The impact of competing efforts (such as employment programs, police patrol strategies) may be difficult to separate from the diminutive effects of typical crime prevention projects.
(6) Often, successful anticrime projects arise out of informal control mechanisms that govern the quality of social interactions within local communities. There is no definite way to measure when these informal patterns initially emerged and, hence, when the "treatment" actually began.

As suggested above, calls for better community crime prevention evaluations should not be made without an adequate consideration of the true costs of such research. Generating reliable, objective information demands a high level of coordination, planning, and technical expertise that frequently exceeds the resources, capabilities, and interests of the agencies responsible for program funding and implementation. Unlike the evaluations showcased in this volume, run-of-the-mill studies in the field generally are not conducted by premier investigators who are well funded or well versed in research design and statistics, and who remain disinterested parties.

SUMMARY AND CONCLUSIONS

The present chapter offers an appraisal of the overall quality of community crime prevention evaluations. We launched our critical assessment of findings in this area by invoking four component aspects of research validity. By applying this touchstone, we identified a number of prevalent shortcomings. First, program objectives, ingredients, and procedures are often poorly articulated and operationalized. Second, typical research designs are weak, and subject to threats that stand as plausible rival explanations for project results. In other words, evaluations are not always powerful enough to permit the attribution of observed effects to project activities. Third, the replicability of the available results is largely unknown and the job of attempting replications in this field is difficult because of the uncertainties surrounding the interventions themselves. Hence, reported successes or failures must be scrutinized carefully on a program-to-program basis before extending the results to other contexts or locations. Finally, in many studies, the measurement of outcome variables is often unreliable, and the statistical analysis of data is either completely lacking or inappropriately applied.

These sobering conclusions must necessarily cast some doubt on the credibility of reported effectiveness. However, we cannot lose sight of the inherent and often unavoidable difficulties that beset these types of studies, nor can we relinquish the knowledge that many of the weaknesses we have identified may be overcome through a conscious effort on the part of evaluators to adopt more rigorous approaches to design, measurement, and analysis.

REFERENCES

Bickman, L., Lavrakas, P. J., & Green, S. K. (1977). *National Evaluation Program— Phase 1 summary report: Citizen Crime Reporting Projects.* Washington, DC: Law Enforcement Assistance Administration.

Campbell, D. T., & Stanley, J. C. (1966). *Experimental and quasi-experimental designs for research.* Chicago: Rand McNally.

Cirel, P., Evans, P., McGillis, D., and Whitcomb, D. (1977). *An exemplary project: Community crime prevention program, Seattle, Washington.* Washington, DC: Law Enforcement Assistance Administration.

Conklin, J. (1975). *The impact of crime.* New York: Macmillan.

Cook County Criminal Justice Commission (1979) *A guide to crime prevention through citizen participation.* Chicago: James H. Lowry & Associates.

Cook, T. D., & Campbell, D. T. (1979). *Quasi-experimentation: Design and analysis issues for field settings.* Chicago: Rand McNally.

DuBow, F., & Emmons, D. (1981). The community hypothesis. In D. Lewis (Ed.), *Reactions to crime.* Beverly Hills, CA: Sage.

Greenberg, S., Rohe, W., & Williams, J. (1983). Neighborhood conditions and community crime control. In *Community crime prevention.* Washington, DC: Center for Responsive Governance.

Heinzelmann, F. (1981) Crime prevention and the physical environment. In D. Lewis (Ed.), *Reactions to crime.* Beverly Hills, CA: Sage.

Heinzelmann, F. (1983). Crime prevention from a community perspective. In *Community crime prevention.* Washington, DC: Center for Responsive Governance.

Heller, N. B., Stenzel, W. W., & Gill, A. (1975). *National Evaluation Program—Phase 1 summary report: Operation Identification Projects.* Washington, DC: Law Enforcement Assistance Administration.

Inciardi, J. A. (1978). The Uniform Crime Reports: Some considerations on their shortcomings and utility. *Review of Public Data, 6,* 3-16.

International Training, Research and Evaluation Council. (1977). *National Evaluation Program—Phase 1 summary report: Crime Prevention Security Surveys.* Washington, DC: Law Enforcement Assistance Administration.

Jacob, H., & Lineberry, R. L. (1982). *Governmental responses to crime: Executive summary.* Washington, DC: National Institute of Justice.

Jacobs, J. (1961). *The death and life of great American cities.* New York: Vintage.

Judd, C. M., & Kenny, D. A. (1981). *Estimating the effects of social interventions.* New York: Cambridge University Press.

Lavrakas, P. J. (1981) On households. In D. A. Lewis (Ed.), *Reactions to crime.* Beverly Hills, CA: Sage.

Lavrakas, P. J. (1985). *The nature and magnitude of RDD panel attrition.* Unpublished manuscript, Northwestern University Survey Lab, Evanston, IL.

Lavrakas, P. J., & Lewis, D. A. (1980). The conceptualization and measurement of citizens' crime prevention behaviors. *Journal of Research in Crime and Delinquency, 17,* 254-272.

Levine, J. P. (1975). The ineffectiveness of adding police to prevent crime. *Public Policy, 23,* 523-545.

Lockhard, J. L., Duncan, J. T., & R. N. Brenner (1978). *Directory of community crime prevention programs: National and state levels.* Washington, DC: Law Enforcement Assistance Administration.

Podolefsky, A., & DuBow, F. (1981). *Strategies for community crime prevention.* Springfield, IL: Charles C Thomas.

Riecken, H. W., & Boruch, R. F. (1974). *Social experimentation.* New York: Academic Press.

Roehl, J. A., & Cook, R. F. (1984). *Evaluation of the Urban Crime Prevention Program.* Washington, DC: National Institute of Justice.

Rosenbaum, D. P., Lewis, D. A., & Grant, J. A. (1985). *The impact of community crime prevention programs in Chicago: Can neighborhood organizations make a difference?* Evanston, IL: Northwestern University, Center for Urban Affairs and Policy Research.

Sechrest, L., & Redner, R. (1979). Strength and integrity of treatments in evaluation studies. In *Review of criminal justice evaluation: 1978.* Washington, DC: Law Enforcement Assistance Administration.

Silberman, C. E. (1978). *Criminal violence, criminal justice.* New York: Random House.

Skogan, W. (1979). Community crime prevention programs: Measurement issues in evaluation. In *Review of criminal justice evaluation: 1978.* Washington, DC: Law Enforcement Assistance Administration.

Suttles, G. (1972). *The social construction of communities.* Chicago: University of Chicago Press.

Tien, J. M., O'Donnell, V. F., & A. Barnett (1979). *National Evaluation Program— Phase 1 summary report: Street Lighting Projects.* Washington, DC: Law Enforcement Assistance Administration.

U.S. Department of Justice, Bureau of Justice Statistics. (1983). Report to the nation on crime and justice: The data. Washington, DC: U.S. Department of Justice.

Weiss, C. H. (1972). *Evaluation research.* Englewood Cliffs, NJ: Prentice-Hall.

Wilson, J. Q. (1975). *Thinking about crime.* New York: Basic Books.

Yin, R. K. (1977). *Evaluating citizen crime prevention programs.* Santa Monica, CA: Rand Corporation.

Yin, R. K. (1979). What is citizen crime prevention? In *Review of criminal justice evaluation: 1978.* Washington, DC: Law Enforcement Assistance Administration.

Yin, R. K., Vogel, M. E., Chaiken, J. M. (1977). *National Evaluation Program—Phase 1 summary report: Citizen Patrol Projects.* Washington, DC: Law Enforcement Assistance Administration.

II

CITIZEN EFFORTS TO
PREVENT RESIDENTIAL CRIME

Chapter 3

CITYWIDE COMMUNITY CRIME PREVENTION
An Assessment of the Seattle Program

BETSY LINDSAY
DANIEL McGILLIS

THE CASE FOR
COMMUNITY CRIME PREVENTION

A study of "index" crimes in Seattle, conducted by the Law and Justice Planning Office in 1972, found that more citizens were concerned about becoming victims of burglary than of any other crime. The Seattle Community Crime Prevention Program was developed in response to this problem. In this chapter we describe the components of this pioneering endeavor and then summarize the results of evaluation research that examined its impact on crime and community responses.[1]

Burglary has been a major problem throughout the United States. Many communities have responded to the problem of increased crime by calling for increased police personnel. The assumptions are that law enforcement agencies are most qualified to combat crime and their effectiveness is directly related to the number of police officers available for patrol and investigation. Yet, the prevalence of residential burglary in particular makes it mathematically improbable that even greatly increased police patrols would deter many crimes, or that an investigations unit could follow up each report properly.

Moreover, the nature of residential burglary makes it particularly elusive to traditional police methods. The crime requires only stealth and opportunity. Because the police patrol officers are, after all, nonresidents in a patrol neighborhood and outnumbered by households, they are greatly hampered in their ability to recognize either stealth or opportunity.

Clearly, to make an impact on the burglary rate, the citizenry must be mobilized. This point was underscored in the FBI's *Uniform Crime Reports* (1975):

> Criminal justice professionals readily and repeatedly admit that, in the absence of citizen assistance, neither more manpower, nor improved technology, nor additional money will enable law enforcement to shoulder the monumental burden of combating crime in America.

Fortunately, the very facts about burglary that can confound police methods make it particularly amenable to citizen prevention. Only a resident can make certain that his or her household is secure. Only alert neighbors can recognize suspicious activity at the back door, even when the police cruiser is at the front door. Two other facts about residential burglary suggest that citizen action is an appropriate response. Most victims are unable to provide identifying numbers on stolen property; and most household burglaries occur in daylight hours when it is possible to witness them.

THE COMMUNITY CRIME PREVENTION PROGRAM IN SEATTLE

In 1972, the city of Seattle's Law and Justice Planning Office (LJPO) undertook a program to put in order of priority certain index crimes as targets for developing prevention programs. The method of identifying the priority crimes was not limited to the usual single measure of frequency. Rather, a total of three variables were considered:

(1) *Frequency of occurrence.* Data were taken from the Seattle Police Department's reports of crime incidents.
(2) *Severity and level of public fear and tolerance.* This element was added to allow the rating plan to weigh an aggravated assault more heavily than a shoplifting incident. Data were collected through interviews with city residents.
(3) *Potential for crime reduction.* Priority crimes must also be amenable to prevention strategies. For example, homicide is not a priority crime. Despite the fact that it scores high on other measures, research indicated that the bulk of homicides occurred between acquaintances and the crime is not particularly amenable to reduction strategies.

The three crimes that emerged from the 1972 study as deserving priority attention were burglary, rape, and robbery.

Burglary in Seattle

In 1972 there were 11,339 burglaries (defined as the illegal entrance into a structure for the purpose of committing a theft or other felony) reported in Seattle. Although this marked a decrease from 1971, demographic and economic factors led planners to anticipate an increase in 1973 (which in fact occurred). LJPO staff identified the following facts concerning burglary in Seattle:

(1) Approximately 75% of all burglaries were residential (rather than commercial) in nature, resulting in property losses exceeding $4 million.
(2) The majority occurred in single-family dwellings.
(3) Arrests for 70% of daylight burglaries and 30% of burglaries committed in darkness were of persons under the age of 19.
(4) Of those entries into dwellings that were locked, the vast majority were accomplished by brute force, not skilled lock-picking.
(5) The bulk of stolen property was disposed of by direct sale (not through a "fence") to the public.
(6) Over 90% of the burglaries were not witnessed.
(7) Arrest and/or return of property occurred in fewer than 10% of all cases.
(8) However, in those cases in which there was an arrest and/or return of property the vast majority were witnessed.

The result of this analysis was a grant application to the Law Enforcement Assistance Administration (LEAA) for funds to hire a staff of civilians to organize target communities and implement surveillance and target-hardening strategies.

Start-Up and Site Selection

Initially, intensive delivery of Community Crime Prevention Program (CCPP) services was planned to occur in two of Seattle's eleven police patrol sectors, with selective testing in a third sector of the effects of mass media exposure. The two sectors selected as target areas comprised approximately 27% of the city's population. Both sectors had areas with a high incidence of burglary and residents included many lower-income families.

After several months of operation, it became obvious that the original goal of delivering services to residents of two sectors in one year was unrealistic in relation to the actual implementation time available and the relatively small project staff. Hence, revisions in delivery goals were made.

Essentially, CCPP decided to provide a systematic, block-by-block service delivery sweep, targeting single-family and duplex dwellings in neighborhoods with significant levels of burglary. Multiple dwellings were generally excluded as the staff research had indicated that a much higher proportion of burglaries occurred in single-family dwellings. Additional factors leading to exclusion of multiple dwellings were the difficulty of organizing a potentially more transient population in such dwellings and the burden of involving landlords in any security improvements.

The decision to concentrate activities in high-risk burglary areas was made not only to provide target hardening where it was most obviously appropriate, but also to test and evaluate project methods more effectively.

The process of site selection provided occasion for early contact between the staff and the police and helped to lay the groundwork for the mutual respect and cooperation so necessary to program success. Throughout the project's history, project staff accompanied police in patrol vehicles through the target area to become familiar with the neighborhoods and police patrol patterns. In this early phase of the program their escorts were the two sector patrol sergeants, both of whom were seasoned patrol veterans and somewhat skeptical of civilian involvement in any enforcement-related endeavors.

After surveying the two sectors, staff indicated their census tract preference for program start-up. Their choice was the "toughest" census tract in the sector, the one with the highest burglary and overall crime rate.

Fully expecting their opinions to fall on deaf ears, the patrol sergeants strongly opposed the choice of the "toughest" areas for program start-up. They suggested that as "rookies," project staff should "get their feet wet" in safer, quieter neighborhoods before tackling the tough ones. Not ony would they need as much experience and expertise as possible in order to make an impact on the tougher neighborhoods, but meeting that problem head-on without experience and prior success would be demoralizing to staff and might start the entire effort off on the wrong foot. Somewhat to the sergeants' surprise, the staff accepted their suggestion.

The anecdote illustrates the nature of the project's relationship with the police: Patrol officers of each tract were among the first contacted and their impressions were highly valued. The police and CCPP staff were fully aware that it was not an exercise in courtesy and public relations, but rather an expert consultation.

While no hard-and-fast formula was applied, considerations in selecting sites for service delivery included absolute burglary rates for the past year, a graph of that rate across an eight-year period, the ratio of burglaries to occupied dwelling units, the percentage of single- and two-family dwellings, and the population turnover rate. Census tracts with relatively and steadily high burglary rates were targeted for CCPP services and, where possible, those areas were matched with control census tracts having comparably high burglary trends.

Community Contact

After an area was targeted to receive CCPP services, the first step in delivering those services involved making contact with the police and the local civic organizations. Police contact, as noted above, included riding a few evenings with the police patrol in order to get their impressions of the neighborhood's crime problem and particularly vulnerable areas, as well as suggestions regarding issues that might be of particular concern to the residents. It also provided the staff with an opportunity to become familiar with the general geography of the neighborhood.

Local civic groups and church organizations were also contacted. This step enabled the staff to take advantage of any strong community ties (when they existed) and channel their energies toward burglary reduction activities. The support lent by such groups helped the staff gain entry into the homes of their membership. Generally, this support merely led to an announcement either at meetings or in mailings that the area had been targeted for CCPP involvement and that residents could expect a visit—a very simple but enormously helpful aid. At times, more active involvement took place. Typically, this included coordinating law enforcement speakers and public involvement programs with CCPP activities in order to heighten awareness and concern. However, *under no circumstances* were block watches held at or organized around such meetings. Staff felt that it was critical for block watch meetings to focus solely on the CCPP mandate and that they be held on the block.

At the same time that the community was being contacted, the CCPP staff developed a "community profile," which included crime data and demographic information about its residents.

Resident Contact

The first actual citizen contact occurred by mail. This contact was made at the same time the community was being "prepped" (as described above) or immediately afterward. Thus, contact occurred either by phone or by mail, and, more typically, by both. In either instance it was important to indicate the municipal aegis of the program and the fact that it was without charge or commercial affiliation. The letterhead and envelope logo used in the mailing was conspicuously marked with the Seattle Police Department's official seal and helped to dispel any doubts regarding the program's official nature.

After being informed that in 1975, 1 out of every 24 homes in Seattle was burglarized (this information is updated annually), the receiver of the letter was also informed that the city now provided "three free burglary prevention services" of which he or she could soon avail himself or herself. The letter described the three primary services of property identification, home security checks, and neighborhood block watch organizing. Finally, the letter stated that CCPP staff would be calling in person or by phone in about a week to register participation, answer any questions, and recruit a host for the block watch meeting. The letter included the signature of each CCPP staff member. Each resident of the targeted neighborhood received such a letter.

The next contact phase was the "door-belling" program. The community organizers canvassed the neighborhood as a team. Usually, their work was done in the early evening when most residents were at home. As they progressed through the streets, they filled in a log with the house addresses and degree of interest indicated by the residents. That information was later transferred to a master log at headquarters. The log also noted those not at home, and follow-up visits or calls were made to them if they did not attend the block watch meeting. The initial door-belling contact lasted about three minutes and reminded, reviewed, or presented the resident with the mailing. Residents were encouraged to participate in all program services but, most important, in a block watch. As neighbors became interested in a watch, this positive support was mentioned to the next contact. This same process was successfully accomplished over the phone as well.

All fieldwork, starting with the contact phase, was coordinated on a rotating basis by one of the community organizers who served as team coordinator. No group of nine or ten individuals performs effectively without a coordinator. Normally, the team coordinator served throughout the delivery of service to one or more complete census tracts and then another community organizer rotated into that duty, which demanded additional work and planning beyond that required of the other team members. This rotational team leadership was an important factor in the smooth field implementation of the CCPP.

In short, the operating assumption of the CCPP was that a systematic, block-by-block "sweep" of a target neighborhood was more likely to yield a high quantity and quality of participating citizens. This assumption relies heavily on the professionalism of the project field staff. It must be remembered that although the ultimate acts of crime prevention were borne by the citizen, the organizing responsibility rested with the professional field staff, who bore the approval and support of both the city government and police. In addition to the official posture lent by the project's municipal and police affiliation, and the resulting willingness on the part of citizens to allow city organizers into their homes, a professional staff guaranteed the full-time commitment necessary to the saturation methods of the project's operations.

It is, of course, unrealistic to expect 100% participation in any block or neighborhood. For a variety of reasons (including wariness, lack of concern, and unavailability), many citizens were unable or unwilling to participate. The project at inception sought to achieve a level of 30% participation for each service of all single- and two-family households per target area, participation being defined as any household's partaking of at least one of the three primary services. In fact, the program achieved a minimum of 40% participation in target areas and therefore raised its minimum participation objective to the 40% level. In some census tracts participation easily exceeded 40%.

Primary Services

By far, the most important function of CCPP was to perform the primary services. These included the three main tactics (block watch organizing, property marking, and household security inspections) that CCPP used to help citizens reduce their vulnerability to burglary. These services were delivered in a deliberate way *only* to target neighborhoods.

Staff time charts for the third year of operations indicated that 90% of the staff's time was devoted to primary service delivery. A description of each of the three tactics that constituted the primary services follows.

THE BLOCK WATCH

This was the single most important feature of the Community Crime Prevention Program. All other services were delivered only as a complement to this one indispensable service. The block watch is an organization of a group of neighbors, usually at least 10, and no more than 15, who are interested in mutual protection against burglary. As the community organizer canvasses a neighborhood, each individual expressing interest in the block watch is asked to host an initial meeting in his or her home. If no host is found but interest exists, the residents are invited to a meeting held in the project's mobile unit. Once a host is found, he or she is asked to invite all the neighbors and is supplied with printed invitations.

Each community organizer averaged two block watch meetings per week involving about 10 households each. To prepare for the meeting, the organizer composed packets of handouts for the participants. These packets included the most recent monthly newsletter, which contained the following information:

(1) census tract description and definitions by street boundaries;
(2) number of burglaries within the tract, during the last month and the same time period the year before, the type of residence burglarized, and time of day and week;
(3) inventory of items stolen;
(4) entry description, including place and method; and
(5) a map of the tract with the burglary locations identified.

Also included was a household inventory list for engraving identification, instructions for using the engraving tool, and the home security checklist. Most important, each member of the block watch was asked to write his or her name, address, and phone number on a blank map of the block prepared in advance by the community organizer. Later, at CCPP headquarters, all members' names, addresses, and telephone numbers were entered onto a consolidated map. Copies were then sent to the block captain for distribution to all block watch members.

The organizing meeting usually began between 7:00 and 7:30 p.m. The organizer introduced himself or herself, reviewed the nature of CCPP, and briefly indicated a few facts about burglary in Seattle that were particularly relevant to citizen action—specifically, that the majority of burglaries occur during daylight hours when it is possible for citizens to witness them, and that in 40% of Seattle's burglaries entry is gained through open doors and windows. The community organizer explained that increased police patrol—the traditional response—could not be expected to have more than a minimal impact on such a situation. However, residents were told that neighbors not only stand a better chance of knowing who belongs in the neighborhood, but, more important, they are there to see or question those who might not. Thus, properly organized and informed neighbors can effectively combat crime.

The intent of the block watch was to work in cooperation with the police. *Under no circumstances was vigilantism or self-help encouraged.* Rather, the community organizer discussed in detail the uses of the 911 emergency phone line, the proper protocol, and the need for that protocol. Many times the patrol officers were able to drop in on the block watch meeting and reinforce remarks made concerning law enforcement cooperation. Above all, residents were informed to call the police when suspicious incidents occurred. Anyone with a legitimate reason for being in the area would quickly be identified as such and would not be hassled by the police. Of course, the beauty of block watch was that one alert resident could mean one alert neighborhood in a matter of minutes by means of pyramiding phone calls, easily facilitated by consulting the block watch map.

Residents were then counseled in some of the methods that burglars might employ—"Has anyone ever rung your doorbell and then appeared surprised to find you home?" Of particular importance, the community organizer discussed some of the measures to combat burglaries that were provided in the materials. The phone, of course, is a primary method. After calling the police, participants were encouraged to inform neighbors of suspicious activity. Furthermore, unusual activity in a neighbor's house could easily be checked by phone. Other suggestions included exchanging vacation schedules and performing certain safeguards for those neighbors on vacation, such as rotating the lights that are on, mowing the lawn, collecting mail and newspapers, using the driveway, and filling the trash cans.

The other component of the block watch was the demonstration of operation identification and security measures. First, the organizer briefly described the contents of the Home Security Guide and the use of the engraving tool. The organizer then scheduled times for its use and encouraged the block watch to purchase one of its own for future use. The demonstration then included types and uses of various locks, reinforcement techniques, and the particular security weaknesses of certain kinds of doors and windows—all included in the Home Security Guide distributed to each household in attendance.

At the conclusion of the meeting, the participants elected a block watch captain, who becomes the neighborhood's liaison between the watch participants and CCPP.

PROPERTY MARKING

Available to each block watch was an engraving instrument for marking property. Window decals to warn intruders that property is marked were issued to neighbors only after an organizer had seen one marked item during a follow-up visit. This avoided the practice of using decals only, which may cease to act as a deterrent to potential burglars if property is not, in fact, marked. Indelibly marked property has a significantly diminished value in the stolen goods market, and provides a method for identification and reclamation should a house be burglarized. The staff performed the marking tasks in the first three years of operations; the organizers then encouraged the participants to mark their own possessions. This arrangement not only allowed the staff to be available for more demonstrations, but also bolstered participation by immediately involving the neighborhood in a positive antiburglary activity that combined individual initiative— the actual engraving—with group activity.

The suggested identifying mark for engraving property in Seattle was a Washington state driver's license number. This was far superior (as would be any state driver's license number) to other identifiers because of the ease with which police could trace the number through the Department of Motor Vehicles and the National Criminal Information Computer. (Through the computerized system, police in Seattle were able to identify the owner within two minutes, compared to three months for Social Security numbers.)

HOME SECURITY INSPECTION

During the weeks following the block watch meeting, and after sufficient time had elapsed for residents to use the engraver and implement any other security measures that were discussed, the organizer visited the participant's home. The organizer and the homeowner spent about 10 minutes walking methodically through and around the outside of the home, discussing weaknesses observed and options for correcting those weaknesses. To ensure that items were not overlooked during the inspection, the organizer reviewed the contents of the Home Security Guide, which listed the most common burglary vulnerabilities along with recommendations (usually including illustrations) for specific remedial actions.

A copy of a Home Security Checklist with recommendations noted was left with the resident. The list familiarized the homeowner with basic terminology of security hardware and could be carried to a locksmith's shop to help the homeowner describe precisely what he or she needed to secure his or her home. As was the case with the property marking, the organizers assisted those unable to implement changes themselves.

Maintenance Services

Originally, the primary technique for maintaining block watch activities and interest during the first two and one-half years of project operation was the distribution of the project's newsletter. Block watch captains were expected to deliver the newsletters personally to each member of the block watch and, during that contact, keep interest in the block watch alive. Distribution of the newsletter was generally not sufficient to keep the block watches alive, however, and many block captains neglected to deliver the newsletters or had their children drop them off on the neighbors' porches.

In response to this problem, the program later developed a maintenance component. Operationally, maintenance service is principally a reapplication of the earlier primary service sweep at a fixed time interval. It provides periodic opportunities for staff and block watch members to (a) reinforce the antiburglary focus of the block watch through meetings of block captains and members; (b) recognize the contributions of block watch members toward reducing residential burglary through awards, newsletter features, and media coverage; and (c) replace block watch captains who, for whatever reason, have ceased to serve effectively as neighborhood coordinators.

Advisory Service

In order for the project to respond to a heavy demand for CCPP services in nontarget neighborhoods, advisory services were offered. This was necessary to insulate and sustain the project's systematic operation. At that time, one community organizer was assigned to this function, which consisted primarily of training community volunteers to introduce and establish CCPP-type activities among their neighbors. However, to maintain the integrity of the evaluation, advisory services were not allowed in either the experimental or control areas.

Summary

In sum, the Community Crime Prevention Program benefited from a clear and relatively singular *focus*. The scope was limited to the prevention of one crime—residential burglary. The strategy relied on three tactics, two of which (the household security inspection and property marking services) were secondary to the block watch. The method of primary service delivery was to select a target neighborhood and saturate it. Finally, project staff developed two other program components: maintenance and advisory services. The former was designed to ensure the maintenance of the block watch organizations developed by project staff, and the latter to encourage community residents to organize CCPP-type activities under their own initiative. Of these two components, only the early stages of maintenance, involving the distribution of newsletters, was included in the experimental intervention that was evaluated.

EVALUATION RESULTS

The Seattle program was unique in the degree of rigor with which its accomplishments were evaluated. The Law and Justice Planning Office of the city of Seattle conducted an intensive series of studies to explore both the operations and impact of the CCPP. This section draws from these studies to report on the program's level of success in reducing burglaries, increasing burglary-in-progress calls, and meeting service objectives.

Reduction of Burglary

On the surface, it would appear to be simple to assess the impact of the Community Crime Prevention Program upon burglary. A researcher would simply need to check police records of burglaries before and after the program delivered services to an area and see if the number of burglaries was reduced. This approach is severely flawed, however, because in addition to reducing burglaries in the target area more than in a control area, the program has a second goal of increasing citizen reporting of burglaries to the police. Victimization surveys show that only about half of the burglaries committed are actually reported to the police due to citizen apathy or belief that the police cannot help anyway. Using police statistics, program success in increasing citizen reporting of burglaries could mask its crime reduction impact and might even produce an increase rather than decrease in burglary reports in neighborhoods receiving the services of the CCPP. Given that the program goals had opposite effects on police burglary data, an independent source of data was needed to assess the program's impact on burglary. Victimization surveys provided that source, and both telephone and door-to-door surveys of citizens were conducted to evaluate CCPP. In these surveys, which included both program participants and nonparticipants, respondents were asked whether they had been recently burglarized and, if so, whether they reported the burglary to the police.

The SEA-KING Victimization Survey

This survey was carefully designed as a rigorous measurement of the impact of the CCPP. The survey was conducted in five Seattle census tracts (four in west Seattle and one in the Green Lake area of Seattle). The first survey was conducted in mid-1975 and dealt with crime victimization during 1974. To collect these preproject data, 1,474 residences were surveyed in person. The second survey was conducted in mid-1976 and dealt with crime occurring in 1975. Included in this postproject survey were 1,216 residences. Drawing from all census tracts, it included residences randomly selected from among those known to have received CCPP services, and an approximately equal number of residences that had not received project services. This survey had a number of features that made it a rigorous evaluation of the CCPP program:

(1) Project tracts were selected randomly rather than for high crime rates. The statistical phenomenon of regression toward the mean, which is typically expected when extremes (here, unusually high crime rate areas) are the focus of study, was avoided because project tracts had relatively low preproject burglary rates. A "spontaneous" reduction in burglary in any one of these tracts independent of the project's impact was not to be expected.

(2) Data were collected for both program and nonprogram participants on a comparable pre-post basis, allowing an assessment of pretreatment burglary rates of the two groups and an estimate of general changes in the burglary rate.

(3) Data were collected by researchers independent of the CCPP project, reducing the likelihood of unintentional biases.

(4) The use of adjacent census tracts as comparison groups enabled an assessment of displacement of burglary to adjoining

census tracts. Many studies of community prevention programs have failed to attempt to study displacement of burglaries. These particular comparison tracts were especially well suited for studying displacement because they were also bordered by Puget Sound, reducing the possibilities for displacement to be distributed to other (noncomparison) adjacent census tracts.

(5) Artifacts due to highly victimized individuals moving out of the target area between pre- and postsurveys were controlled by inclusion of both treated and untreated residences.

(6) Additional police activities did not occur in project tracts. Often evaluations of the impact of community crime prevention programs are confounded because cities develop coordinated programs for crime reduction providing both increased police services and other community crime program services to an area simultaneously. The problems in disentangling the individual effects of the police and the community crime prevention program are obvious and usually insurmountable.

(7) Victimization data rather than the less reliable police reporting data were used, as was noted earlier.

Table 3.1 presents a summary of the results of the SEA-KING victimization survey. The findings are highlighted below.

Burglary Rates. The analysis of burglary victimization data revealed the following:

(1) Within experimental tracts pretreatment burglary rates of the CCPP-treated homes and nontreated homes were virtually identical (6.18% versus 6.45%).

(2) A comparison of the posttreatment data for CCPP and non-CCPP residences within experimental tracts shows a statistically significant lower burglary rate for CCPP participants (2.43% versus 5.65%, $p < .05$). The reduction in burglary in CCPP residences was 61% (from 6.18 to 2.43).

(3) A marginally significant overall reduction in burglary rates occurred within the experimental tracts when CCPP residences and non-CCPP residences were combined (6.34% in 1974 versus 4.04% in 1975, $p < .07$).

(4) Within adjacent control tracts pretreatment burglary rates were higher than those in experimental tracts (10.43% versus 6.34%, $p < .01$).

(5) Control tract burglary rates were not significantly different between 1974 and 1975 (10.43% versus 9.95%).

TABLE 3.1 SEA-KING Victimization Data: Burglary Victimization per Twelve Months

Area	Total	Not Burglarized	Burglarized[a] N	Burglarized[a] %	Reported Yes N	Reported Yes %	Reported No
Pretreatment (January-December 1974)							
Control (federal tracts 96 and 105)	575	515	60	10.43	28	47	32
Experimental (federal tracts 97 and 98)							
CCPP members	356	334	22	6.18	15	68	7
Non-CCPP members	543	508	35	6.45	14	40	21
Total	899	842	57	6.34	29	51	28
Posttreatment (January-December 1975)							
Control (federal tracts 96 and 105)	442	400	42	9.95	24	57	18
Experimental (federal tracts 97 and 98)							
CCPP members	247	241	6	2.43	6	100	0
Non-CCPP members	248	234	14	5.65	7	64	4[b]
Total	495	475	20	4.04	13	76	4[b]

a. Burglarized one or more times.
b. Does not include three cases for which reporting data were unknown.

Reporting Rates. The analysis of reporting data can be summarized as follows:

(1) Reporting rates did not differ significantly between experimental and control tracts in the pretreatment period, or between 1974 and 1975 for control tracts. Reporting rates between 1974 and 1975 increased at a marginally significant level for experimental tracts (50.9% versus 76.5%, p < .06).

(2) Within experimental tracts pretreatment reporting rates differed significantly between CCPP participants and nonparticipants (68% versus 40%, p < .05). A statistically valid comparison of posttreatment reporting rates for the CCPP and non-CCPP groups was not possible due to the small number of burglary cases. All of the six burglaries to CCPP residences were reported, however.

Burglary Displacement. Analyses were performed to test the displacement hypothesis. Data from the SEA-KING survey do not support the hypothesis that deferred burglaries are displaced to non-CCPP residences. It might be expected that non-CCPP residences in the same census tract as CCPP residences would become the most likely target of displaced burglaries. These census tracts showed a 12% decline in burglary, however (from 6.45% to 5.65%). Burglary rates in the adjacent census tracts also declined by 5% (from 10.43% to 9.95%). These data are not conclusive, but suggest that displacement is not occurring. These decreases compare to a 61% decline in burglary in treated residences.

The LJPO Telephone Survey

A telephone survey was conducted by the Law and Justice Planning Office to supplement the SEA-KING study. This survey was conducted in August and September 1976, and included victimization data for the preceding 6 months from both project and nonproject residents in five census tracts, plus an additional 790 households citywide. A total of 1,970 CCPP members and 1,322 non-CCPP members responded to the survey. The five tracts were chosen on the basis of recent treatment (having been completed no more than 18 months, nor less than 6 months prior to the survey), and meeting CCPP criteria for successful treatment (that is, 30% or more of the single and duplex residences received burglary reduction services).

Table 3.2 presents a summary of the results of the LJPO telephone survey. This survey provided valuable supplementary information to that of the SEA-KING survey because the latter survey included only 247 CCPP participants and 248 CCPP "refusers" in experimental tracts in the postproject survey. The telephone survey covered the two SEA-KING experimental tracts plus three additional census tracts. As was noted above, data in the LJPO telephone survey were collected for a 6-month period. Combined data from the SEA-KING and LJPO telephone surveys appear in Table 3.3. Highlights of the LJPO survey findings follow.

Burglary Rates. The analysis of burglary victimization data revealed the following:

(1) CCPP members reported a slightly lower level of burglary (5% for 6 months) compared to non-CCPP members (6.1%), but this difference is not statistically significant.

(2) When LJPO data were combined with SEA-KING posttreatment data, a significantly lower burglary rate was found for CCPP participants compared to non-CCPP residences (9.2% versus 11.1%, $p < .05$).

(3) Unexpectedly, non-CCPP participants had a significantly higher reporting rate than CCPP members for the combined LJPO and SEA-KING survey data (83% versus 72%, p<.01). These non-CCPP participants lived in CCPP-treated census tracts and may have increased their burglary reporting in the SEA-KING data, individuals in control census tracts have particularly low reporting rates (47%).

Length of Time of Project Impact. LJPO survey data allowed for an estimation of the duration of project effects, because various tracts surveyed had received services at different periods of time. Tracts served at periods of 14, 12, and 9 months prior to the survey showed significant differences between CCPP and non-CCPP residences, with CCPP residences having lower burglary rates. Tracts served 17 and 18 months prior to the survey did not show a significant difference between CCPP and non-CCPP residences, and CCPP members were burglarized at a slightly higher rate than non-CCPP members (4.9% versus 3.3%). Thus, the LJPO research tentatively suggests that project effects last from 12 to 18 months. Althouth the results were not significant, the research team pointed out that with the passage of time, CCPP members may begin to become burglary-prone and that some sort of retreatment may be necessary.

TABLE 3.2 LJPO Telephone Survey, Summary of Results: Residential Burglary Rate
for Preceding Six Months at Time of Call

Census Tract	Date Completed	CCPP Members						Non-CCPP Members					
		No Burglary	Burglary N	%	Reported[b] N	%	Not	No	Burglary N	%	Reported[b] N	%	Not Reported
87	5/75	177	12	6.4	8	67	4	143	9	5.9	5	56	4
89	7/75	335	23	6.4	15	65	8	176	20	10.2	19	95	1
95	12/75	424	29	6.4	22	76	7	370	36	8.9	28	76	9
97	9/75	445	13	2.8	8	67	4	251	9	3.5	7	100	0
98	4/75	490	22	4.3	16	76	5	302	6	2.0	4	67	2
Total		1871	99	5.0	69	71	28	1242	80	6.1	63	80	16

a. Federal census tracts.
b. Totals of "reported" and "not reported" may not add up to total "burglary" because, in some cases, respondents were not sure. ((Tract 95 may contain a numerical error of one or two cases.)

TABLE 3.3   Combined SEA-KING and LJPO Telephone
Victimization Survey Data

	Total Interviewed	No Burglary	Burglary		Reported		Not Reported	
			N	%	N	%	N	%
CCPP members	2217	2013	204	9.2	144	72	56	28
Non-CCPP members	1570	1396	174	11.1	140	83	29	17
Total	3787	3409	378	10.0	284	77	85	23

In conclusion, the CCPP was apparently successful in reducing the burglary victimization of its participants. The two surveys discussed, plus an earlier, more limited survey conducted by the project staff, support this conclusion. As has been noted, alternative explanations for the results can never be ruled out totally, but the present data are strongly supportive of the program.

Burglary-in-Progress Calls. As was discussed above, the Community Crime Prevention Program was expected to result in increased numbers of burglary-in-progress calls. In order to assess this impact, the Law and Justice Planning Office collected data on burglary-in-progress calls using the police department's computerized dispatch records. Areas treated by the CCPP were compared to non-CCPP areas. A number of problems occurred with these comparisons because the dispatch system uses car beats rather than census tracts to record location and the two units are not comparable. Highlights of the data include the following:

(1) A significant increase in the proportion of burglary-in-progress calls to all burglary calls in treated car beats was observed (9.1% pre- versus 11.6% postprogram, $p < .05$). No significant difference in nontreated car beats was observed (8.5% pre- versus 8.8% postprogram).

(2) Data support the assertion that the calls were of high quality, as arrests resulting from the calls increased slightly (from 17.5% to 19.2%), and the amount of suspect descriptive information also increased nonsignificantly from 60.5% to 65.6%.

Service Goals. The Community Crime Prevention Program set and achieved the following goals for its operations:

(1) formation of neighborhood block watch groups in 30% of all occupied single-family and duplex dwellings in test communities;

(2) completion of the marking of property for identification in 30% of all target households;

(3) completion of security inspections in 30% of all target households;

(4) provision of at least 70% of all target households with information about burglary and ways to reduce it; and

(5) outside the test communities, on request, provision of all possible aid regarding burglary reduction.

Summary

A number of general conclusions regarding the program can be drawn:

(1) The CCPP was apparently successful in reducing the burglary victimization of its participants. All three victimization surveys support this conclusion.

(2) The CCPP influence apparently lasted from 12-18 months, at which point some "decay" effects occurred, and retreatment was sometimes necessary.

(3) Reporting rates for both CCPP members and nonmembers tended to increase in treated areas.

(4) Burglary-in-progress calls as a proportion of all burglary calls to police increased significantly in treated areas and their quality was relatively high as measured by presentation of suspect information and the occurrence of subsequent arrests.

IMPLICATIONS FOR
FUTURE RESEARCH OR POLICY

The Seattle Community Crime Prevention Program's evaluation was designed to provide a rigorous assessment of the program's achievements. The victimization survey design helped to rule out alternative explanations associated with regression to the mean, atypical burglary levels of participants in the pretreatment period, covarying increases in police activity, displacement, general trends toward burglary reduction, and potential biases in data collection due to project control of the survey. Each of these issues is noted above. Obviously, it is never possible to rule out all alternative explanations for the findings, but the steps taken in the evaluation helped to reduce the credibility of many possibilities.

The steps taken to make the study relatively rigorous are familiar to researchers. We believe that few studies incorporate as many detailed safeguards, and one major reason for this is the scarcity of resources for evaluation research. The Law and Justice Planning Office study was conducted with local Law Enforcement Assistance Administration funds. These funds were sufficient to enable the LJPO research team to conduct the needed victimization surveys and related research. The termination of the Law Enforcement Assistance Administration has resulted in a sharp reduction in funds available nationally for ambitious studies of criminal justice programs. Many studies lack rigor because the researchers cannot afford to perform the costly tasks required to achieve highly reliable findings.

In some cases improvements in research designs can increase the rigor of a study without significant cost implications. The obverse is also often true, and the availability of large sums of money for research has never been the guarantee of sound research design. In this regard, the Law and Justice Planning Office researchers deserve considerable credit for conducting a sound and useful evaluation of the Seattle Community Crime Prevention Program.

The evaluation suggests that the Seattle program is very effective and worthy of replication in other jurisdictions. The National Institute of Law Enforcement and Criminal Justice (now the National Institute of Justice) has endorsed the Seattle Community Crime Prevention Program as an exemplary project and has urged its replication across the United States. Clearly other jurisdictions need to tailor the program's components to their situations. Some jurisdictions may lack sufficient funds to duplicate the program's model of intensive use of professional staff and may need to rely more heavily on volunteer assistance. Such an approach is likely to reduce a program's effectiveness, although the actual impact remains an empirical question. In this regard, it would be very useful to conduct an experimental study in a single jurisdiction in which different areas of the city received varying combinations of professional and volunteer assistance in implementing community crime prevention programs. The results of the differing approaches could be assessed in a manner similar to the Seattle study to determine the minimal requirements for professional assistance.

NOTE

1. The evaluation study reported in this chapter was conducted by the Seattle Law and Justice Planning Office, and the study was directed by Dr. Kenneth Mathews. His work in designing and implementing the study was outstanding. Portions of this chapter are drawn from a report for the U.S. Department of Justice entitled *An Exemplary Project: Community Crime Prevention.* Authors of the report were Paul Cirel, Patricia Evans, Daniel McGillis, and Debra Whitcomb (1977).

REFERENCES

Federal Bureau of Investigation. (1975, September). Uniform crime reports. Washington, DC: U.S. Department of Justice.

Cirei, P., Evans, P., McGillis, D., & Whitcomb, D. (1977). *An exemplary project: Community crime prevention* (Report for the U.S. Department of Justice). Washington, DC: Government Printing Office.

Federal Bureau of Investigation (1975, September). Uniform crime reports. Washington, DC: U.S. Department of Justice.

Chapter 4

NEIGHBORHOOD-BASED ANTIBURGLARY STRATEGIES
An Analysis of Public and Private Benefits from the Portland Program

A N N E L. S C H N E I D E R

Most publicly funded efforts to reduce or control crime can be categorized as prevention, rehabilitation, or deterrence.[1] The purposes of these programs are to prevent persons from developing criminal careers, or, for those who are already engaged in crime, to retrain them, modify their behavior, or incapacitate them. If prevention, treatment, or deterrence efforts are effective in reducing crime, then it is generally assumed that a "public good" has been produced—that is, that the entire public will benefit from the increased safety (Shoup, 1976; McKenzie & Tullock, 1975; Wilson & Schneider, 1976).

Programs that seek to reduce crime by focusing on the potential victims usually are designed to educate residents in the techniques of crime prevention or to supply them with the training and equipment that would reduce the probability of their own victimization. Environmental design programs are similar in that they focus on the built environment of a specific household or area and seek to reduce the likelihood of its victimization.

The victim-oriented approach, however, does not necessarily produce a "public good." If some residents in an area undertake self-protection activities and successfully reduce the probability that they

AUTHOR'S NOTE: *Funding for the research upon which this chapter was based was provided by Grant 74-NI-99-0016-G from the Oregon Law Enforcement Council and the National Institute of Law Enforcement in Criminal Justice, Washington, D.C. Points of view or opinions stated in this document are those of the author, and do not necessarily represent the official position or policies of the Department of Justice.*

will be victimized, offenders may select other residents in the area as their victims (Maltz, 1972; Mattick, Olander, Baker, & Schlegel, 1974). Thus, the total volume of crime may not be reduced. It is possible that crime will be shifted from one victim to another, from one area to another, from the inner city to the suburbs, or even from the urban areas to the rural areas of the nation.

When public funds are spent on programs that successfully reduce the criminal activities of offenders or potential offenders, few would criticize the expenditures because the benefits of crime reduction are, for the most part, distributed to everyone as increased safety. On the other hand, if a city government supplies funds to a victim-oriented program, and if that program shifts the monetary and social costs of crime from one set of people (participants) to another (nonparticipants), then one might legitimately question the fairness of the program.

Publicly funded crime prevention efforts also may have the effect of redistributing the amount of protection among different socioeconomic classes. It is generally believed that persons in the higher-income groups are able to purchase better protection for themselves (Weicher, 1976). This has not become much of a political issue, however, because in a free-market economy most acknowledge the right of individuals to spend their money in whatever manner they choose. However, when public funds are used to purchase additional protection for some citizens but not all, then their allocation among socioeconomic groups is an important consideration.

At the time the Portland, Oregon, burglary prevention program was implemented in 1973, very little was known about the impact of these programs, much less the extent to which they would produce private rather than public benefits or result in a more (or less) equitable distribution of protection among different socioeconomic groups.

THE PROGRAM

The Portland burglary prevention program was implemented during the summer of 1973 as part of the Law Enforcement Assistance Administration (LEAA)-funded Impact Cities initiative. The program was operated by the Crime Prevention Bureau (CPB), which was a civilian-staffed component of the police department.

The program was based primarily on a neighborhood prevention strategy. The CPB staff identified several high crime target areas for door-to-door canvassing of residents. This effort was followed by neighborhood meetings, usually sponsored by local residents, in which the program was explained, engraving equipment distributed, and decals signifying participation were given to those who attended.

The private prevention techniques recommended by the program included information about types of locks, alarms, use of outside lighting around entrances to the residence, removal or trimming of hedges to increase the visibility of the residence, and special precautions to take during vacations.

Residents were encouraged to mark their property with an engraver supplied by the Crime Prevention Bureau. These engravers were available at the meeting, directly from the CPB headquarters, and from public libraries. A crime prevention decal was to be posted in a conspicuous place near the front door. It informed potential burglars that items in the household were engraved and could be traced.

The neighborhood prevention efforts included information on the methods of operation that burglars tended to use, information on suspicious behavior, actions to take if suspicious behavior or a crime in progress was observed, and general exhortations for the residents to watch out for the safety of each other.

In the early phases of the program, the CPB designated certain areas of the city for high-priority efforts on the part of CPB personnel. Two census tracts (36.02 and 19), both of which had high burglary rates, were designated for major work in terms of block meetings, door-to-door coverage with the engraving equipment, and the dissemination of information. In addition, an area that also was selected for street lighting (one that had the highest burglary rates in Portland) was designated as an area of special activity.

Several months after the program began, the CPB altered its strategy and began implementing the program citywide on the basis of requests received from residents throughout the city. CPB staff did not canvass these other areas, but they did speak at neighborhood meetings, which were organized by the community. They also initiated a massive television advertising campaign, which produced a dramatic increase in the number of persons obtaining information, engravers, and decals from the CPB offices. This strategy was reversed after the first evaluation reports were produced. These reports sparked a discussion about displacement effects (which program staff strongly suspected were occurring) and how such effects might be minimized. Thereafter, the CPB returned to its canvassing, neighborhood-based strategy in an effort to saturate an entire area bounded by natural barriers to minimize displacement.

Logic of the Program

The rationale underlying this type of neighborhood burglary prevention program is that burglars wish to incur the smallest possible risk when selecting a home to burglarize. The burglar is expected to avoid homes with burglar alarms or dogs, as well as those in which the neighbors can see the entrances easily. Property that has been marked with an identification number is presumed to be more difficult to fence, more easily recovered, and more apt to be traced back to the burglar. Neighborhoods in which most of the residents know each other and in which residents have been encouraged to help watch for suspicious behavior or strangers should be less attractive to potential burglars, because their presence is more apt to be noticed. The CPB specifically sought to increase not only the protection of individual households, but the protection of the entire neighborhood.

EVALUATION PURPOSE AND METHODOLOGY

The evaluation of Portland's Impact City Program—for which I served as principal investigator and which included the neighborhood burglary prevention effort—was contracted by the Oregon Law Enforcement Council (OLEC) to the Oregon Research Institute after a competitive bidding process. Because the study had to serve several purposes, OLEC had already decided that a multiple-purpose design should be developed and that one aspect of the design would include a victimization survey.

The purposes of the evaluation were as follows:

(1) to measure the private benefits of the burglary prevention program by examining its effect on the burglary rates of participating households compared with nonparticipants;

(2) to assess the public benefits of the program by estimating the change in burglary rates for the entire city;

(3) to measure the effect on the recovery rates of marked property;

(4) to examine the change in "private-oriented" crime prevention behavior versus "collective" crime prevention behavior that could be attributed to the neighborhood burglary program; and

(5) to assess the effect of the program on the distribution of private protection among different socioeconomic groups.

The Data

Three sources of data were available for the evaluation.

A victimization survey specifically designed to assist in the evaluation of the burglary prevention program was conducted in the summer of 1974 (covering a recall period from May 1973 through April 1974) in the Portland metropolitan area (see Schneider, 1975c). Of the approximately 3,950 interviews, 1,909 were within the city limits of Portland and the remainder were in the suburban areas. All of the interviews were conducted in person.

The sample was developed in such a way as to oversample residents in three target areas identified by the CPB: the street-lighting area (which received extensive coverage by the CPB, as well as the addition of street lights); the northeast Portland area; and one other high-priority neighborhood in the inner city. The remaining households were selected randomly from throughout the city.

The victimization survey instrument contained extensive questions regarding knowledge of and participation in crime prevention activities, attitudes toward crime, actions taken to avoid being victimized, and so forth. These questions were asked first and were then followed by the victimization portion of the interview. The victimization screening and follow-up questions were the same as those used in LEAA-sponsored surveys.

The second source of data was another victimization survey, this one conducted in 1972 by LEAA as part of its City Victimization plan. This survey was extremely limited, however, in its contribution to the evaluation because Census Bureau rules prevented the data from being broken out to subareas within the city. The rules also prohibited the Bureau from providing individual-level data, which could have been used to create a historical control group. Nevertheless, the LEAA study was used for in the pre-post examination of change in the citywide burglary rates, as will be explained below.

Police statistics on the offense rates, by month, for burglaries and other Crime Index offenses on a citywide basis were the third set of data used in the evaluation.

The Design

Two issues present extraordinary problems in developing a valid research design for community crime prevention programs such as the one implemented in Portland. One of these is the simultaneous impact of the program on burglary rates and on the reporting of burglaries to the police. The other is the displacement effect.

If the program increases the probability that burglaries will be reported to the police, then time-series or pre-post designs using official police statistics will not be able to determine the true effect. If the program is effective in reducing burglaries and also increases the probability of reporting, then the analysis may show no change at all. The two victimization surveys conducted in Portland indicate an increase in reporting of burglaries (from 50% in the 1972 survey to 65% in 1974). Furthermore, the later survey indicates differences of a similar magnitude between participants and nonparticipants (Schneider, 1975a).

The fact that the program probably increased the reporting of burglaries precluded the use of official statistics either in time-series or concurrent comparison group designs.

In relation to displacement effects and collective benefits, the problems emerge only if the program is effective in reducing burglaries for participating households. If so, then any one of three outcomes may occur.

First, some burglars and potential burglars abandon crime entirely within the area due to the deterrent effects of the program. Others are not concerned about the new protections and continue their activities without distinguishing between participating and nonparticipating households.

With this scenario, the burglary rate for participating and nonparticipating households in the area would decline at approximately the same rate. No displacement has occurred within the area being considered, and the program has positive private effects and positive collective effects as well.

Second, some burglars and potential burglars abandon crime in the area entirely due to the program and others shift their activities toward the nonparticipating households.

In this instance, the burglary rate for participating households would decline markedly whereas the rate for nonparticipants would decline some or remain the same as before the program, or even increase slightly depending on how many burglars were permanently deterred. In this example, the benefits to participating households are greater than the benefits to nonparticipating households, but the overall effect of the program may be positive for both participants and nonparticipants.

Third, no burglars or potential burglars abandon crime in the area and all shift their choices toward the nonparticipating households. If this occurs, the rate for participating households would decline and the rate for nonparticipants would increase by approximately the same amount because the latter households are selected as victims instead of the participating ones.

Displacement has occurred in this situation and the program has positive private benefits, but negative (or no) collective benefits. The cost of the entire volume of burglaries has been shifted to the nonparticipants. If the program had not existed, this cost would have been shared more equitably among households in the area.

Which of these outcomes occurs may depend on the proportion of residents who are participating. As the percentage of participants increases, the first or second outcomes discussed above may become more likely, but no research has been done to determine this. If participation reaches close to 100% within an entire urbanized area, then the burglars must move to another city, abandon crime, or begin burglarizing the participating households. If the latter choice is made by a substantial number of burglars, then the private benefits of participating (as well as the collective benefits) may decline as a function of exceptionally high participation.

The implication of the displacement phenomena, if it occurs, is that the private effects of the program must be measured by comparing participating and nonparticipating households. To measure the public effects, it is necessary to compare the burglary rate of an area large enough to include both the private effect and its displacement.

To assess the effectiveness of antiburglary programs for participating households (that is, the private benefits), one must ascertain what the burglary rate for participants would have been if they had not participated in the program. Through comparison of the expected rate (the rate they would have experienced if they had not participated) with the actual rate, the impact of the program can be estimated.

Similarly, to estimate the public (collective) benefits of the program, it is necessary to estimate the burglary rate of the entire area (including participants and nonparticipants) and to compare this with the rate the area would have experienced if there had been no program. Unfortunately, there were no simple ways to obtain an expected rate either for the participants or for the area as a whole. Because households were not randomly selected for inclusion in the program, there are only two possible estimates of the expected burglary rate. One of these is the preprogram rate for households that later participated and the other is the concurrent burglary rate of nonparticipating households. There are problems with both of these.

As noted above, preprogram victimization data were available only on a citywide basis and, therefore, could not be divided into those who later participated in the program and those who did not. The only source of data for determining the preprogram rates of persons who later participated or did not were the official police statistics. However, there were two reasons not to use these. First, participation in the program clearly increased the probability of reporting crimes to the police. This would have produced an increase in the official (reported) burglary rate for participating households. Second, households that experienced a burglary were especially motivated to participate in the program. In fact, police officers often informed burglary victims about the program and sought their participation. Thus, the use of historical burglary statistics for the participating households would have shown an abnormally high burglary rate prior to their participation and an almost automatic decline afterward. This presented a classic regression to the mean problem.

There also were problems, however, in assessing the private effects by comparing participating and nonparticipating households using the 1974 victimization survey data. The most obvious problem was the possibility of a selection bias, in which the participants differ systematically from the nonparticipants prior to their inclusion in the program. If so, then there is every reason to expect a difference in their burglary rates that is independent of the program.

There is no perfect solution to this problem of research design, but the strategy that was used involved comparing participants with nonparticipants who lived in the same section of the city and introducing statistical controls for other variables within each area that were related both to participation and to the burglary rate. In effect, the assumption was made that the burglary rate for participants within Area X of the city would have been the same as the rate for nonparticipants in Area X if the former had not participated in the program.

If a difference exists between participating and nonparticipating households that appears to be related to the program, then it is necessary to determine whether the reduction in crime for participants was matched by an increase for nonparticipants, or whether there were some collective benefits. For this part of the analysis, the preprogram victimization survey rates for the entire city were compared with the postprogram rates. In addition, the official burglary statistics from the police, both pre and post, were adjusted for differences in reporting percentages (as reflected in the two victimization surveys). Although neither of these designs, alone, is a very good one, it was believed that the two in conjunction might shed some light on the issue of collective versus private benefits.

The examination of the other propositions did not present nearly such complex design issues. The question of whether the program resulted in increased recovery rates was examined using the 1974 victimization survey data in which comparisons were made of the recovery rates for engraved and nonengraved items.

The impact of the program on "private" versus "collective" protection was examined by dividing the various types of actions reported in the victimization survey into those that benefited the individual and those that benefited the entire neighborhood. (These scales are discussed below.) Using multiple regression analysis, the independent effect of attending block meetings on these types of activities was assessed.

The redistributive effects of the program were studied by comparing the correlation of socioeconomic variables with the amount and type of protection. This analysis was conducted within the randomly selected portion of the sample, which included self-selected participants in the program and within the CPB-selected participants. We would expect an income or social-class bias to be present in the first group, given that those who are better off tend to purchase more private protection. This could be the case either because they have a greater demand for protection or because they are able to afford it, or both.

Within the CPB group, however, the service was, in effect, delivered directly to the consumer at no charge. Hence, there is no reason to think that those who are better off would avail themselves to a greater extent of this "free" good unless, of course, those who are better off prefer more protection even when it's free.

EFFECTS OF THE PROGRAM

Effect on Participating Households

Homes that participated in the CPB program, as indicated by the display of an antiburglary decal, had lower burglary rates than homes that did not (see Table 4.1). The use of the decal was selected as the primary indicator of participation because this was one of the few aspects of participation that was readily visible to a potential burglar. Most homes that displayed the decal also had taken numerous other preventive actions.

For the entire city, the difference between participants and nonparticipants was about 30 burglaries per 1,000 households. If it is assumed that participating households would have had the same rate as

TABLE 4.1 Effect of Participation on Burglary Rates of
Participating Households (in percentages)

Area	Participating Homes	Nonparticipating Homes	All Homes
Portland (totals) (N = 1,959)	6.87*	10.1*	9.65
Street-lighting area (N = 311)	8.4*	24.0*	21.0
CPB high-priority area (N = 115)	7.7*	21.0*	17.3*
N.E. Portland (N = 43)	7.9	11.3	10.8
Remainder of city (N = 1,015)	6.6	9.4	9.0
Special CPB participant sample (N = 87)	n.a.	n.a.	n.a.

NOTE: The entries in the cells are the proportion of households that had one or more burglaries, corrected to an annual rate, after they began displaying a CPB sticker signifying that they had engraved their property and were participating in the neighborhood watch program. The street-lighting area and the high-priority area were targeted for house-to-house canvassing and neighborhood meetings. Participants from other areas were primarily self-selected.
*Indicates a statistically significant difference using a Z-test of proportions.

nonparticipants in the absence of the program, then the "reduction" in burglaries is about 32%.

The most marked differences were in the two census tracts designated as high-priority areas for the Crime Prevention Bureau and in the Street Lighting Area of Portland. These areas had the highest levels of participation. In the CPB area, 30% of the residents reported that they had attended a meeting, and in the street-lighting area 16% said they had attended.

The information in Table 4.1 was obtained by calculating the percentage of homes with stickers that were burglarized one or more times after the stickers were displayed. The number of months of opportunity for burglaries to occur was calculated (based on the dates when the stickers were displayed), and the rate was then adjusted to a yearly equivalent.

The lower burglary rates for participating households could be attributed to the antiburglary program, but other factors must be considered. First, it is possible that a self-selection process was operative and that persons less apt to be burglarized were more apt to participate in the program. The logic of this is not self-evident, however, and it is just as likely that people who had been burglarized recently were more apt to participate in the program. In addition, the Seattle study found no evidence of a consistent bias introduced by self-selection of participants (Matthews, 1975). Also, this sort of bias is even less likely in Portland within the target areas of the city, because the CPB was actively "recruiting" these individuals.

Another possible confounding factor is that there was some type of socioeconomic variable producing both the higher participation rate and the lower burglary rate. Bivariate and multivariate analyses did not detect any evidence of this, however. Participants within each area tended to have slightly higher educational levels than nonparticipants, but these differences were not statistically significant and there were no significant differences in income. Analysis of the race of participants indicated that they were more likely than nonparticipants to belong to a minority group and that minorities, on the whole, had higher victimization rates. Thus, this variable could not have produced a spurious positive effective.

Effect on Citywide Burglary

No baseline victimization data were available for specific areas within the city. However, the LEAA-sponsored survey of 1972 can be used to estimate the collective benefits of the antiburglary program for city residents as a whole. And official records for these time periods can be adjusted for differences in reporting (as indicated by the victimization surveys) to produce a second pre-post estimate of the overall impact.

In 1974, the total burglary rate for the city was 127 per 1,000 households, if all burglaries at the same house were included in the calculation of the rate. The rate was 96.5, if calculated in terms of the proportion of households with one or more burglaries. The equivalent rates in the 1972 data were 151 (including multiple burglaries at each household), and 115 if using the prevalence measure of households with one or more burglaries. These figures indicate that there may have been a citywide decline in burglaries.

The official burglary statistics obtained from the Portland police department, however, portray a vastly different picture as they show an increase from 68.6 per 1,000 in early 1971 to more than 90 per 1,000 by the end of 1973 and early 1974 (see Table 4.2). The victimization survey data, however, can be used to estimate the proportion of

TABLE 4.2   Effect of CPB Program on Citywide Burglary Rates[a]

Month	Official Burglary Rate per 1,000	Proportion of Burglaries Reported to Police	Corrected Burglary Rate
1971			
January-April	68.6	ND	
May-August	75	.50	150
September-December	80	.50	160
1972			
January-April	74	.50	148
May-August	77	.50	154
September-December	77	ND	
1973			
January-April	66	ND	
May-August	83	.66	123
September-December	100	.79	127
1974			
January-April	90	.67	134
May-June	85	ND	

a. The first column contains the official burglary rate, per 1,000, as recorded by the Portland Police Department. The second column shows the proportion of victimization burglaries reported to the police—according to survey respondents. The final column shows the estimated "true" number of burglaries found by dividing the reported burglaries by the percentage of all burglaries that were reported. These corrected figures are very close to the estimated burglary rates obtained from the survey data, which were 151 per 1,000 in 1971-1972 and 127 per 1,000 in 1973-1974. ND = no data.

all burglaries reported to the police and these figures can then serve as an adjustment for the official statistics.

It is commonly known that victimization data from a single survey covering a 12-month period cannot be used to examine trends or change in the crime rates during that same time period because of telescoping and forgetting effects. However, examination of the proportion of burglaries reported in each month of the series did not reveal any pattern that would suggest telescoping or other kinds of recall biases. The forward records check undertaken later on these same Portland victimization data confirmed the fact that there was no relationship between the time lag from interview to incident and any of the details of the crime, provided that the respondent remembered the incident at all (Schneider, 1978).

With the adjustments in the official statistics to take into account the changes in reporting, the official burglary rates showed a drop between 1971-1972 and 1973-1974. If these figures are reliable, the program not only produced significant private benefits, but also benefited the nonparticipants in terms of a citywide decline in burglary rates.

Effect on Reporting

Persons who participated in one or more of the antiburglary activities (attending a meeting, marking property, or displaying a decal) were considerably more apt to report burglaries to the police than were nonparticipants. In the entire city, the percentage increased from 65% (for persons with no information and no involvement) to 80% and above for participants. The same pattern was apparent within each section selected for special analysis, although the smallest effect was observed in the street-lighting area of northeast Portland. The figures for small areas were based on very small numbers of participants and very few burglaries, but the pattern is consistent enough to justify some confidence in the conclusion.

Recovery Rates

The recovery rate for stolen items was extremely low. Less than 5% of the stolen television sets and auto accessories (such as tape decks) were recovered. It is quite difficult with these data to test the proposition that engraved property is more apt to be recovered than property that is not engraved because of the low frequency with which engraved items were stolen. For example, only six engraved television sets were stolen. The recovery rate for unmarked sets was only 5% and, therefore, 20 engraved televisions would have to be stolen before it would be reasonable to expect that a *single one* would be recovered. There was no evidence that engraved clocks or radios or other small items were more likely to be recovered than unmarked ones.

Bicycles were the only item that seemed to have an improved chance of recovery if they had been engraved. Of the engraved bicycles, 44% were recovered, compared to 15% of the unmarked bicycles. It should be noted that the recovery rate referred to here is measured by whether the stolen item was returned to the owner—regardless of whether it was recovered by the owner personally, by the police, by a neighbor, or by some other person.

Level of Participation

Within the city of Portland, an estimated 27% of the residents engraved some of their household property, 12% displayed an antiburglary sticker, 19% lived in an area where a block meeting (sponsored by the CPB or other group) had been held, and an estimated 10% attended such a meeting. The participation levels were highest in those sections of the city that were designated as high-priority areas. The level of participation in the one area where door-to-door canvassing was used (the CPB area) was almost twice as high as in other parts of the city.

Even without CPB intensive activity, however, a substantial proportion of the citizens apparently were willing to invest their own time and effort to obtain the property markers and stickers.

People were more inclined to engrave their property than to display stickers—only about half of those who engraved property said they put stickers on their doors or windows. Many persons who engraved but had not displayed stickers said they did not have stickers and others said they just had not gotten around to displaying them. In either case, there was a possibility that people did not fully understand the rationale of the program—that the sticker was the initial deterrent.

Private Versus Collective Actions

Four variables were developed to examine whether participation in the CPB program had a more dramatic impact on actions that would benefit the individual household or on those that might have a collective effect. These were (a) protective neighboring, (b) bystander helpfulness, (c) private protection, and (d) the use of antiburglary stickers.

Protective Neighboring. Protective neighboring was defined as the extent to which respondents said that persons in the neighborhood would assist in protecting one another's property. There were four questions related to this issue and an additive scale was formed from them.

The questions used in the scale were as follows:

- Do you think the people who live near here would help watch out for your property when you are not home?
- During the last year have you asked a neighbor to watch your home while you were gone?
- During the last year has a neighbor asked you to watch his or her home while he or she was gone?
- If you were being attacked or robbed, do you think your neighbors would come to your assistance, or what would they do?

One point was given for a positive response to each of the first three questions. For the last question, a point was given if the respondent said that neighbors would come to assist, another point was given if the respondent said that neighbors would call the police, and a point was deducted if the respondent said neighbors would ignore it.

Bystander Helpfulness. Bystander helpfulness was defined as the number of appropriate actions the respondent actually took as a fraction of the total number of opportunities revealed in the survey. Persons who did not have the opportunity to take an appropriate action were excluded from this part of the analysis.

The appropriate actions were found through three questions. One of these asked the respondents whether they had witnessed a crime in progress, another asked whether they had seen or heard something that made them think a crime was being committed, and the third inquired whether they were aware of any burglaries or property theft that had occurred at a neighbor's home while the neighbor was gone. In each instance, if the respondent said that the opportunity had existed, he or she was asked what action was taken. Appropriate actions were scored as one point each and summed to create the index.

Private Protection. An index of private security action was created from questions indicating whether the household had a gun or weapon for use in crime prevention, an alarm, theft insurance, outside lights (excluding decorative lights), or a watchdog.

Antiburglary Stickers. The fourth variable was whether the household had displayed antiburglary stickers.

Multivariate analysis was undertaken for each dependent variable, controlling for length of time in the neighborhood, income, renter or homeowner status, prior victimizations, household density (number of persons per room), age of respondent, and physical upkeep of the block.

The results indicated a substantial impact of the antiburglary program for all four variables in the multivariate analysis (see Table 4.3), although the effect on private protection appeared to be less dramatic. Participation in CPB programs appears to have enhanced both public and private protection activities.

Effect on Distribution of Protection

Two strategies were used to estimate the effect of the program on the distribution of private protection. First, the multiple regression analysis reported in Table 4.3 shows that income and homeowner

TABLE 4.3   Effect of Attending CPB Neighborhood Meetings
on Public and Private Protection Activities

	Protective Neighboring	Bystander Helpfulness	Private Protection	Use of Stickers
Attendance at CPB meeting	.21**	.22**	.06*	.28**
Length of time at residence	.06*	−.08	−.06	.03
Income	.13**	.06	.24**	.04
Homeowner (rather than renter)	.15**	.00	.19**	.04
Prior victimization				
burglary	−.04*	.11*	−.01	.02
violent	.03	.09	−.01	−.03
theft	−.03	.06	.03	.05*
Crowdedness	.01	−.04	−.04	−.01
Age	−.02	.10	−.05	.10*
Upkeep of area	.09**	−.06	−.07*	.01

NOTE: Entries in the cells are the standardized regression coefficients for each independent variable with each dependent variable when the other variables listed in the table were controlled.
*Statistically significant at .05 level, two-tailed test.
**Statistically significant at or beyond .01 level.

status were related to private protection but not to the use of the antiburglary stickers promoted by the program. Similar relationships were found for other indicators of program participation (such as attendance at block meetings), and for other indicators of socioeconomic status (such as education). Race, in fact, was inversely related to program participation in that minorities were more likely to participate. This reveals that the distribution of the protection offered by CPB was free of the type of social-class bias that characterizes privately purchased protection.

A second analysis was undertaken to determine whether this phenomenon existed only for participants who were recruited through the door-to-door canvassing and neighborhood efforts or whether it held for the self-selected participants from throughout the city. A multiple regression analysis was conducted of the relationship between socioeconomic variables and the use of antiburglary stickers for the citywide sample and then compared with a similar analysis of CPB participants.

The results showed that relatively strong relationships, significant beyond the .01 level, existed in the citywide sample between socioeconomic variables and the use of stickers, the engraving of property, and most other types of private protective behavior (Wilson & Schneider, 1976). However, when the analysis was repeated, for the CPB participant sample, the relationships between socieconomic variables and property engraving or use the sticker dropped to zero or were negative and nonsignificant. The implications of these and other findings merit some discussion.

POLICY IMPLICATIONS

There are two important policy issues that should be addressed. One of these is whether the results in this study are strong enough to indicate that a positive effect was, in fact, found or whether the apparent effect was actually produced by some unidentified variable. The second has to do with the issue of public versus private benefits and the choices that the communities have in how they operate a burglary prevention program.

The results of this evaluation are certainly clear: The neighborhood-based burglary reduction program in Portland, Oregon, reduced burglaries for those who participated. In the high crime areas of Portland more than 20% of the homes could expect to be burglarized at least once a year. This was reduced to about 8% for participating households in those areas—a rate approximately the same as for participating households throughout the city.

Critics can identify many shortcomings in the design of this study. There were no surefire methods for ensuring that differences between participating and nonparticipating households were not produced by some type of selection bias or by displacement of crime from participants to nonparticipants. However, a search for some other variable that could be producing a spurious relationship between program participation and the decrease in burglaries did not uncover any possibilities.

There also was no good technique for determining whether or not a citywide burglary reduction occurred (which would indicate a public, as well as private, benefit from the program), but the comparison of victimization surveys showed a decline from 151 per 1,000 to 127 per 1,000 between 1971-1972 and 1973-1974. The official statistics, after correcting for a major increase in the probability of reporting burglaries, also showed a decline of about the same magnitude. Two tests do not, of course, prove the point, but they contribute to the evidence that the program actually reduced burglaries rather than simply distributed them differently among the population. If the decline in participating households had been produced entirely by displacement to nonparticipating households, then there should have been no change in the citywide rates.

The evaluation also suggests that studies that rely on official statistics will not provide valid results because participation clearly increased the probability of a burglary being reported to the police.

Further investigation of the private versus public impact of the Portland program suggested that attendance at the neighborhood meetings was associated rather strongly with several different types of actions designed to benefit the entire neighborhood, not simply the private protection of the individual. Similarly, the results suggest that the usual positive correlations between socioeconomic status and levels of private protection did not occur in the sample of participants who were "recruited" into participation by the program.

Alternatively, and very important, the results indicated that in the sample that contained the self-selected participants, there was a social-class bias: Those attending meetings, engraving their property, and displaying the decals tended to be in the higher socioeconomic groups.

In retrospect, this study did not settle all policy issues, nor did it establish beyond doubt that the Portland program was effective. It certainly did not show that this model would be effective in all cities under all sorts of conditions. The evaluation, however, did show that the bulk of the evidence favored a positive impact and it showed that the focused, door-to-door canvassing, with a heavy emphasis on neighborhood rather than individual protection, was important.

NOTE

1. This chapter is a summary and compilation of the results from many reports about the Portland Crime Prevention Bureau and other Impact Cities programs during the years 1974 through 1977.

REFERENCES

Buchanan, J. M. (1970). *The public finance.* Homewood, IL: Richard D. Irwin.
Ehrlich, I. & Becker, G. S. (1972). Market insurance, self insurance, and self protection. *Journal of Political Economy, 80,* 623-648.
Maltz, M. D. (1972). *Evaluation of crime control programs.* Washington, DC: National Institute of Law Enforcement and Criminal Justice.

Mathews, K. E., Jr., (1974). *Evaluation of first-year results of community crime pre-vention: Burglary reduction*. Seattle: Seattle Law and Justice Planning Office.

Mattick, H. W., Olander, C. K., Baker, C. G., & Schlegel, H. E. (1974). *An evaluation of operation identification as implemented in Illionis*. Chicago: University of Illinois at Chicago Circle, Center for Research in Criminal Justice.

McKenzie, B., & Tullock, G. (1975). *The new world of economics: Explorations in the human experience*. Homewood, IL: Richard D. Irwin.

Schneider, A. L. (1975a). Crime and victimization in Portland: Analysis of trends, 1971-1974 (Tech. Rep.). Portland: Oregon Research Institute.

Schneider, A. L. (1975b). *Evaluation of the Portland neighborhood-based anti-bur-glary program* (Tech. Rep.). Portland: Oregon Research Institute.

Schneider, A. L. (1975c). The 1974 Portland victimization survey: Reporting on proce-dures (Tech. Rep.). Portland: Oregon Research Institute.

Schneider, A. L. (1977). *Citizen response to environmental crime prevention programs*. Paper prepared for the National Institute of Justice.

Schneider, A. L. (1978, December). *The Portland forward records check of crime vic-tims*. Washington, DC: Government Printing Office.

Shoup, C. S. (1976). Standards for distributing a free governmental service: Crime pre-vention. In L. R. McPheters & W. B. Stronge (Eds.), *The economics of crime and law enforcement*. Springfield, IL: Charles C Thomas.

Weicher, J. C. (1976). The allocation of police protection by income class. In L. R. McPheters & W. B. Stronge (Eds.), *The economics of crime and law enforcement*. Springfield, IL: Charles C Thomas.

Wilson, L. A., & Schneider, A. L. (1976). *Investigating the efficacy and equity of public initiatives in the provision of private safety*. Paper presented at the annual meetings of the Western Political Science Association.

Chapter 5

A THREE-PRONGED EFFORT TO REDUCE CRIME AND FEAR OF CRIME
The Hartford Experiment

F L O Y D J. F O W L E R, J r.
T H O M A S W. M A N G I O N E

OVERVIEW OF THE PROJECT

Asylum Hill is a residential area near the business and insurance centers of Hartford, Connecticut. In the early part of the 1970s this attractive area, consisting primarily of low-rise buildings and multiunit frame structures, was in danger of becoming an undesirable neighborhood. Landlords were reluctant to maintain the housing stock. Long-time residents were leaving. Major factors in this incipient decline were thought to be rising rates of robbery and burglary and the fear they engendered.

In 1973, an interdisciplinary team of specialists began an assessment of the nature of crime in Asylum Hill and the factors that contributed to it. An innovative aspect of their charge from the National Institute of Law Enforcement and Criminal Justice (NILECJ), now the National Institute of Justice (NIJ), was to give special attention to the way that the physical environment contributed to crime, either by aiding offenders or by making the task of protection more difficult for police and residents.

From this analysis emerged a plan to reduce crime and fear in the northern half of the area, North Asylum Hill, where crime was a greater problem than in the southern part of the neighborhood. The plan outlined an integrated, three-pronged approach to reducing criminal opportunities. It included proposals for changing the physical environment, in addition to changes in the delivery of police services and efforts to organize residents to improve their neighborhood.

Community organization efforts began in the fall of 1974. Police reorganization began early in 1975. Work was begun in the summer of 1976 on the physical environment part of the program, consisting primarily of changes in the traffic flow on streets of North Asylum Hill, with the final construction completed in November 1976. The effect of the program on the neighborhood, with a focus on crime and fear, was evaluated in 1977 and again in 1979. This chapter describes the findings of these evaluations.

A real strength of the project was the extensive data collected in order to permit evaluation of the impact of the program. The most important data were from household surveys of Asylum Hill residents in 1973, 1975, and the spring of 1976 (which we combined to provide preprogram values), and in 1977, and 1979. Parallel surveys were carried out in the rest of Hartford to provide control data. Those surveys provided the main measures of such key issues as crime rates, fear of crime, and informal social control. In addition, systematic physical design observations, pedestrian and traffic counts, questionnaires completed by police officers, police record data, and interviews with police and community leaders were collected both before and after the program was implemented. Data from these sources were used in planning the program and in monitoring what actually happened.

BACKGROUND OF THE PROJECT

The idea that a neighborhood crime control effort must be multifaceted and should include attention to the physical layout of a neighborhood and how it is used emerged from a variety of sources. Although prior thoughts about crime control had largely focused on police and, to a lesser extent, citizen action, the limits of what police and citizens could do had begun to be recognized in 1973. Neither police action nor citizen action alone had been shown able to reduce crime rates without displacement, or to be effective over an extended period of time. Hence one simple impetus for the Hartford project was a felt need for a new and better strategy for attacking crime.

Four research efforts were the primary sources of insight about the role of the physical environment in crime. Jacobs (1961) observed that certain neighborhoods were relatively immune to crime, despite being located in highly urban settings where crime rates were high in surrounding neighborhoods. Her conclusion was that two factors contributed to this situation. First, two such neighborhoods had commercial and residential properties mixed together, producing a considerable number of people on the streets and opportunities for surveillance. Second, the residents cared about the quality of their neighborhoods and watched out for one another.

Angel (1968) reached a related set of conclusions regarding the role of the physical environment in street crime. His concept of "critical density" was essentially that use of space should be organized so that there were quite a few people on the most used streets. His contention was that robbery targets were created when there were streets that had only a small number of people using them—enough to provide targets without too much waiting, but not enough to serve as a deterrent to criminals.

Newman's work (1972) focused on residential crime in the public housing environment. He found that crimes in public housing projects occurred in places that could not be observed. He also found that if buildings and spaces were structured to increase the number of doorways and other spaces that could be observed easily from windows and public spaces, the amount of crime was reduced.

Repetto (1974) looked at residential crimes in 17 neighborhoods. Although proximity to offender populations was an important predictor of crime rates, like Newman, he found that opportunities for surveillance made a difference; like Jacobs, he found evidence that neighborhood cohesion had a deterrent effect on crime.

This set of observations and conclusions was the basis of the ideas that the Hartford project team brought into the initial problem analysis and planning phases of its work. Since then, the implications of these ideas have been more fully developed and articulated than they were in 1973.

Stated abstractly, the approach focuses on the interaction between human behavior and the (physically) built environment. It was hypothesized that the *proper design and effective use* of the built environment can lead to a reduction in crime and fear. It is the combination of proper design and effective use that leads to a synergistic outcome, in which the combination of the parts is more effective than any of the parts alone (see Tien, 1975).

More concretely, criminals operate in an environment that includes police, citizens, and a physical environment. All three affect criminal opportunities. The total set of relationships among offenders, the police, and citizens, structured by the physical environment, should be considered in analyzing the nature of crime and in trying to reduce it. Some of these relationships are implicit in the research described above and may be outlined briefly as follows:

(1) *The physical environment* directly affects the movement of offenders by providing places where they can be concealed or be inconspicuous, as well as defining escape routes.

(2) *Offenders* are deterred by the physical proximity of *police*. However, given typical police resources, police must choose either frequent presence in a few areas or less frequent presence over a wider area.

(3) *Offenders* are deterred by *citizens* who use the spaces in their neighborhoods, thereby exercising surveillance, and who exercise control over who uses the neighborhood, thereby making extended waiting for an opportunity less comfortable.

(4) The *physical environment* affects the task of *police* to the extent that opportunities for crime are structured. To the extent that there are fewer places where offenders may operate freely, because of environmental effects on either offenders or citizens, the task of police patrol is made easier. The more familiar police are with the distribution of crime over an area, the more effectively they can allocate patrol resources.

(5) The *physical environment* affects *citizens'* ability to reduce criminal opportunities in several ways. To the extent that physical surveillance is easy, the citizens' ability to exercise surveillance is improved. To the extent that the environment encourages residents to use their neighborhood, their opportunities for surveillance are increased. In addition, the amount of social interaction among neighbors is affected by the arrangement of housing spaces. A high degree of interaction should increase residents' ability to distinguish between neighbors and strangers. It may increase the likelihood that residents will concern themselves with criminal opportunities, as interaction often leads to increased cohesion. Finally, the physical appearance of the neighborhood may affect the likelihood that residents will care about, or take pride in, what happens in their neighborhood.

(6) *Police* and *citizens* can each facilitate the other's success in opportunity reduction. Citizens can communicate to police places or events where police are needed. In turn, if police are aware of citizens' fears and concerns, they can be responsive in ways that may reduce fear and increase citizens' use of the neighborhood.

Each of the above points could be elaborated extensively. However, the last two begin to give the flavor of what is meant by synergism: the idea that each relationship, if it is improved, can affect criminal opportunities directly and, in addition, may produce other results that, in turn, may further reduce opportunities. The interdependence described means that to neglect the police, or citizens, or the physical environment, will limit the potential of any program to reduce criminal opportunities.

PROGRAM DESCRIPTION

Before 1973, no approach combining police, citizens, and the physical environment had been applied to an existing residential neighborhood. However, the failures of more limited approaches, together with the untested but persuasive nature of the rationale outlined above, suggested the need for an empirical test of its applicability and utility.

Hartford, Connecticut, was chosen as the site for this test for three reasons. First, there were neighborhoods in Hartford similar to those in many cities where crime is a major problem. It seemed essential to test the approach in the kind of areas where extensive crime control efforts were most needed and most likely to be attempted. Second, there existed a local organization that was ideal to carry out such an experiment—the Hartford Institute of Criminal and Social Justice. As a nonprofit institute outside the city government, with strong working relationships with city officials, the police department, and the business community, it offered a potential that did not exist in many cities for successfully coordinating and implementing a complex experiment. Third, the project required independent funding of the proposed crime control program, including any physical design changes required. NILECJ could fund only the planning and evaluation components of the experiment. In Hartford, there was an expressed willingness on the part of private and public interests to make capital investments in an existing neighborhood, if a feasible and convincing plan could be developed.

Planning the Program

In 1973, an interdisciplinary team was assembled. It included experts in urban design and land-use planning, as well as criminological, police, and research experts. Using existing police record data, data from a sample survey of residents, site analysis, and the results of interviews with offenders, police officials and other knowledgeable people, this team assembled a composite picture of crime and fear in the target areas. The principal focus of the analysis was the way the

neighborhood environment contributed to the creation of criminal opportunities. The analysis also included an assessment of the roles, current and potential, of citizens and police in opportunity reduction.

The area chosen as a target was Asylum Hill, a residential area a
few blocks from the central business district of Hartford. The 5,000
residents lived mainly in low-rise apartment houses and some two- and
three-family houses. The area was racially mixed and consisted largely
of single residents, young and old. It had a high rate of transience and
street crime.

Briefly, the analysis concluded that this neighborhood had become
nonresidential in character because of the large amount of vehicular
and pedestrian traffic that passed through each day. Residents
avoided their streets and yards, did not know their neighbors, and
could not exercise any control over who used their neighborhood or
for what purpose. Offenders could comfortably wander residential
streets in such an environment. Although the composition of the
neighborhood and the nature of the housing contributed to this situation, the extensive use of the neighborhood by outsiders was considered to be an important contributing factor—and one that could be
changed.

The physical design team proposed the following steps:

(1) to restrict vehicular traffic through the neighborhood and to
     channel most remaining through traffic onto two major streets
     within the neighborhood; and
(2) to define visually the boundaries of the neighborhood and
     subparts of the neighborhood.

These changes were to be realized by creating cul-de-sacs at a few
critical intersections, narrowing the entrances to some streets, and
making other streets one-way. The combination of these changes,
which could be accomplished in a reasonably short period of time at a
modest cost, was intended to make the neighborhood more residential—to make it a place that belonged more to the residents—so they
would feel a part of it and take care of it.

The Hartford police were very well regarded by Asylum Hill
residents. Their pattern of rotating assignments within a centralized
department, however, did not foster intimate knowledge in any given
officer of a neighborhood, its physical environment, the patterns of
crime, or the residents and their concerns.

Therefore, the plan proposed that a decentralized team of police be
assigned permanently to the area. It was felt that police could be more

effective in opportunity reduction if they were familiar with the neighborhood. This also would provide an opportunity for increased communication between citizens and police so that each could support the efforts of the other more effectively. Decisions about policies and procedures would more likely reflect neighborhood priorities.

It was felt that an increased citizen role in opportunity reduction would result from the physical changes and, perhaps, from closer relationships with the police as well. However, an important part of the program entailed encouraging existing community organizations and stimulating the development of others. Community organizations were needed to enable citizens to participate in the planning and implementation of the physical changes. Their approval of the plans was required before the physical improvements could be funded. In addition, such groups provided a mechanism for establishing a Police Advisory Committee, through which citizens and police could discuss concerns, problems, and priorities. Finally, it was thought that such groups might, on their own, initiate activities directly related to crime and fear or to improving the neighborhood in general.

The purpose of the community organization component of the program was not simply or primarily to mobilize citizens to fight crime. Instead, this component was seen as an essential ingredient to implementing all parts of the program. Moreover, the goal of increased citizen involvement in crime reduction was expected to be achieved through the combined efforts of the physical changes, the reorganization of police, and the work of the community groups.

The Program Implementation

Community organization work began in the fall of 1974. At that time, there was one existing resident organization serving the northern part of the neighborhood. Over a period of six months, two more organizations serving other parts of Asylum Hill were formed.

The initial agenda for community meetings was the way the physical environment affected the neighborhood and how changes might improve the neighborhood as a place to live. Later, a Police Advisory Committee was formed that included representatives of the three major community groups. Over time, the groups initiated block watch programs, recreational programs for youth, and improvements in a large neighborhood park, and worked with others in Hartford to try to stabilize the housing situation in Asylum Hill.

The Hartford Police Department created a district that included Asylum Hill early in 1975. Within the district, two teams were created, one of which was designated to serve Asylum Hill. A group of officers was permanently assigned to the area and provided most of the police service. There was a moderate amount of command autonomy for the team leader. A good relationship between the team leader and the Police Advisory Committee developed and led to providing police services that clearly reflected citizen priorities.

The physical design plan underwent a long period of review during which a number of details were modified. Approval was difficult to obtain for several reasons. It was the most radically innovative component in that it proposed closing off several streets to through traffic. The logical connection between closing streets and crime reduction is a subtle one, more so than that between police or citizen efforts and crime reduction, and is, therefore, more difficult to communicate. The proposed street closings necessarily affected more people directly than the other two program components, including residents and those with businesses on the streets to be closed, city departments providing services in the area, and political officials of the city. Therefore, more people had to be consulted and convinced of the value of the changes.

Eventually a plan was approved that entailed 11 changes in the public streets, all in the northern half of the neighborhood. Two key east-west streets were closed to through traffic. A number of other streets were narrowed at intersections—one was made one-way. One north-south street and one east-west street were left open to carry traffic not routed around the neighborhood. The goal was to make most of the streets in the neighborhood of use primarily to residents. Some of the street narrowings were also intended to give definition to neighborhood boundaries. The intersection treatments were designed to be attractive—planters and areas for residents use were included. Work began in June 1976. The majority of the street closings were finished in the summer of 1976; all were completed by November 1976.

Changes in the Program
from 1977 Through 1979

For the most part, the physical design treatment remained stable from its initial implementation through 1979. One of its most direct consequences was the impact on traffic in the neighborhood. Vehicular traffic through the neighborhood dipped markedly in the first year and continued to decline through 1979.

The police program and the community program did not remain stable during the three-year period after implementation. Police initially developed good relationships within the neighborhood, and they reported improved feelings about the neighborhood. In response to residents' requests, they launched efforts to control loitering men and prostitutes, who had been continuing neighborhood irritants. Most striking, arrests for burglary and robbery increased markedly by 1977.

There was a significant erosion of the police team component of the program between 1977 and 1979. Police officers cited a reduction in personnel as the principal problem. For whatever reason, officers often were assigned to work districts other than their "home" district. The team leader in Asylum Hill seldom attended Police Advisory Committee meetings. There were virtually no special police activities, beyond patrol and calls for service, as there had been in 1975 through 1977. The district leaders generally spent less time in the district field offices than before and more time at the central headquarters.

The police officers, in their questionnaire responses, reported a decline in their effectiveness in responding to calls for service and in clearing cases. A concrete indication of this was a sharp drop in the number of arrests of offenders committing crimes in Asylum Hill. Arrests had more than doubled in the first year of the police team. Arrests in 1979, however, were only about 60% of those in 1977, or only slightly higher than before the program began.

The community organization component of the program also changed between 1977 and 1979. In 1977, the efforts of the three organizations in North Asylum Hill relied entirely on voluntarism. A good deal of effort was devoted to planning and implementing the street changes and working with the police. There was also an active block watch program at some periods of the year, as well as a park clean-up effort.

By 1979, there had been a notable shift in the nature of the community organization in Asylum Hill. One group was nearly inactive. The block watch program, while still extant, was having increased difficulties recruiting volunteers. On the other hand, there had been two major positive events in the area. First, the Police Advisory Committee, in conjunction with that of another district, applied for and was granted significant funding for five different anticrime programs. These programs together composed the Community Crime Prevention Program (CCPP). There was staff for the CCPP that was paid for by the grant. Second, there was an infusion of new money for housing rehabilitation. Neighborhood residents worked with leaders from banks and insurance companies to get public and private monies to help improve the housing stock in Asylum Hill. They also called city inspectors regarding houses that were not maintained and exerted influence on the way buildings were used.

In addition, it is important to note that the Police Advisory Committee was as strong, or stronger, in 1979 as it was in 1977. However, its strength was no longer exerted solely through the neighborhood team police leader. Rather, it was able to exert political influence directly on central police headquarters and on other appropriate agencies in city government.

Ideally, for evaluation purposes, the program and other relevant aspects of the community should remain stable. It is not surprising, however, that in a neighborhood-scale experiment there were salient changes in the program. These changes obviously must be considered when attempting to assess the effects of the program.

EVALUATION RESULTS

If the changes made in the neighborhood were successful, we expected to find improvements in three groups of indicators: Informal social control would be increased within the neighborhood, burglary and robbery rates would be lower, and fear of these crimes would have decreased.

In Tables 5.1-5.3, we use pooled data from 1973, 1975, and, in some cases, the spring of 1976 to provide preprogram values. Although some activities began earlier, we considered the program "in place" in the fall of 1976, when the street changes were completed.

Informal Social Control

Changes in measures related to informal control were modest after one year of program implementation, but after two more years had passed almost every relevant indicator showed significant increases. Residents used their neighborhood more, walked more often both during the day and evening hours, used the nearby park more often, and spent more days per week outside in front of their homes (see Table 5.1).

One important precursor to exercising informal social control is knowing who belongs in a neighborhood and who does not. The program planners hoped to improve stranger recognition in two ways. First, if people used the streets more, they were more likely to become familiar with their neighbors. Second, to the extent that congestion was reduced, it would be easier to become familiar with people who belonged in the neighborhood. In 1979, ease of stranger recognition had increased significantly—35%—compared to preprogram levels—25% (see Table 5.1).

Territoriality is a concept introduced by Newman (1972). His idea is that there are some spaces, pieces of turf, for which individuals take responsibility, and that they will supervise and control. In some areas, people feel responsible for only small spaces—for instance, their own housing units and spaces quite adjacent to them. In order to have informal social control operating effectively at a neighborhood level, residents must feel responsibility for larger spaces. To the extent that residents will take control of the sidewalks in front of their homes, of their neighbors' yards, of the parking lots near their buildings, in short, for areas that do not strictly belong to them but rather belong to the neighborhood, the potential for effectively controlling the area is markedly increased.

There were two measures directly related to the extent to which residents were taking responsibility for, or were concerned about, what went on in their neighborhood and what happened to their neighbors. One question in the survey asked whether or not people had made arrangements with neighbors to look out for one another's houses. They were also asked whether these were regular arrangements or occurred only on special occasions. In 1977, there was a significant increase over preprogram figures in the rate at which there were routine arrangements between North Asylum Hill residents to look out for one another's homes. This significant increase was maintained in 1979 (see Table 5.1).

A second measure asked whether or not respondents had observed any suspicious event in their neighborhood in the year preceding the interview. If so, they were asked if they had done anything about it. Responses were coded into three main categories: those who essentially did nothing or ignored it; those who intervened directly, either by asking the person what he or she was doing or by calling a neighbor; and those who called the police. There is probably no measure that more directly captures the concept of "territoriality" than the rate of intervention.

There was no apparent change in the rate at which "territorial" behavior was reported between 1976 and 1977. However, the 1979 interviews revealed a significant increase in the rate at which respondents reported having intervened in a suspicious event in their

TABLE 5.1   Use of the Neighborhood and Territoriality
in North Asylum Hill, 1975-1979

	Year		
	Preprogram[a] (N = 167)	1977 (N = 232)	1979 (N = 218)
Use of neighborhood			
Walk in the neighborhood during the day at least several times per week.[b]	53	70	64*
Walk in neighborhood at night at least several times per week.[b]	22	18	27**
Like to use nearby park.[b]	26	37*	36*
Average number of days per week outside of residents' homes'	1.7	1.6	2.2**
Territoriality			
Have regular arrangements with neighbors to watch each other's houses.[b]	16	26*	29*
Easy to recognize a stranger.[b]	25	32	35*
Have intervened in a suspicious situation in neighborhood.[b]	21	20	30**

a. Combination of data from 1973, 1975, and 1976.
b. In percentages.
*Significantly different from preprogram levels.
**Significantly different from 1977 levels.

neighborhood (see Table 5.1). In this case, though, there was also a parallel change in the rest of the city for which we have no explanation.

Obviously, informal social control of a neighborhood is a two-way street. Not only were we concerned about the extent to which residents reported doing constructive things, we were also interested in the way they viewed their neighbors as resources with respect to neighborhood crime control. A number of questions were asked that related to the general topic of the way North Asylum Hill residents felt about their neighbors. To simplify the analysis, as well as to produce a more reliable indicator of residents' feelings, seven items were combined into a single index. The index ranged from a low of 1.0 to a high, positive view of 5.0.

When the program was evaluated in 1977, the index of resident perceptions of "neighbors as a resource" had not changed from preprogram levels, 2.85 to 2.88. However, between 1977 and 1979, there was a statistically significant increase in the way North Asylum Hill residents saw their neighbors in a helping role, 2.88 to 3.18.

Another component in developing informal social control in a neighborhood is the degree of resident confidence in the area. Unless people feel that some good can come from their efforts and that problems can be solved, they are unlikely to persist indefinitely. Before and after the programs, residents were asked whether they thought their neighborhood would get better, get worse, or stay about the same in the upcoming five years. Again we saw a pattern in which a significant shift in opinion came between 1977 and 1979. Before the program was instituted, only 26% thought the neighborhood could get better. In 1979, 57%, more than a twofold increase, thought the neighborhood would get better. A similar pattern was observed for the question asking whether or not the neighborhood had gotten better in the past year. Only 16% thought it had gotten better before the program; in 1979, 39% thought it had improved.

Burglary and Robbery Rates

Burglary is the crime of breaking and entering with intent to commit a felony, most often grand larceny or theft. For some accounting purposes, "attempted burglaries" are grouped with burglaries. Attempted burglaries are instances in which there is evidence of effort to enter a home illegally, but entry is not successful, and, of course, nothing is taken. Because of the difficulty of knowing when such events actually occur, and hence the unreliability of reporting, attempted burglaries were not included in our analysis.[1]

One of the most fundamental questions to be answered in this project was whether or not the rate of burglary victimization was different in North Asylum Hill than it would have been if the program had not been implemented. We calculated the proportionate change based on citywide trends and applied this trend to the rates in North Asylum Hill to get an expected rate. In 1977, the burglary rate was much better than expected. The expected burglary rate in North Asylum Hill in 1977, adjusting for the experience in the rest of Hartford, was more than 22 burglaries per 100 households (see Table 5.2). The observed burglary rate in North Asylum Hill in 1977 was fewer than 11 per 100 households, a statistically significant reduction.

However, in 1979 burglary rates had increased markedly. Between 1977 and 1979 burglary victimization rates for the rest of Hartford declined. An adjustment for the city experience yields an expected

TABLE 5.2 North Asylum Hill Crime Rates, Observed and Expected

Type by Year	Crime Rates per 100 Households	
	Burglary	Robbery/ Purse-Snatching
Preprogram rate	17.5	4.0
Observed rate, 1976-1977	10.6	4.2
Expected[a] rate, 1976-1977	22.4	5.9
Significance of difference[b] observed-expected, 1976-1977	.01	.13
Observed rate, 1978-1979	19.3	6.6
Expected[a] rate, 1978-1979	19.1	5.1
Significance of difference[b] observed-expected, 1978-1979	NS[c]	NS[c]

a. Expected calculated by applying citywide trend to observed value in preceding time period.
b. Based on one-tailed t-test. Usual   probability required for statistical confidence is .05 or lower.
c. Significance levels that exceed .20 are reported as NS.

burglary rate in North Asylum Hill of 19 burglaries per 100 households for 1979. The observed rate in North Asylum Hill was exactly the expected rate of 19 burglaries per 100 households.

Robbery is the crime of taking something from someone by force or threat of force. Purse-snatching is akin to robbery in that the victim is present and some force is used. The line between robbery and purse-snatching depends on the amount of force used to grab the purse and on the amount of confrontation between the victim and the offender. Because of the basic similarity of the two crimes, we chose to combine these two street crimes in our analysis.

In 1977, the observed robbery/purse-snatching rate was lower than would have been expected, and this difference approaches the standard level of statistical significance. In 1979, the observed rate for robbery/purse-snatching in North Asylum Hill was not different from the level one would have predicted without the program.

Perceptions and Fear of Crime

Fear, in some ways, is a worse problem than crime. While victims suffer the direct consequences of crime when it happens, fear can affect the quality of life of victims and nonvictims over an indefinite period of time.

Measures of fear are presented in two general groups. One group deals with personal concerns about crime. People were asked how worried they were about various crimes occurring to them in different situations, how safe they felt in different situations, and how likely they felt they were to be victims of various crimes. These measures turned out to be highly intercorrelated. They were combined into two indices, one of which combined all the items with concerns about burglary, which we labeled "fear of burglary," and another that combined items related to street crime, which we labeled "fear of robbery."

A second set of items uses resident ratings of the extent to which various crimes are a "problem," using the neighborhood, rather than the person's own concerns, as a referent. Again, an index was constructed combining the ratings of a number of different crime problems into a single measure, labeled "crime problem rating." In addition, the items rating burglary and robbery as problems were analyzed separately, as were the answers to a question about whether crime was going up, going down, or staying about the same in the neighborhood. The same approach to modeling expected values was used as in the case of crime rates.

Table 5.3 presents the values of the index of fear of burglary for North Asylum Hill. If one looks at the data for North Asylum Hill alone, the value of the index was extremely constant during the experimental period. However, in the rest of Hartford there was a steady increase in the index since the preprogram period. As a result, based on the experience in the rest of Hartford, we would have expected a rise in fear of burglary in North Asylum Hill. Thus, although there was not a decline in the fear of burglary in North Asylum Hill, in the context of what was happening in the rest of Hartford one must conclude that the responses to this index were significantly lower in 1979 than would have been expected from the citywide trend, and almost significantly lower in 1977.

Table 5.3 also presents the index of fear of robbery. The findings were almost identical to those presented above. The value of the index was almost constant across the years in North Asylum Hill. However, in the rest of Hartford there was a steady increase in fear of robbery since the preprogram period. When we calculated the values expected in North Asylum Hill by applying the citywide trend, we found that fear of robbery in 1977 was lower than expected, approaching statistical significance. The 1979 figure was significantly lower than we would have expected.

Respondents were asked whether they considered burglary to be a "big problem, some problem, or almost no problem" in their neighborhood. There was a marked shift in the rate at which North

TABLE 5.3 North Asylum Hill Fear Levels, Observed and Expected

Type by Year	Mean Fear of Crime	
	Burglary	Robbery/ Purse-Snatching
Preprogram	2.29	2.48
Observed, 1977	2.30	2.48
Expected,[a] 1977	2.37	2.56
Significance of difference[b] observed-expected, 1977	.15	.10
Observed, 1979	2.32	2.50
Expected,[a] 1979	2.44	2.64
Significance of difference[b] observed-expected, 1979	.02	.01

a. Expected calculated by applying citywide trend to observed value in preceding time period.
b. Based on one-tailed t-test. Usual probability required for statistical confidence is .05 or lower.

Asylum Hill residents considered burglary to be a problem after the experimental program was implemented. In this case, a reduction from preprogram values was observed in 1977 that was almost statistically significant (40% compared to 31%); an even more significant reduction was observed in 1979 (down to 26%).

Also, we asked about the extent to which robbery was considered to be a problem in the neighborhood. The findings were similar to what we observed with respect to fear of robbery. There was no absolute change in the rate at which respondents considered robbery to be a problem in North Asylum Hill. Once again, though, the data can be interpreted in the context of what was going on throughout the city. In the rest of Hartford, there was an increase in the rate at which robbery was considered a problem between 1977 and 1979. When one adjusts for that fact, the observed rating in North Asylum Hill in 1979 was significantly lower than we would have expected.

Finally, we asked whether residents thought crime was going up, staying about the same, or going down in their neighborhood. There was an absolute improvement in resident perceptions in North Asylum Hill. The striking change occurred between 1977 and 1979 (17% compared to 32%). Although the responses from people throughout the city of Hartford also improved slightly in the extent to which they saw crime going down, adjusting for the citywide experience does not diminish the statistical significance of the change observed in North Asylum Hill. Very clearly, North Asylum Hill residents were more likely to see crime as declining than one would have expected from preprogram responses and from the experience in the rest of Hartford.

CONCLUSIONS AND IMPLICATIONS

The experimental program evaluated in this project has the potential to contribute to our understanding of community crime prevention issues in a variety of ways. In this closing section, the main conclusions and implications are summarized and discussed.

Certainly one of the most significant results of this evaluation is the documentation of change in the measures thought to be related to informal social control and territoriality. The combination of people using the streets more, recognizing strangers more easily, taking more initiative, and feeling more confident that their neighbors were a resource against crime adds up to "territoriality" or "informal social control." These measures showed significant improvements between 1977 and 1979 in North Asylum Hill.

A critical question is the extent to which one can attribute these changes to the "program." We cannot prove in a statistical sense that the program caused the changes. There was only a single experiment. The experiment took place not in a vacuum, but in an ongoing neighborhood within a city over several years, with a variety of events going on around it. However, there are several important points that can be made.

This program was an effort to solve some problems that were thought to exist in North Asylum Hill. Essentially, catalytic mechanisms were established. These mechanisms included establishing several community organizations, a neighborhood police team, and an environment (a neighborhood that was less thoroughly inundated with outside traffic) that would enhance the likelihood that problem solving would occur. The program was not intended as the solution to problems but as the means to solve problems. The solutions to problems, if they occurred, would emerge from the actions of police and residents within the neighborhood environment over a period of time.

The exact role of the program in strengthening territoriality and informal social control is hard to document. Two concrete links can be established. First, introduction of the street changes was associated with decreased traffic and increased use of the neighborhood by residents. It also corresponded with increases in stranger recognition and an increased likelihood of informal arrangements to watch houses. Second, the neighborhood organizations involved more people in neighborhood problems in 1979 than in any previous year, and those organizations were judged to be more effective than in the past.

Certainly events outside the program occurred that helped produce progress. Some middle-class suburban people moved into the neighborhood and provided leadership. The rising prices of housing in the neighborhood made it possible to fix up and rehabilitate housing that at former levels could not have been restored. There probably was good fortune in the leadership that was available to the neighborhood police team in its first years of operation. The relationship with the police provided neighborhood leaders with a real problem-solving capability early in the program when, perhaps, the capabilities of the community groups themselves to solve problems were not as great.

On the other side, political difficulties that delayed implementation of the physical changes detracted from program momentum and undoubtedly reduced the likelihood of success. There was continual vocal opposition to the program from businesspeople and a few residents. The police department had problems throughout, both with internal political problems and with resources. The transient nature of the neighborhood certainly made it a difficult one for a program such as this.

Altogether, this experiment seems to have been neither distinctively blessed nor distinctively disadvantaged. The idea that the neighborhood might have become stronger in the ways observed without the program is plausible. However, it seems likely that the program as a whole, and particularly the street changes, had a critical role to play.

There is no doubt that the people in North Asylum Hill were significantly less fearful and concerned about crime after the program was implemented than one would have expected given the trends in the rest of the city. This finding was absolutely clear in the 1979 data for all relevant measures.

The patterns of fear observed in North Asylum Hill are consistent with the notion that the degree of social control and organization in a neighborhood and the degree of fear and concern about crime are connected (Lewis, Szoc, Salem, & Levin, 1980; Skogan & Maxfield, 1981). When people see incivilities, when they feel that there is no help available, then the crime that exists in the neighborhood is problematic for them, and they are frightened. When they see their neighbors as a resource against crime, when they see police, when the incivilities such as drunken men and teenagers hanging out are at a minimum or under control, the problems of crime seem less severe and people are less afraid.

In North Asylum Hill the incivilities did not improve; they may have gotten worse. The visibility of police remained unchanged. However, there was a clear and significant increase in the extent to which North Asylum Hill residents saw themselves and their neighbors banding together to control the neighborhood and to control crime in the neighborhood. It seems hard to believe these changes did not play a role in the amelioration of the fears and concerns about robbery and burglary. Moreover, the fact that the positive results regarding fear occurred in the face of a rising crime rate, and possibly some increase in apparent incivilities, makes the importance of the neighborhood's cohesion for determining fear levels take on added significance.

And what about crime? The victimization data clearly show that burglary dropped significantly below its expected levels immediately after the program was implemented, but then rose significantly during the following two years. The data are slightly less clear with respect to robbery/purse-snatching, but probably the same general pattern applies to that crime as well.

If that indeed is what happened to those crimes, there are several conclusions that follow. First, it means that a program such as the one implemented in Hartford can affect the rate of crime in a neighborhood. This is a very important conclusion, and one that has rarely been demonstrated.

Second, the fact that the victimization patterns do not correspond very well with our measures of fear and concerns about these crimes is one more piece of evidence that fear of crime and the actual prevalence of crime are not necessarily closely related.

Third, the most critical aspect of the data is that burglary and robbery apparently went up between 1977 and 1979 at the same time that various measures of informal social control and territoriality were indicating a significant improvement. There are at least two explanations for the increase in crime. First, there is reason to believe that the pressure from offenders on the area increased between 1977 and 1979. Second, there seems to be little doubt that the effectiveness of police service in the area peaked in 1977, then declined in the subsequent two years.

Police success in arresting people for burglary and robbery declined after 1977. Recent research by Wilson and Boland (1979) suggests that aggressive arrest policies may deter crime. In addition to making arrests, the police team also attended to the drunks and loitering men. Although they did not feel they "solved" these problems, they certainly attempted to control them. Such efforts were among the casualties of reduced police service in Asylum Hill. It is quite plausible that the reduction in police service is the key explanation for reduced arrests, for perceptions of a greater problem with loitering, drinking men, and for the increased crime rates of 1979.

Perhaps the best way to fit the pieces together is the following: What was needed and established in North Asylum Hill was some problem-solving capabilities that were not there before. Day-to-day supervision of neighborhood activities is necessarily an ongoing, informal process. However, for some problems—such as obtaining housing financing, cleaning up the park, or mobilizing police efforts—some kind of residents' organization is needed. Moreover, there are some problems with which only the police can deal effectively. Arresting criminals, dispersing groups of men, and controlling public drinking are among these.

In 1977, the police component of the program was working well, and the citizen efforts—formal and informal—were gaining strength. In 1979, the police were no longer effective neighborhood problem solvers in their sphere, but the residents were doing a better job than ever before. One could surmise that what the residents were doing was helpful to reducing fear levels, but that the police component was essential to affecting crime rates. We also would expect that had the police component remained strong in 1979, there would have been a continued reduction in crime rates and more dramatic positive effects on fear.

One particularly important conclusion is clearly supported by these data: Informal social control by itself is not enough to reduce burglary and robbery/purse-snatching in a neighborhood such as Asylum Hill. Despite the striking improvements in these respects observed in North Asylum Hill, some set of additional factors worked to create an increase in burglaries and robberies.

Finally, we need to address the question of whether or not this is a good kind of program for other communities to attempt to implement. In our view, however, that is the wrong question to ask. In essence, this experiment should not be exported *in toto* to some other community. Rather, it was a project in which neighborhood problems were analyzed and solutions to those problems that were feasible in the particular context were designed and implemented. A crime control program such as this must be custom fit to a particular set of circumstances. What one would want to derive from the Hartford project is not a program design, but rather an approach to problem analysis and strategies to affect them. This approach would incorporate the following observations:

(1) Measures of informal social control and territoriality can change significantly over time in response to a program such as this.

(2) There apparently is an intimate relationship between people's fears and concerns about crime and the degree of social organization and informal social control in a neighborhood.

Helping residents control a neighborhood seems to be a critical and effective way to reduce fear of crime.

(3) Burglary rates and robbery rates increased significantly despite increased social control. Police efforts to arrest offenders and control incivilities appeared to play a role in deterring crime. Maintaining social order is not always a popular role for the police, but it may be more important than previously appreciated in reducing crime rates.

(4) Victimization rates or objective risks of crime have little relationship to resident concerns and fears. The latter are much more closely tied to people's perceptions of the conditions of the neighborhood.

(5) Change in the physical environment can be an important lever for producing significant changes in the character of a neighborhood. Although the street changes were not a sufficient condition, there can be little doubt that they played a necessary and crucial role in catalyzing the improvements that were observed.

NOTE

1. For our analysis of crime rates, we rely only on the victimization experiences reported by survey respondents. Because of various internal changes in the Hartford Police Department, we did not feel that the incidence of burglaries from police records constituted a reliable indicator of the rate at which these crimes occurred.

REFERENCES

Angel, S. (1968). *Discouraging crime through city planning.* Berkeley: University of California Press.

Fowler, F. J., Jr., & Mangione, T. W. (1982). *Neighborhood crime, fear and social control: A second look at the Hartford program.* Washington, DC: U.S. Department of Justice.

Fowler, F. J., Jr., McCalla, M. E., & Mangione, T. W. (1979). *Reducing residential crime and fear: The Hartford neighborhood crime prevention program.* Washington, DC: U.S. Department of Justice.

Jacobs, J. (1961). *The death and life of great American cities.* New York: Vintage.

Lewis, D. A., Szoc, R., Salem, G., & Levin, R. (1980). *Crime and community: Understanding fear of crime in urban America.* Evanston, IL: Northwestern University, Center for Urban Affairs.

Newman, O. (1972). *Defensible space: Crime prevention through urban design.* New York: Macmillan.

Newman, O., & Franck, K. (1980). *Factors influencing crime and instability in urban housing developments.* New York: Institute for Community Design Analysis.

Reppetto, T. A. (1974). *Residential crime.* Cambridge, MA: Ballinger.

Skogan, W. G., & Maxfield, M. G. (1981). *Coping with crime: Victimization, fear and reactions to crime in three American cities.* Beverly Hills, CA: Sage.

Tien, J. M., Reppetto, T. A., & Hines, L. F. (1975). *The elements of CPTED.* Arlington, VA: Westinghouse Electric Corporation.

Wilson, J. Q., & Boland, B. (1979). *The effect of police on crime.* Washington, DC: U.S. Department of Justice.

Chapter 6

NEIGHBORHOOD-BASED CRIME PREVENTION
Assessing the Efficacy of Community Organizing in Chicago

DENNIS P. ROSENBAUM
DAN A. LEWIS
JANE A. GRANT

Millions of Americans are now participating in both individual and collective actions to protect themselves, family members, belongings, and neighbors from crime, and to create a sense of safety and social integration in their communities. Given all the excitement about citizen participation in voluntary crime prevention activities, many policymakers, service providers, community leaders, and funding agencies are interested in knowing whether these strategies are effective mechanisms for fighting crime, reducing fear of crime, and building a sense of neighborhood in urban areas. Unfortunately, we know very little about the effectiveness of citizen or police crime prevention programs.

The Ford Foundation has recently funded both community-based programs in this area and evaluations of these programs. One of the major initiatives supported by the Ford Foundation was a multineighborhood crime prevention program, directed by the Citizen Information Service in Chicago, Illinois. Ford also funded an evaluation of this program, which we conducted at Northwestern University's Center for Urban Affairs and Policy Research. The purpose of this chapter is to describe and interpret the major results of this evaluation.

AUTHORS' NOTE: *The research described here was funded under Grant 820-1104 from the Ford Foundation. We wish to thank Sharon Rowser of the Ford Foundation for her comments and advice in the early stages of this research. Points of view or opinions stated in this chapter are those of the authors and do not necessarily represent the official position or policies of the Ford Foundation.*

109

OVERVIEW OF THE PROGRAM
AND THE EVALUATION

The Citizen Information Service of Chicago (CIS), a branch of the League of Women Voters, directed and monitored the Organizing Neighborhoods for Crime Prevention project. The project was a continuation and expansion of programs previously funded by ACTION and the Law Enforcement Assistance Administration as part of the Urban Crime Prevention Program (UCPP). With new funding from the Ford Foundation and assistance from CIS, community organizations in Chicago were able to reach new areas of the city and continue their crime prevention activities.

The new UCPP included funding for nine Chicago community organizations to develop and implement neighborhood crime prevention programs within their own service areas. The "treatment" or intervention was an attempt to organize residents of selected neighborhoods through door-to-door contacts, block meetings, neighborhood meetings, the distribution of educational materials, and related strategies. Unlike the original UCPP, which included a wide variety of crime prevention strategies (such as arson prevention, consumer fraud, and dispute settlement), the new project focused on establishing and maintaining block watches and/or youth-focused activities. CIS encouraged participating organizations to adopt the block watch model, but the extent to which this strategy was actually adopted varied considerably across the groups. (For a detailed discussion of the interventions, see Lewis, Grant, & Rosenbaum, 1985.)

The Evaluation. The evaluation of these projects was a two-year assessment funded by the Ford Foundation. The central question addressed by our evaluation was whether or not local community organizations—with some outside funding, but with no substantial help from law enforcement—could introduce programs that would have a significant impact on local residents and the neighborhood as a whole. Could these programs significantly influence residents' perceptions, attitudes, and behaviors in a manner consistent with reducing crime and enhancing the quality of neighborhood life? Much has been written in recent years about the importance of community organizations as vehicles for community crime prevention, but little is known about whether or not *citizen-based* programs can make a difference in the community. This is one of the few quasi-experimental evaluations of exclusively citizen-based programs.

Previous Research. In the mid-1970s, community crime prevention scholars were entering an era of research marked by in-depth analyses of individual and collective citizen reactions to crime. As a result of this work, our theoretical understanding of community crime prevention was significantly advanced, along with our ability to measure these processes and their effects (DuBow, McCabe, & Kaplan, 1979; Greenberg, Rohe, & Williams, 1982; Lavrakas, 1982; Skogan et al., 1982; Taub, Taylor, & Dunham, 1982; Taylor & Bower, 1980).

This line of research, however, has not adequately addressed questions related to the effectiveness of individual or collective responses to crime. The major data sets have been cross-sectional rather than longitudinal. The real question is whether or not *change or improvement* is noted over time in the amount of neighboring, perceptions of crime, and so forth, within target neighborhoods relative to areas that do not receive community crime prevention programs. The bulk of previous research in community crime prevention has generated little evidence regarding the impact of neighborhood organizing or police activities on fear of crime, neighborhood deterioration, and related problems. *Processes,* rather than *programs,* have been the focal point. However, the growing need for answers to important questions about effectiveness has thrust us into a period of renewed emphasis on *program-focused* research and evaluation, with the hope of better understanding and improving the efficacy of police and citizen crime prevention efforts. With a few exceptions, the evaluation research in this field has been of low quality and does not incorporate the types of controls necessary to produce compelling evaluation results (see Lurigio & Rosenbaum, Chapter 2, this volume).

Advances in Measurement. Recently, criminal justice scholars have conducted considerable research to conceptually refine and validate measures of fear of crime (Rosenbaum & Baumer, 1981), neighborhood attachment and social interaction (Riger & Lavrakas, 1981), protective behaviors (Lavrakas, 1979), participation in organized neighborhood activities (Skogan & Maxfield, 1981), incivility (Lewis & Maxfield, 1980), and other dimensions relevant to program evaluation in this field. However, evaluations utilizing these advancements in theory and measurement were virtually nonexistent in the field of community crime prevention until 1983, when both the Ford Foundation and the National Institute of Justice initiated several major evaluations.[1] The present evaluation was built on this decade of cumulative experience. The outcome measures employed in this evaluation cover many of the attitudinal, perceptual, and behavioral dimensions to emerge from this research on community crime prevention.

Statement of Hypotheses

Aside from statements about crime reduction, rarely have we seen the expectations for community crime prevention programs described for the benefit of both theoretical and empirical scrutiny. DuBow and Emmons (1981) have described what they call "the community hypothesis" to specify the community benefits that should result from collective crime prevention activities and to identify the underlying mechanisms. Greenberg et al. (1982) have sought to clarify the role of informal social control processes in explaining community crime prevention outcomes. To help us clarify our thinking about this evaluation, we combined this type of theorizing with the stated objectives of the UCPP projects to generate some testable hypotheses about the consequences of citizen crime prevention. Although we will not propose any unifying theory of impact, we hope the collection of hypotheses stated here will bring us a few steps closer to an integration of previous theoretical statements.

A general "community crime prevention hypothesis," which serves as the umbrella for other hypotheses and predictions, can be stated as follows: When citizens voluntarily come together to share and discuss neighborhood problems or issues (including crime), and work collectively toward resolving or preventing these problems, such participatory actions can enhance the psychological and social well-being of the community and eventually reduce both the perceived and actual incidents of such problems. This hypothesis assumes, in the present context, that voluntary community organizations can serve as effective vehicles for stimulating the citizen participation necessary to effect these changes. While the above hypothesis is clearly a global statement, it provides us with a framework for examining more specific and testable predictions. The seven primary hypotheses that served to drive this evaluation conceptually can be stated as follows:

- *Hypothesis 1:* Local community organizations intent on organizing citizens around the issue of crime reduction will, as a first step, be able to improve residents' awareness of local opportunities to participate in crime prevention activities and, second, stimulate actual participation in these activities.

- *Hypothesis 2:* Exposure to the program—especially through participation in neighborhood or block meetings—will enhance feelings of efficacy about individual and collective actions, as well as increase personal responsibility for these actions. Although less likely, informational exposure to crime prevention literature, such as newsletters or flyers, may produce these effects.

- *Hypothesis 3:* At the core of community crime prevention theorizing is the expectation that organizing efforts will produce behavioral changes among citizens in terms of both attempts to regulate social behavior in the neighborhood and prevent future victimization via protective actions.

- *Hypothesis 4:* Collective activities and efforts to prevent crime will enhance social cohesion in the neighborhood.

- *Hypothesis 5:* If, indeed, these programs are able to enhance individual and collective actions that produce fewer opportunities and more social sanctions for deviant behavior, then we would expect a reduction in crime and other forms of social disorder.

- *Hypothesis 6:* Fear of crime and related perceptions of crime should decline as a result of reductions in victimization and disorder *or* as a direct product of the changes in neighborhood social processes discussed in previous hypotheses.

- *Hypothesis 7:* Residents' general perceptions of the neighborhood's future and attachment to the community as a place to live will be improved by collective action.

This evaluation was structured as a test of these seven hypotheses to determine if the interventions being studied would have any of these anticipated effects. The theoretical rationale for these hypotheses is articulated in Rosenbaum, Lewis, and Grant (1985).

METHODOLOGY

Research Design

The basic research design used in this evaluation is what Cook and Campbell (1979) call the "untreated control group design with pretest and posttest." That is, measurement was taken before and after the implementation of the crime prevention program in the "treated" neighborhoods, and identical measurement occurred at the same time in "untreated" (comparison) neighborhoods, as well as in a citywide sample of Chicago residents. A one-year lag was scheduled between the pretest and posttest, with most of the quantitative data collected in February and March of 1983 and again in 1984. Fieldwork, however, was continued throughout the implementation period.

Types of Samples. Two types of samples were employed in this evaluation: panel and independent samples. The primary thrust of the evaluation was to assess the impact of these programs on neighborhood residents over a one-year time period. A panel design—involving repeated measurement on the *same* respondents over time—provided a strong test of the individual change hypothesis. Error variance was reduced as each respondent served as his or her own control. Thus, the panel data were given special attention in this evaluation.

However, while a panel design (with proper control groups) is generally stronger than an independent samples design on "internal validity" (that is, the extent to which it allows a strong inference that x caused y), it can be weaker on "external validity" (that is, the extent to which the results can be generalized to other settings, populations, and so on) because of panel attrition between the pretest and posttest.

Selecting Treated
and Untreated Neighborhoods

Treated Neighborhoods. Nine well-established volunteer community organizations agreed to work with CIS and seek funding from the Ford Foundation to develop and implement community crime prevention programs. This self-selection and funding process occurred prior to the start-up of the evaluation, and, therefore, was not under the control of the evaluators.

We selected five of these nine organizations for inclusion in the evaluation. This reduction was necessary to maintain a high-quality evaluation given the resources available. Using program documents, interviews with organization leaders, and neighborhood census data, we selected the communities most interested in pursuing a block watch-type program and having the resources or support available to do so. We also attempted to maintain some variety along ethnic and socioeconomic dimensions, but the neighborhoods tended to be middle- or lower-middle-income areas. One predominantly black neighborhood discontinued the program after being selected, leaving us with only two neighborhoods having a sizable percentage of minorities.

Our influence over the selection of target areas *within* the five chosen neighborhoods was limited to setting two restrictions on the community organizations making these decisions: (1) The programs should be implemented in areas where their organization had not carried out any community organizing in the past two years, especially crime prevention activities, and (2) the programs should be implemented in contiguous areas whenever possible.

Untreated Comparison Neighborhoods. As noted earlier, our research design called for two primary types of control groups: (1) untreated comparison neighborhoods that were similar to the treated neighborhoods on some basic characteristics, and (2) a citywide comparison group that was not vulnerable to local history and should detect citywide changes.

To avoid the shortcomings of using a single location as a comparison neighborhood, we decided to use a *pooled* control group that would contain data from three separate locations within the city. We reasoned that this strategy would give more stability and robustness to the findings. The following procedures were used to identify and select untreated comparision areas:

(1) Each of the treatment sites was profiled using 1980 census data on median value of owner-occupied units, median contract rent, percentage of rentals, racial composition, and age distribution.
(2) For each of these distinct profiles, the pool of more than 800 census tracts in Chicago was searched to identify a group of 10 to 15 sites that were similar to the treatment area profile.
(3) For each treatment site, 3 census tracts were randomly selected from this group of 10 to 15 census tracts.

Data Collection Methods and Procedures

Several data sources and methodologies were employed in this evaluation. The primary methodologies were telephone surveys of neighborhood residents, fieldwork focused on participant observations, and interviews with community organization leaders and staff. The telephone surveys generated the primary data for assessing changes in residents' perceptions, attitudes, feelings, and behaviors over time and, thus, determining the extent and nature of program impact. In the context of impact assessment, the fieldwork results were used to assist in the planning of survey analyses and the interpretation of survey results.

Sampling Strategy. In the absence of prior knowledge about whether the activities would be implemented at the block or neighborhood level, we utilized a multilevel sampling scheme.

Blockfaces (that is, pairs of adjacent sides of two city blocks) were randomly selected to represent neighborhood areas and then households were randomly selected to represent each of these selected blockfaces (we will refer to blockfaces as "blocks" for ease of discussion).

With emphasis on measuring change in small geographic areas, rather than estimating population parameters, our main sampling frame was the list of published telephone numbers in these target areas. However, to generate our citywide control group, a random digit dial (RDD) telephone survey was conducted.

The last defining characteristic of our sampling plan is the method of respondent selection. For all telephone surveys (both RDD and directory based) we used the head-of-household selection technique with adults who were 19 or older.

Completion Rates and Sample Sizes. At *time 1,* a total of 3,357 interviews were completed, with a completion rate of 65.8%. At *time 2,* we were able to reinterview 1,652 respondents from the original sample (49.2%) to create our panel sample. In addition, 1,172 new "posttest only" residents were interviewed, bringing the total time 2 sample to 2,824. There were 1,301 "refusals" at time 2 (including over 500 respondents who had moved since time 1), thus producing a completion rate of 68.0%.

Measurement

The survey instrument contained more than 200 items measuring a variety of constructs. A careful attempt was made to incorporate "proven" items from previous research on reactions to crime and fear of crime. Instruments from several major studies were reviewed and different measures were compared. In addition to building upon earlier research, we expanded the scope of measurement to include variables in such areas as perceived efficacy.

Given the number of survey items employed, extensive data reduction was necessary. This effort focused on the development of multi-item scales that could demonstrate the properties of unidimensionality and strong internal consistency. Factor analysis and reliability analysis were performed on all scales for the entire set of pretest data and then replicated for each neighborhood. A high degree of success was achieved. The overall alphas ranged from .59 to .91, indicating that the items "hang together" to an acceptable degree.

The scales employed covered a broad range of theoretical constructs pertinent to the hypotheses being tested. In total, 23 separate scales were used to assess both the extent of program implementation and the intermediate effects of the intervention on a wide variety of perceptions, emotions, attitudes, and behaviors.

RESULTS

Analysis Strategy

The overall analysis strategy was to test the seven primary hypotheses articulated earlier, looking for *differential change* over a one-year period between the "treated" and "untreated" areas. More than one level of analysis was utilized because of differences in the way the treatment was administered. We performed neighborhood-level analyses on all neighborhoods, using neighborhood as a dummy variable to represent the treatment (0 = untreated neighborhood, 1 = treated neighborhood). Block-level analyses (0 = untreated blocks, 1 = treated blocks) were conducted on the one neighborhood that implemented the program on a block-by-block basis.

The primary analysis of program impact was conducted within a hierarchical multiple regression framework using the panel data. The posttest scores on the variable of interest were used as the dependent variable and predictor variables were entered into the regression equation in three distinct groupings: (1) pretest scores, (2) important covariates, and (3) the treatment dummy variable. The following covariates were used for virtually all regression analyses: the respondent's sex, age, race, educational level, occupancy status (owner or renter), victimization history, and vicarious victimization history (knowledge of other victims).If the presence or absence of the crime prevention program (as represented by different neighborhoods or blocks) added significantly to the amount of variance in the posttest already explained by the pretest and other covariates, we would be inclined to say there was a "treatment effect"; that is, the program made a difference in the outcome variable of interest.

TESTING THE MAIN HYPOTHESES: NEIGHBORHOOD COMPARISONS

The results will be presented as they pertain to each of the seven main hypothesis guiding this evaluation. The results reported in this section are based on neighborhood-level comparisions of treated and untreated area. Although we collected data from both panel and independent samples, in this chapter we will report only the panel results, due to lack of space and because these data were considered a much stronger test of program impact. However, the reader should note that the independent sample results were consistently nonsignificant, showing virtually no program impact across a wide variety of measures (see Rosenbaum et al., 1985). We will return to this fact later.

Hypothesis 1:
Increased Exposure and Participation

Exposure/Awareness. The results suggest that organizations were quite successful at exposing local residents to the program, that is, making them aware of opportunities to get involved in crime prevention activities. There were significant "treatment effects" in seven of the eight comparisons. That is, after controlling for pretest differences and other covariates, treated neighborhoods showed significant gains relative to untreated neighborhoods over a one-year period in terms of having "heard or read about" and having had the "opportunity to attend" a "neighborhood crime prevention meeting" or "block watch program on your block."

Participation. It is one thing to make citizens aware of crime prevention meetings, but another to get them to attend and participate. While the effects on participation were not as strong as the effects on exposure (as would be expected), nevertheless, the data showed fairly consistent support for the first hypothesis. All four neighborhoods were able to distinguish themselves on participation levels from one of their two control groups, but none was able to distinguish itself from both control groups. Figure 6.1 shows the direction of these changes over time. Indeed, all four treated neighborhoods demonstrated significant *increases* in participation levels among local residents relative to at least one control group.

These participation findings should be tempered by our assessment of the amount and prevalence of participation. For example, the unadjusted percentages indicate that treated areas *as a whole* showed only a 3.9% increase in participation, from 12.3% of the residents in 1983 to 16.2% in 1984. The citywide control group showed an increase of 7.0% (from 6.1% to 13.1% of Chicagoans) and the neighborhood control groups showed a 1.4% rise in participation (from 8.1% to 9.5%). Moreover, our fieldwork clearly suggests that only one organization seriously adopted the block watch philosophy and pro-

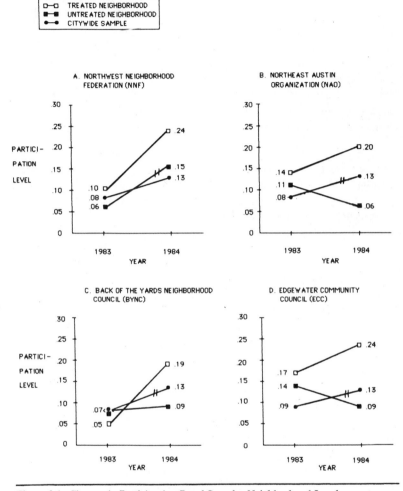

Figure 6.1 Changes in Participation Panel Sample—Neighborhood Level

gram. Two other groups preferred to implement the program via neighborhood meetings geared to the entire community or to specific audiences (such as church groups). Holding a few neighborhood meetings over the course of the year may have been sufficient to produce a significant increase in neighborhood participation (as measured by our surveys). Even the organization that vigorously pursued the block watch model overestimated what it could accomplish in one year.

In sum, we found some consistent, albeit qualified, support for Hypothesis 1. Residents in treated neighborhoods showed significant increases in awareness of, and participation in, crime prevention meetings relative to certain untreated areas. While these data stand as encouraging evidence that the organizations did, in fact, implement some type of program, there remain serious doubts about the strength/dosage of the treatment given the limited number of people involved, number of meetings held, and number of blocks organized during the implementation period.

Hypothesis 2:
Greater Efficacy and Responsibility

Efficacy of Block Action. Did the interventions help to "empower" the local residents and make them feel that people on their blocks can make a difference in the neighborhood? For some, the answer is yes, but for others the answer is no. In fact, the results indicate that feelings of efficacy about block-level action unexpectedly *declined* in two neighborhoods (relative to comparision neighborhoods), although it *increased* in two others as predicted.

Efficacy of Collective Crime Prevention Behavior. Did the programs change residents' attitudes about the efficaciousness of collective crime prevention behavior, such as block watches and citizen patrols? The results indicate no effects across all comparisons. Overall, residents' beliefs about the helpfulness of collective citizen action in preventing crime were not altered by these programs.

Efficacy of Individual Target Hardening. Did the interventions persuade residents to believe more strongly in the efficacy of individual home protection measures, such as installing alarm systems or special locks? This was not the case. Only one treatment neighborhood showed a marginally significant effect, and the direction of change was counter to the hypothesis, that is, decreased efficacy in comparison to the citywide sample.

Attribution of Responsibility. Did the programs influence residents to think that preventing crime is more the responsibility of citizens than of police? The treatments generally had no effect on attributions of responsibility for crime prevention. However, for the one neighborhood where significant effects were observed, the results again ran counter to the hypothesis. Specifically, residents attributed *less* responsibility to citizens and *more* responsibility to the police in comparison to both control groups.

In sum, the support for Hypothesis 2 regarding enhancement of efficacy and responsibility is weak, at best. With few exceptions, attributions of responsibility for crime prevention and the perceived efficacy of collective crime prevention were unaffected by the treatment. The third outcome measure—efficacy of block-level action—showed contradictory results, as some neighborhoods increased and others decreased. It is worth noting that a decline in efficacy occurred in the one neighborhood that followed the block watch model and implemented the program on a block-by-block basis.

Hypothesis 3:
Behavioral Changes

Community crime prevention programs are expected to produce behavioral changes among citizens both in terms of efforts to prevent future victimization and efforts to regulate social behavior. In this section, we will summarize the results from five separate behavioral scales pertinent to this hypothesis.

Home Protection Behavior. We hypothesized that programs would increase individual home protection behaviors, such as installing better locks, engraving valuable property, or having a home security survey. Two of the four neighborhoods showed increases in home protection behavior relative to the citywide sample, but they did not differ from their comparision neighborhoods, which were also experiencing increases between the pretest and posttest.

Street Avoidance Behavior. We hypothesized that having more information about crime or having crime become a silent issue might increase personal protective behaviors, such as watching out for suspicious persons or avoiding certain types of strangers. In general, this was not true. None of the comparisons showed any program effects.

Victimization Reporting. Crime prevention programs typically encourage citizens to report crime to the police, especially their own experiences with victimization. We hypothesized that programs would produce an increase in the percentage of victimizations reported to the police. There was little consistent support for this hypothesis. One neighborhood showed an increase in reporting relative to Chicago, and another neighborhood showed a marginally significant decrease.

Collective Surveillance. Central to the block watch concept is the notion of "neighboring," whereby block residents take a territorial interest in their immediate environment and collectively protect each other and their property from criminal intruders. In this context, we hypothesized that residents in the treated areas would show increases in the tendency to ask neighbors to watch their homes while they were away. The results indicate almost no support for this hypothesis. Only the neighborhood that fully adopted the block watch model was able to show a marginally significant increase in requests for neighbors to watch their homes.

Taking Action Against Neighborhood Problems. Assuming that these programs encourage the exercise of informal social control and enhance citizen efficacy, we hypothesized that local residents, when faced with identifiable neighborhood problems, would be more inclined to intervene and take some form of action to help solve these problems. Looking at the percentage of "big problems" in the neighborhood for which residents took some action (10-item scale), we found little support for this hypothesis. In fact, the one significant finding was in the opposite direction, showing a *decrease* in the tendency to take action among neighborhood residents relative to the control group.

In sum, the total picture with regard to behavioral changes is not supportive of Hypothesis 3. The vast majority of comparisons were nonsignificant. Furthermore, some of the significant findings showed no consistent pattern across neighborhoods.

Hypothesis 4:
Social Integration

A central tenet of community crime prevention theorists is that collective activity has the capacity to enhance social integration among community residents, thus making the neighborhood a better social environment in which to live. Two measures of social integration were used to test Hypothesis 4—the self-reported frequency of spontaneous verbal interaction with neighbors on the street and the proportion of block residents that they know by name.

Chatting with Neighbors. There was no support for the hypothesis that these programs could increase the frequency of informal "chatting" on the street among neighbors.

Residents Known by Name. Residents in three of the four neighborhoods showed no evidence of an increase in the proportion of block residents they know by name. The one neighborhood that did change provides evidence against the hypothesis, namely, a significant *reduction* in the proportion of residents known by name relative to both control groups.

Hypothesis 5:
Reduced Crime and Incivility

Assuming that all the mechanisms and processes posited in earlier hypotheses are in place, two major outcomes that should be expected are (1) a reduction in criminal victimization and (2) a reduction in various types of incivility or disorder. To test this hypothesis, we examined the impact of the programs on five different scales—two measuring victimization and three measuring different forms of disorder.

Victimization Experience. The results show an interesting mixture of changes in victimization experience. Three of the four neighborhoods showed significant changes in the average number of victimizations per respondent, but two of these three run counter to the hypothesis. Specifically, two neighborhoods showed significant *increases* in the number of victimizations per respondent between 1983 and 1984, and one showed a marginally significant *decrease* in victimization experiences. Interestingly enough, the neighborhood showing the decline in victimization was the only one that organized a sizable number of block watches. These changes are illustrated in Figure 6.2. Victimization levels in Chicago remained very stable between 1983 and 1984.

Vicarious Victimization. Indirect or vicarious victimization was measured by asking respondents if they "personally know anyone" (other than themselves) who had been a vitcim of serious crime in the past year (respondents were asked about a cluster of personal and property crimes in two items). The result showed *increases* in the number of vicarious victimizations in one neighborhood and unfavorable differential change in two others. In these latter neighborhoods, vicarious victimization was actually decreasing, but not as rapidly as the comparison neighborhoods. In sum, there is no support for the hypothesis that programs will yield reductions in vicarious victimization, and some evidence to the contrary.

Youth Disorder. The amount of youth disorder in these neighborhoods (for example, "hanging out," grafitti, drugs, gangs) was expected to decline as another indicator of program success. Change was evident in only one neighborhood, and the results revealed an increase in youth disorder relative to the comparison neighborhoods.

Youth Rejection of Social Control. Another measure of disorder, which more directly examined the success of social control efforts, is the extent to which neighborhood youths are viewed as respectful of property and people, law abiding, and responsive to parental requests.

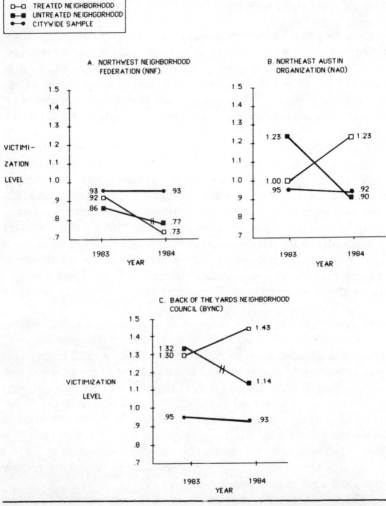

Figure 6.2 Changes in Victimization Experience Panel Sample—Neighborhood Level

Consistent with the hypothesis, two neighborhoods showed significant reductions in the perceived amount of youth rejection of social control or youth deviance.

Neighborhood Deterioration. In addition to addressing social disorder, community crime prevention programs often seek to improve the physical environment because of the close connection between neighborhood deterioration and crime. Using a 3-item neighborhood deterioration scale (covering abandoned buildings or vehicles, garbage or litter, and disinterested landlords), we sought to measure residents' perceptions of the physical environment in a way that might detect disinvestment in the community. Only one neighborhood was able to show any perceived improvement in the physical environment and this change was in relationship to the citywide sample.

In sum, we found no consistent support for Hypothesis 5 regarding reductions in crime, social disorder, and "physical" disorder. In fact, the significant changes were generally in the direction of *increases* rather than decreases in these problems areas. Specifically, there were more increases than decreases in both direct and vicarious victimization levels, as well as youth disorder. Scales measuring youth rejection of social control and neighborhood deterioration were generally unchanged.

Hypothesis 6:
Reduced Fear and Perceived Crime Rates

According to Hypothesis 6, one of the major outcomes of community crime prevention programs should be a reduction in residents' fear of crime and a drop in the amount of crime they perceive in their neighborhood.

Fear of Personal Crime. This fear scale measured individual concern about being harmed or threatened while walking alone in one's own neighborhood. Contrary to the hypothesis, the results show significant *increases* in fear of personal crime in three of the four neighborhoods.

Fear of Property Crime. This scale measured residents' fear of being victimized by property crime, primarily their concern about residential burglary. The results do not support the hypothesis. The data show only one significant effect, and this was an increase in fear relative to the comparison neighborhoods.

Perceptions of Neighborhood Crime. A 4-item scale measured residents' perceptions of the *amount* of crime in their neighborhood. Contrary to the hypothesis, the results indicate that residents in two of the four treated neighborhoods experienced *increases* in their perceptions of the amount of crime in their immediate environments.

In sum, the available evidence from three outcome measures not only failed to support Hypothesis 6, but showed unexpected changes in the opposite direction. Specifically, there were some consistent findings in the panel samples that showed *increases* in fear of personal crime and *increases* in perceptions of local crime rates.

Hypothesis 7: Increased Optimism and Attachment to Neighborhood

Hypothesis 7 addresses the final outcome of these interventions. If all goes well, the programs should improve residents' optimism about the future of their neighborhoods and increase their attachment to the areas as places to live. Two scales were used to test this hypothesis—a 2-item scale measuring residents' optimism about neighborhood change in the past year and in the two years ahead (that is, whether the neighborhood is getting "better," "worse," or "staying about the same"), and a single-item scale asking residents about their likelihood of moving in the next two years.

Optimism About Neighborhood Change. Contrary to the hypothesis, the results show significant *declines* in residents' optimism about neighborhood change in three of the four neighborhoods. In other words, residents were more inclined after one year to report that their neighborhood was getting "worse" rather than "better." Although control groups also showed declines in optimism, the treatment areas were declining at a significantly faster rate.

Likelihood of Moving. Changes in the likelihood of moving out of the neighborhood also ran counter to the hypothesis. Residents in two of the four neighborhoods revealed significant increases in their likelihood of moving relative to both control groups.

In sum, the available evidence goes against Hypothesis 7. Three of the four neighborhoods showed *decreases* in optimism about changes in the neighborhood, and residents from two of the four neighborhoods showed a greater likelihood of moving.

Summary of Neighborhood-Level Results

Several facts about the neighborhood-level results should be highlighted. First, the large majority of comparisions revealed no differential change between the treated and untreated areas, thus failing to support most of the main hypotheses. Second, patterns of significant changes are apparent by neighborhood, with some neighborhoods showing very little change and others showing change on a number of outcome variables. Third, the majority of significant findings ran *counter* to the main hypotheses. Of the 59 statistically significant findings, 36 were against the initial predictions.

The differences in outcomes between the target neighborhoods are noteworthy. The two areas where "programs," per se, were *not* implemented showed very few changes relative to control groups. (One of these discontinued the program early on, and was not included in our discussion of the results.) In contrast, the remaining three neighborhoods showed a number of significant unexpected changes. The one neighborhood that initiated a number of block watches showed fewer of these unfavorable results and, in fact, showed some encouraging effects along the lines of reductions in victimization, as well as increases in surveillance and home protection behavior. Still, most of the changes in this neighborhood were unexpected, such as increases in fear of crime.

Finally, the consistent absence of significant findings in the independent samples analyses (not reported here) suggests a limit on the external validity of the panel results, but only on the issue of treatment implementation. As it turns out, there was little evidence of successful treatment *implementation* in the independent samples (which contained more renters and younger residents than the panel sample), and this may account for the absence of program effects.

TESTING ALTERNATIVE EXPLANATIONS

Should we attribute the unexpected neighborhood changes in the panel sample to the various treatments or can we propose some plausible alternative explanations for these seemingly unfavorable outcomes? Specifically, why did three of the treatment neighborhoods show significant *increases* in various problems, such as fear of crime, perceptions of the crime problem, vicarious victimization, and concern about future changes in the neighborhood? Although it is possible that the intervention heightened these concerns and fears among residents, another possibility is that the neighborhoods selected for these programs were already on the decline at the time of program implementation and this trend simply continued after the programs were initiated. Our fieldwork offers some support for this interpretation, as organizers sometimes spoke of working in "front-line" neighborhoods and fighting the battle against "residential transition." In addition, our survey data suggest that these neighborhoods were worse off than the control groups on some of these critical outcome measures at the time of the pretest, although most of the pretest comparisons between treatment and control groups were nonsignificant.

If these neighborhoods were, in fact, experiencing a process of decline, such changes may have resulted in a greater volume of crime and more victimizations—outcomes that are not easily explained by the treatment (that is, one would be hard pressed to specify how programs work to produce increases in victimization). There is a real possibility, however, that significant increases in victimization experience between the pretest and posttest—both direct and indirect victimization—could account for the increases in fear of crime and other perceptual changes. We tested this differential victimization hypothesis and found no evidence to support it.

Returning to the question of "residential transition," another rival hypothesis is that increases in fear of crime are directly due to residents' growing concern about transition. We tested this hypothesis as well and found no evidence to support it.

In sum, we have posited several alternative hypotheses to account for the unexpected outcomes observed at the neighborhood level, and found no empirical support for them. However, concluding that we can find no reasonable alternative explanations is not the same as totally accepting the original hypothesis that the treatment is causing the observed effects. Fortunately, we have more compelling data (described below) to address the question of whether community efforts make a difference, for better or worse.

BLOCK-LEVEL ANALYSES: THE NNF TEST CASE

Evaluations can test a theory of impact only when there is little doubt about (1) the nature of the treatment and (2) the "dosage" of the treatment. For one community crime prevention program—run by the Northwest Neighborhood Federation (NNF)—we could identify and clearly define the treatment, and we were fairly confident that the "dosage" of treatment was higher than what we had observed in other neighborhoods.

Specifically, as noted earlier, NNF pursued the block watch approach to community crime prevention. A minimum of two meetings was necessary before NNF organizers would consider a block "organized." Because community organizers were able to organize only about half of the blocks in the treatement area, this created a unique opportunity for us to compare *treated* and *untreated* blocks within the *same* neighborhood, and apply the pretest-posttest control group design used earlier.

This NNF test case did not suffer from the same type of (unmeasured) nonequivalence between treated and untreated areas that probably existed with neighborhood comparisons (despite our best efforts to control it), because both groups of blocks were in the same geographic area. Also, there was little evidence that organizers systematically selected certain blocks and not others to receive the program. Residents who lived on treated and untreated blocks did not differ on a number of demographic characteristics, such as sex, age, and race. There were marginally more homeowners living on treated blocks, but our analysis controlled for occupancy status by using it as a covariate.

Implementation Results. The first basic question was whether residents on treated blocks would report more exposure to (awareness of) the program and be more likely to have participated in crime prevention meetings than residents on untreated blocks. The results indicate that NNF organizers were highly successful at stimulating citizen awareness of, and participation in, local meetings. Dramatic increases were observed between the pretest and the posttest for the treated blocks, but untreated blocks remained unchanged. Furthermore, there were no significant *pretest* differences in exposure or participation between residents on treated and untreated blocks that might suggest a selection bias or contribute to selection by treatment interactions.

Outcome Results. The important question is, Did these organizing efforts make a difference? Did residents of treated and untreated blocks display differential changes in attitudes, perceptions, and/or behaviors as a result of known differential participation in the block watch program? Across 21 separate outcome measures, the results indicate that neighborhood organizing had very few effects on local residents. Only one scale registered significant change. Specifically, residents on treated blocks were more likely than residents on untreated blocks to attribute responsibility for crime prevention to citizens instead of police. Three marginally significant findings were produced: Residents of treated (versus untreated) blocks showed (1) an increase in home protection behaviors, (2) an increase in action taken against neighborhood problems, and (3) a decrease in optimism about change in the neighborhood. However, when viewing the block-level results *as a whole,* the general conclusion must be that organizers were very successful at implementing a program, but that this intervention produced few of the hypothesized effects.

DISCUSSION

This evaluation generated little empirical support for the seven main hypotheses that we felt embodied the primary objectives of these community crime prevention programs. Most of the findings were nonsignificant and another group of findings were significant in the direction opposite to the hypotheses. The basic question we are left with is, Why did this happen? Did these programs fail or is there a better way to interpret the findings?

When evaluators do not observe program effects that are expected, there are many possible reasons for this failure. As Suchman (1969) and Weiss (1972) have noted, there are two general categories of reasons: Either (1) the program did not set in motion the "causal process" that would produce the desired goals (referred to as "program failure") or (2) the program activated the supposed "causal process" but this process did not produce the desired effects (referred to as "theory failure"). In the context of interpreting evaluation results, there is a third general category of reasons for observed failure, namely, measurement or research problems that cause the evaluators to overlook significant program effects. In an attempt to shed some light on the present evaluation results, we will briefly discuss these three categories of reasons as they apply to the circumstances in Chicago.

Program Failure. One explanation for nonsignificant findings is "program failure," sometimes referred to as "implementation failure." In the field of evaluation research, we continually experience this problem. Often, evaluators are unable to test the underlying theory of impact because the program was not implemented as planned or never implemented at all.

Although we have reported some evidence of successful program implementation, we would have to conclude that the level of implementation success was marginal, at best. Our fieldwork indicates that only one of the five organizations used the outside funding primarily for organizing block watches. Aside from the intent of community organizations, one of the evaluation issues is, How much "treatment" is needed to show an impact? Increasing community participation in crime prevention meetings from 12% to 16% hardly seems sufficient to produce communitywide effects. Holding several meetings over a 12-month period, with few additional activities, would appear to be a very weak treatment.

Although the argument can be made that the treatment dosage was quite weak for most comparisons, the NNF case study (with treated and untreated blocks) contained a much stronger implementation, and, therefore, offered a stronger test of the hypotheses. Even though the experienced NNF organizers followed the suggested model, the expected outcomes did not occur. Hence, these particular data encourage us to conclude that the problem lies not with the program, but rather with the theory itself. Also, given the unfavorable neighborhood findings, these *nonsignificant* block-level results can be viewed as marginally good news for block watch supporters. These data suggest that the observed declines at the neighborhood level were *not* the untoward effects of block watch, per se, even though they may have been a by-product of other components of the treatment in these neighborhoods (such as neighborhoodwide meetings).

Measurement Failure. Another possible explanation for the observed findings is that evaluation research simply failed to detect the real changes that occurred or falsely detected "changes" that run counter to the hypotheses. We do not feel this is a defensible explanation. The use of statistical significance criteria ($p < .05$), the best possible quasi-experimental design, and measures with known reliability and validity all help to render measurement explanations less compelling.

Theory Failure. The third possible explanation for the findings is theory failure. The available data have caused us to reexamine the theoretical underpinning of our current thinking about community crime prevention programs. Specifically, the counterhypothesis findings at the neighborhood level and the nonsignificant findings at the block level raise a serious question about whether the theory of impact is defective in specifying one or more of the following: (1) the amount or dosage of treatment needed to produce the desired effects, (2) the content of the treatment needed to produce these effects, or (3) the content of the effects themselves (that is, the appropriate outcome measures).

In terms of treatment dosage, we must ask ourselves whether or not a one or two hour meeting that occurs only once a month or every few months, and is attended by only a few local residents, should be expected to change the quality of life in a neighborhood. We do not believe such expectations are realistic.

Issues about the *quantity* of the treatment concern us less than those pertaining to the *nature* of the treatment. At the heart of any solid theoretical statement is the specification of causal, intervening, and outcome variables, as well as the relationships among them. Although a complete impact theory for community crime prevention has yet to be developed, one can question whether the current thinking (as represented by the hypotheses stated earlier) is defensible. For example, what reasons do we have for thinking that block watch activities will reduce fear of crime, increase perceived efficacy, or improve perceptions of the neighborhood? One could easily predict just the opposite outcome given that the intervention entails citizens coming together in small groups (often without the aid of law enforcement) to discuss the crime problems in their neighborhoods. Frequently such discussions take the form of exchanging victimization stories or validating one another's assessments of the severity of the local crime problem.

The current state of theorizing in community crime prevention is still rather primitive. Greater specificity in prediction could be obtained through continued observations of the actual social processes involved and through greater utilization of existing research and theory in relevant disciplines. Over the few past decades, for example, there has been extensive social psychological research on small group processes (such as conformity, group conflict, leadership) and individual-social processes (such as social comparision, social influence, social judgment, coping with stress) that could be applied to the topic of community crime prevention, and may help to clarify some of the underlying mechanisms that are operating to produce the observed effects.

In sum, there is a clear need for more research in this field to clarify the processes and impacts of community crime prevention programs. The current results force us to address seriously the possibility of both theory failure and program failure in this field. We have suggested how each could be deficient. Before we implement or evaluate more community crime prevention programs, we should rethink the principles and expectations that guide our actions. The problem may lie more in our way of thinking about community crime prevention than in the actions of local community organizations.

NOTE

1. The Ford Foundation and the National Institute of Justice, U.S. Department of Justice, have funded important programs and evaluations in the past two years. In addition to the current Chicago project, Ford has supported the Eisenhower Neighborhood Anti-Crime Self-Help Program in ten U.S. cities and Northwestern's evaluation of this program via the Eisenhower Foundation. NIJ has funded the Police Foundation's evaluation of the Fear Reduction Program in Houston and Newark. Both of these projects are still ongoing.

REFERENCES

Cook, T. D., & Campbell, D. T. (1979). *Quasi-experimentation: Design and analysis issues for field settings.* Chicago: Rand McNally.

DuBow, F., & Emmons, D. (1981). The community hypothesis. In D. A. Lewis (Ed.), *Reactions to crime*. Beverly Hills, CA: Sage.

DuBow, F., McCabe, E., & Kaplan, G. (1979). *Reactions to crime: A critical review of the literature*. Washington, DC: U.S. Department of Justice, National Institute of Law Enforcement and Criminal Justice.

Greenberg, S., Rohe, W., & Williams, J. R. (1982). *Safe and secure neighborhoods: Physical characteristics and informal territorial control in high and low crime neighborhoods*. Washington, DC: U.S. Department of Justice, National Institute of Justice.

Lavrakas, P. J. (1979). The measurement of property protection behaviors. *Bellringer: Review of Criminal Justice Evaluation, 12,* 11-13.

Lavrakas, P. J. (1982). *Factors related to citizen involvement in personal, household and neighborhood anti-crime measures*. Washington, DC: Government Printing Office.

Lewis, D. A., Grant, J. A., & Rosenbaum, D. P. (1985). *The social construction of reform: Crime prevention and community organizations* (Final Report, Vol. 2). Submitted to the Ford Foundation.

Lewis, D. A., & Maxfield, M. (1980). Fear in neighborhoods: An investigation of the impact of crime. *Journal or Research in Crime and Delinquency, 17,* 160-189.

Riger, S., & Lavrakas, P. J. (1981). Community ties: Patterns of attachment and social interaction in urban neighborhoods. *Journal of Community Psychology, 9,* 55-66.

Rosenbaum, D. P., & Baumer, T. L. (1981). *Measuring fear of crime: A set of recommended scales* (Prepared for the National Institute of Justice, U.S. Department of Justice). Evanston, IL: Westinghouse Evaluation Institute.

Rosenbaum, D. P., Lewis, D. A., & Grant, J. A. (1985). *The impact of community crime prevention programs in Chicago: Can neighborhood organizations make a difference* (Final Report, Vol 1)? Submitted to the Ford Foundation.

Skogan, W. G., Lewis, D. A., Podolefsky, A., DuBow, F., Gordon, M. T., Hunter, A., Maxfield, M. G., & Salem, G. (1982). *Reactions to Crime Project: Executive summary*. Washington, DC: National Institute of Justice, U.S. Department of Justice.

Skogan, W. G., & Maxfield, M. G. (1981). *Coping with crime: Individual and neighborhood reactions*. Beverly Hills, CA: Sage.

Suchman, E. A. (Ed.). (1969). Evaluating educational programs: A symposium [Special issue]. *Urban Review, 3*(4).

Taub, R. P., Taylor, D. G., & Dunham, J. D. (1982). *Safe and secure neighborhoods: Territoriality, solidarity and the reduction of crime*. Chicago: National Opinion Research Center.

Taylor, R. B., & Bower, S. N. (1980). *Informal control in the urban residential environment*. Washington, DC: National Institute of Law Enforcement and Criminal Justice, U.S. Department of Justice.

Weiss, C. (1972). *Evaluation research*. Englewood Cliffs, NJ: Prentice-Hall.

III

INNOVATIONS IN POLICING: A RETURN TO THE NEIGHBORHOOD

Chapter 7

EXPERIMENTING WITH FOOT PATROL
The Newark Experience

ANTONY M. PATE

Just as the patrol function is operationally central to policing, foot patrol is historically central to patrol. Indeed, the word "patrol" itself stems from the Middle French word for "to walk or paddle in mud or dirty water." In 1829, members of the first bureaucratic police department, the Metropolitan Police of London, were instructed to walk in order to become acquainted with the residents on their beat, and to reach citizens quickly if they needed assistance. Even now, foot patrol is a key element of police activity in many countries. In Japan, for example, police officers are addressed by the public as "Omawari-san," Mr. Walkabout, a description of their primary duties.

In the United States, patrolling was also performed initially on foot (Fogelson, 1977; Lane, 1975; Richardson, 1970). However, the methods of policing began to change dramatically in the 1930s with the increased use of motor vehicles. After World War II, two-way radios were installed in the vehicles in order to increase patrol territory, to allow calls to be dispatched more efficiently, to improve supervision, and—a less publicized intention—to reduce police corruption.

O. W. Wilson, one of the chief advocates of motor patrol, hypothesized that rapid and unpredictable movement of police vehicles, either on a random basis or based on perceptions of hazards, could promote a sense of omnipresence of the police. He believed that such a presence would help prevent crime by causing criminals to think that there was a

AUTHOR'S NOTE: *This chapter is based on my earlier research, which is reported in more detail in Police Foundation (1981),* The Newark Foot Patrol Experiment. *I would especially like to thank my colleagues Minna Ferziger, Michele Lioy, Lawrence W. Sherman, and Mary Ann Wycoff, for their comments and suggestions.*

137

high probability of their being discovered. Further, deploying radio-controlled vehicles in relatively small geographical areas would make the police readily available for rapid response to calls for service and for apprehending criminals. In these ways, he thought, motor patrol would cause citizens to feel safer in their neighborhoods and more satisfied with police service.

By the 1970s, social scientists began to question the effectiveness of motor patrol, calling for more extensive research to determine whether or not frequent patrols actually posed a significant threat of criminal detection and apprehension and how they related to citizen attitudes. Empirical questions about the value of motor patrol began with the work of Reiss (1971), who found that motor patrol seldom dealt with crime-related matters. Those findings were supplemented by the work of Press (1971), who found that reported crime was not consistently affected by increased levels of motor patrol, and supported by interviews with prisoners that suggested the fear of police intervention was not especially pronounced among prisoners (Institute for Defense Analysis, 1966). Experimentation in Kansas City, Missouri, strongly suggested that variations in random motor patrol had no clear effects (Kelling, Pate, Dieckmand, & Brown, 1974). These results were largely reinforced by subsequent research (Schnelle, Kirchner, Casey, & Useltor, 1977).

The basic tenets of rapid response time were challenged by studies that found that victims allow as much as 20 to 40 minutes to elapse before calling the police (Bertram & Vargo, 1976; Kansas City, Missouri, Police Department, 1978). In addition, Pate, Ferrara, Bowers, and Lorence (1976) found that satisfaction with police response to calls for service was more strongly associated with citizens' expectations of how long it would take the police to respond than with the actual length of time it took.

Also during the 1960s, the quality of the relationship between citizens, especially minority citizens, and the police began to deteriorate. Radicals portrayed the police as alien occupying forces in minority and university communities, and residents of those communities became hostile to police, whether they were patrolling in cars or organized into tactical units. Confrontations developed between citizens and the police; arrests often led to more conflict and, on some occasions, to prolonged demonstrations and even rioting. Officers were portrayed as having little or no contact with citizens, except those who were victims of crime or targets of often aggressively conducted pedestrian or car checks. Isolated in their rolling radio-dispatched fortresses, many police seemed unable to communicate with the citizens they were to serve.

To combat the deficiencies of motor patrol, some police departments have increased the number of posts patrolled on foot. Police departments in Boston, Baltimore, Arlington County (Virginia), Fort Worth, Washington, D.C., Nashville, and many cities in New Jersey have reassigned officers to foot beats. In other cities, the high cost of automobiles and gasoline have forced departments to deploy officers on foot. In some areas, inaccessibility to rapid automobile movement has made the foot beat a reasonable alternative.

Despite the reemergence of foot patrol, literature concerning it is limited. Adams (1971) pointed to its importance for certain kinds of problems and areas, suggesting that cars should be used primarily for transportation rather than as a protective shell. Gourley (1974) suggested that police officers on foot could get to know citizens on their beats better, but later dismissed foot patrol as inefficient and obsolete. The International Association of Chiefs of Police (1970) identified the advantages and disadvantages of foot patrol but generally supported the President's Commission's (1967) recommendation that it should serve as an occasional adjunct to motorized patrol.

Even more scarce than general discussions of foot patrol are empirical studies of its effectiveness. In England, Bright (1970) found that, over a three-month period, reported crime rates were significantly reduced by the deployment of one foot patrol officer in an area where none had patrolled before. Subsequent increases to two, three, or four officers per beat resulted in no further change. Bloch and Ulberg (1972) pointed to foot patrol as one aspect of a team policing experiment that helped improve community relations. Schnelle, Kirchner, McNees, and Lawler (1975) found that recorded crime increased significantly as a result of citizens' reporting directly to foot patrol officers.

Pendland and Gay (1972) studied the effects of instituting foot patrol for one year in a high-crime area of Fort Worth and found that recorded crime levels decreased and citizen satisfaction increased. Prefecture de Police, Paris (1973), based mainly on the recorded activities of foot officers in Paris, indicates that foot patrol was useful in dealing with public nuisance problems, stolen vehicles, and citizen relations in general. Hogan and Fagin (1974) reported that foot patrol, supplementing motor patrol, not only reduced crime but also positively affected the attitudes of the citizens in the areas patrolled.

In contrast, a study of foot patrol in Arlington County, Virginia, found no strong effects (Resource Planning Corporation, 1975). Another study, conducted in Isla Vista, California, found strong citizen support for foot patrol but no clear effects on crime (Kinney, 1979).

Research concerning foot patrol has been fragmentary and contradictory. Further, the absence of control over certain variables makes the results from those studies tentative and inconclusive. The Newark Foot Patrol Experiment was designed to produce more definitive answers in this area. This chapter is a description of the Newark experiment, both the program and the evaluation findings.

THE NEWARK EXPERIMENT

Background

The state-supported New Jersey Safe and Clean Neighborhoods Program offered a unique opportunity to conduct a more rigorous evaluation of foot patrol. That program, first passed by the state legislature in February 1973, and made into a permanent program in 1979, attempts to develop and maintain safe and clean neighborhoods by expanding the number of walking police officers in high-crime neighborhoods, and by providing resources to assist in physically upgrading and stabilizing those neighborhoods. The program matches state dollars with local dollars on an equal basis. Two-thirds of the funds are to provide for the salaries, wages, fringe benefits, and equipment (bulletproof vests, walkie-talkies, uniforms) for foot patrol officers.

The goal of the program is to develop safe neighborhoods through the use of walking police officers, based on the assumption that "the uniformed walking patrol officers, by being highly visible on the streets, are not only helping to prevent crime and enforce the laws, but at the same time are also helping to restore confidence in citizens and are improving public relations with merchants and residents" (Collins, 1979, p. 2).

In order to obtain an objective assessment of the effectiveness of foot patrol under the auspices of the Safe and Clean Neighborhoods Program, the state of New Jersey invited the Police Foundation to conduct an independent evaluation of the program. All program costs were to be paid by the state. All evaluation costs were to be paid by the Police Foundation. After discussions with members of specially created task forces in several cities, it was decided to implement different research designs in various cities. In Newark, the biggest city in the state, an excellent data retrieval system and a high level of cooperation made it possible for a quasi-experimental design to be used.

Research Design

To test the effectiveness of foot patrol, geographical areas of Newark were assigned to one of three experimental conditions:

(1) the "Retain" condition, in which foot patrol had existed for at least five years, and was to be continued;
(2) the "Drop" condition, in which foot patrol had existed for at least five years, and was to be eliminated; or
(3) the "Add" condition, in which foot patrol had not existed for at least five years, and was instituted.

To make these assignments, activity logs on all existing foot posts were examined to determine which had been patrolled on foot consistently since the beginning of the Safe and Clean Neighborhoods Program. There were eight such beats, each along a commercial strip, eight to sixteen blocks long, patrolled from 4 p.m. to midnight on Monday through Friday nights. These beats were matched into four sets of two beats each, based on a number of different demographic criteria available from census data. A random selection process was used to determine which beat in each pair would have its foot patrol continued and which would have it discontinued. In addition, foot patrol was instituted in four areas (similar to those previously patrolled on foot) where it had not existed before.

The resulting design is a hybrid combination of a "pretest-posttest control group design" and a "nonequivalent control group design" (Campbell & Stanley, 1966). The research design is shown in Figure 7.1, using the standard graphic representation system. An X represents the exposure of a group to an experimental treatment; an O represents observation or measurement; Xs and Os in different rows apply to different groups; left to right indicates temporal order; Xs and Os vertical to one another are simultaneous; and R indicates random assignment to separate treatment groups. The design took the form shown in Figure 7.1.

Cook and Campbell (1979), in their classic analysis of research designs, suggest that, despite certain threats to internal validity in-

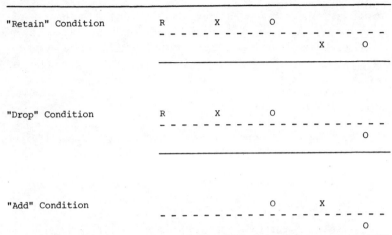

NOTE: X = exposure to experimental treatment; O = observation or measurement; R = random assignment.

Figure 7.1 Research Design for the Newark Foot Patrol Experiment

herent in this approach, creative and exhaustive consideration of the particular circumstances of the administration of treatment, the context of the treatment events, the characteristics of the treatment groups, and how these variables may be expected to interact, "can enhance significantly our confidence in making causal attributions."

Two features of this design pose potential problems for the interpretation of results: (a) the possible nonequivalence of treatment groups and (b) separate pretest and posttest samples.

Nonequivalence of Treatment Groups. As mentioned earlier, the Newark foot patrol evaluation involved some areas of Newark that had a recent history of foot patrol and others that had no such coverage. Therefore, any significant differences between responses could possibly result from preexisting differences between the treatment areas and not from the presence or absence of foot patrol.

More specifically, the Add beats were different from the Drop and Retain beats before the first wave of observations because they had no foot patrol. Since the police department had used distinguishing criteria to make its original foot patrol allocation decisions, this difference could be symptomatic of still greater differences between the beats. Interviews with foot patrol command personnel revealed facts they thought should be considered in allocating foot patrols to areas of cities: level of street activity, number of calls for service, crime rates, population density, and concentration of businesses. If these factors were, in fact, considered, and if need for police services was the basis of assignments, then the Add beats—to which police originally had not assigned foot patrols—would be expected to be characterized by lower levels of street activity, fewer calls for service, lower crime rates, lower population density, and a smaller proportion of businesses among all beat buildings than the Drop and Retain beats.

On the other hand, if assignments of foot patrols were politically determined and highly valued by local residents, it is likely that neighborhoods populated by the relatively disenfranchised—minorities and the poor, with little political power and few resources—would receive less foot patrol coverage. Thus, the Add beats could be expected to have lower income levels, larger minority populations, higher crime rates, greater density, and fewer nonresidential units than the Drop and Retain beats.

Whatever the actual differences among Add, Drop, and Retain beats, they possibly could affect the reception and impact of foot patrol officers in the treatment areas. Interpretations of responses across groups and across time must therefore consider the possible effects of the selective assignment of treatments to nonequivalent groups.

Separate Pretest/Posttest Samples. This design feature was included because it was deemed highly likely that pretest measurement would affect posttest responses in a way that could lead to incorrect inferences about cause, or simply to uninterpretable responses. For example, one important dependent variable in this study was awareness of the presence of foot patrol officers in the neighborhood. Extensive questioning about local foot patrol officers at Time 1 could not fail to make respondents more aware of these officers' presence in the future, rendering biases in the Time 2 awareness responses.

The separate pretest/posttest samples eliminate the problem of contamination of posttest responses from the pretest measurement (Campbell & Stanley, 1966), but it introduces the possibility of another serious threat to internal validity. For this design to yield interpretable results, it is essential that the pretest and posttest samples within treatment groups represent the same population. If this assumption is violated, it is virtually impossible to make causal inferences about differences in the groups' responses over time. For this reason, it was critical that the three sets of beats matched each other on as many different characteristics as possible. In addition to selecting beats based on similar census data, survey results concerning age, race, sex, and other variables were examined for both the pretest and the posttest. Analysis of these variables revealed that it was reasonable to assume that the groups were indeed comparable.

HYPOTHESIZED EFFECTS

The purpose of the research was to determine the extent to which the presence of foot patrol could achieve the following hypothesized effects on residents:

(1) Perceived Disorder Problems in the Area. Because officers on foot patrol are in direct contact with street activity, the level of perceived crime-related activity, such as loitering, disorderly conduct, drug use, and other such behaviors, can be hypothesized to be reduced by the presence, and increased by the absence, of such patrol.

(2) Perceived Crime Problems in the Area. Similarly, the concentrated presence of foot patrol in a relatively small area can be expected, by its deterrent effect, to lead to a reduction in perceived crime problems. The absence of such patrol should be expected to produce higher perceived levels of such problems.

(3) Perceived Likelihood of Victimization in the Area. Assuming the presence of foot patrol achieves a reduction in perceived crime and crime-related problems, a consequence should be that residents of the area so patrolled should think that the likelihood of being a crime victim is smaller. The absence of such patrol should produce increased estimates of the likelihood of crime.

(4) Perceived Safety of the Area. As a consequence of the earlier hypothesized effects, it can be expected that residents in areas exposed to foot patrol will believe that their neighborhood is safer than will residents of areas not provided with such patrol.

(5) Likelihood of Reporting Crimes. Due to the closer proximity of police that is created by foot patrol, and the greater number of opportunities provided to have contacts with police, the presence of such patrol should increase the likelihood of reporting crimes to the police. Its absence should reduce that likelihood.

(6) Evaluation of Police Service. Due to the closer interaction with police officers allowed by foot patrol—and the suggestion of caring that it implies—the presence of such patrol should lead to higher evaluations of police service. The absence of foot patrol should produce lower evaluations.

(7) Victimization. If foot patrol does, indeed, have a deterrent effect, victimization should be lower in those areas with patrols and higher in those areas without it.

(8) Recorded Crime. Although not representative of victimization, it can be hypothesized that recorded crime will be lowest in areas with foot patrol, highest in areas without it.

Because the presence of foot patrol was manipulated after the close of most businesses, few, if any, effects should be expected among the nonresidential establishments.

IMPLEMENTING THE EXPERIMENT

The first step in implementing the Newark experiment was to secure the permission of the Department of Community Affairs (DCA) to alter the conditions of the contract with the police department under which foot patrol was funded. Under that contract, the department must specify the areas to be patrolled, the number of officers to walk the beats, and the times those officers will be present. To ensure that these contracts are taken seriously, DCA sends inspectors without warning to verify that the conditions are being maintained. Violations, if they occur, can lead to the termination of state funding for foot patrol. After several meetings involving state officials, Newark administrators, and Police Foundation representatives, it was agreed that the experimental design described above should be implemented. DCA was to be advised of the changes in foot beats, but the actual decisions about changes were to be made by the Police Foundation evaluators.

State approval obtained, representatives of the Newark Police Department and the Police Foundation met several times to discuss the evaluation design as well as the potential difficulties in carrying it out. It was mutually understood that random assignment was necessary to determine which areas would continue to receive foot patrol coverage and which would have such coverage eliminated. It was also agreed that, to ensure objectivity, the evaluators should make the assignments, rather than the department itself.

It was anticipated that this procedure might create several problems. In the first place, random assignment constituted a clear violation of the usual procedures of decision making in the police department. In addition, having the evaluators, rather than department administrators, make the assignments meant that an intrusion into the usual command structure would take place. Furthermore, when foot patrol was removed from the selected areas, it was reasonable to assume that protests from residents and commercial associations would occur, perhaps channeled through the city council or the mayor's office. If such protests did occur, it was highly likely that the press would publicize them.

In fact, the experiment was much easier to implement and maintain than was anticipated. Police department objections to the random and external nature of the assignment of foot patrol beats were overcome by frequent and intense discussions with the operational commanders most threatened by the intrusions. The needs for objectivity and, therefore, for randomness were made clear. As a result, with the endorsement of managers at the highest levels of the police bureaucracy, such evaluative "meddling" became accepted (and supported) by middle-level operatives as a way of investigating the possible advantages of foot patrol.

Sporadic episodes of public outcry against the loss of foot patrol were dealt with by the police director at public meetings, in which the need for sound evaluations of department policies were reiterated. The director staunchly maintained the experiment, even when members of the city council expressed disgruntlement.

Most significantly, the experiment survived even during an unusually tempestuous period in the Newark Police Department, caused by massive layoffs, sweeping transfers of personnel, abruptly implemented reorganizations of a number of highly revered, specialized units, and dramatic confrontations between the police officers' bargaining agent and the police director regarding contract negotiations.

There seem to have been three basic reasons the experiment was so successfully maintained and each is discussed below.

(1) High-Level Department Support. The Newark experiment was born of discussions among representatives of the Police Foundation, Newark's police director, the chief of police, the deputy chief of the patrol division, and a task force of officers assigned to foot patrol. All department representatives became convinced that a controlled experiment examining the effectiveness of foot patrol was worthwhile, that Newark was a good place in which to conduct such an experiment, and that they were willing to take the risks of possible difficulties that might accompany such an experiment. Throughout the experimental period, no one wavered in this commitment, even in the face of external and internal criticism.

As a result of this support, the rest of the department cooperated fully in the experiment. Any failure to implement it became seen as tantamount to a violation of department procedure, for which officers would be required to answer along the normal channels of accountability.

(2) Strict Enforcement of State Guidelines. It was very fortunate that the mechanisms for deployment of Safe and Clean Neighborhoods foot patrols had been in place in Newark and functioning well for several years before the Police Foundation came on the scene. Moreover, DCA indicates that Newark was among the exemplary cities in terms of compliance with DCA regulations and guidelines. Therefore, no new organization was necessary for the implementation of the experiment—only modification of the geographic assignments of certain foot patrol officers.

State control over the use of Safe and Clean Neighborhoods personnel also presented advantages when, during the latter part of the experimental period, staff shortages in the Newark Police Department became so acute that pressure began to mount for putting foot patrol officers in radio cars on an emergency basis. The Department of Community Affairs refused to allow such reassignments. Because the state provided funds to cover half of the cost of foot patrol operations, the Newark Police Department, although desparate for radio car officers, could ill afford to jeopardize the flow of state funds by ignoring the DCA's decision. The foot patrol officers, because of this significant external funding, became an island of stability in the midst of the tremendous instability that characterized the department at the end of the experimental year.

(3) Perceptions of Foot Patrol as a Peripheral Activity. Despite the strong support and good fortune described above, there is reason to doubt that the experiment could have survived the events that occurred in Newark during the experimental year had it been other than a foot patrol experiment. Foot patrol is commonly viewed as a peripheral activity within the patrol division. Outside intervention concerning foot patrol is therefore much less threatening than attempts to manipulate the deployment of radio cars, for example. In addition, foot patrol occupies the time of relatively few officers in the department. Therefore, few persons had vested interests that might be threatened by an experiment involving foot patrol.

VALIDATING THE EXPERIMENT

In any experiment, it is important to measure the extent to which the desired manipulations are carried out. The presence of several potential problems associated with implementing the experiment suggest that maintaining the desired conditions would be unusually difficult, so that the measurement of compliance to the experiment's guidelines had to be as rigorous as possible.

Fortunately, the Newark Police Department provided the means of determining whether or not foot patrol officers were, in fact, on their posts. At least one of the two officers walking each post always has a walkie-talkie to provide radio contact with the department; the officers also are required to register their presence once an hour by pulling a lever on one of the call boxes located on their posts. This system has been in effect since the late nineteenth century.

Each call box in Newark is assigned a unique identification number. Hourly box pulls (eight pulls for each tour of duty) by foot patrol officers were recorded at respective district stations. A clerk then recorded this information and submitted it daily to patrol division headquarters. These data, collected by the evaluation staff, constituted the core of the empirical verification for the experimental manipulations.

Based on call box pulls, there was no evidence of a foot patrol presence in the Drop posts during the entire experimental period (February 1978 through January 1979). On the Retain and Add posts, the average monthly level of coverage was 81%, ranging from 64% to 91% per month.

The call box data were not the only source of data concerning the validity of the experimental manipulations. Representatives from the Department of Community Affairs continued to make their unannounced inspections of all the Newark foot patrol posts to see that they were patrolled according to the contract. The Internal Affairs Division, at the direction of the police director, made periodic inspections of the foot posts to make certain that officers were where they were supposed to be. And civilian observers, hired primarily to count the number of pedestrians on the sidewalks in the experimental areas, also noted the times when they saw foot patrol officers on the post under observation. All of these alternative sources confirmed the conclusion supported by the call box data that the beats were covered according to the dictates of the research design.

MEASUREMENT AND ANALYSIS

Survey questionnaires were designed to collect information about exposure to the program as well as to measure each hypothesized effect. To increase reliability and to combine interrelated items, separate factor analyses were performed on the Time 1 and Time 2 survey responses. Items that clustered on the same factor at both times, and that were related conceptually, were combined to form scales. In addition, certain types of archival data were collected from police department records.

Each beat was found to contain approximately 150-200 households and 35-50 nonresidential establishmcnts (businesses, churches, schools, and so forth). To ensure representativeness and equal samples per beat, 430 residential and 170 nonresidential respondents (36 and 14 per beat, respectively) were interviewed between November 1977 and February 1978, before the experiment began; separate samples of 430 and 170 were interviewed between January and April of 1979. Responses were analyzed by two-way analysis of variance, with treatment area (Drop, Retain, and Add) and time (before, T_1, and after, T_2) as independent variables. A statistically significant interaction effect indicated a difference across treatment areas in the changes in responses from Time 1 and Time 2. When an interaction effect was found to be significant at the .05 level, multiple comparisons were made to determine which particular differences created the statistically significant result.

Two analyses of variance were conducted on each dependent variable presented in this report. The first analysis used beats as the units of analysis. That is, the mean responses for each of the four beats in each treatment group at both points in time were entered into the analysis of variance. Strictly speaking, because the random assignment of treatments was applied to beats, this is the most appropriate method of analysis. Because there were only twelve beats involved in the experiment, however, the total sample size in such analyses can be only twelve. Because statistical significance is greatly dependent upon sample size, only very large effects can be expected to be significant with such a small number of observations. Analyzing data in this fashion, therefore, tends to bias the results toward the conclusion of "no differences" and the social significance of the findings could be lost.

To counteract this bias, a second form of analysis of variance was conducted, using individual respondents as units of analysis. Such analyses were carried out to provide more powerful tests of differences. This approach is consistent with the admonition in Blalock (1960) that flexibility in drawing inferences, including the justifiable shifting of units of analysis, is desirable.

RESULTS

The extent to which residents of the experimental areas perceived the manipulation of the presence of foot patrol—and the results of the tests of the various hypotheses—are presented below.

Recalled Awareness of Foot Patrol. Among residential respondents, the awareness of foot patrol in the Drop condition decreased noticeably; awareness in the Add condition increased markedly; awareness in the Retain condition decreased somewhat, but the change was less than in either of the other two conditions. No matter whether beats or individuals are used as units of analysis, the interaction effect among conditions was highly significant. Thus, the residents involved in the experiment perceived the experimental manipulations accurately.

Given that foot patrol was manipulated after most businesses had closed, it is not surprising that nonresidential respondents demonstrated no significant experimental effects. Perceived awareness of foot patrol decreased in all three conditions, perhaps because of the widely publicized massive layoffs.

Perceived Disorder Problems in the Area. None of the four analyses (with the four different disorder scales) using beats as units of analysis found statistically significant differences among residential respondents. However, three of the four analyses using individuals as units of analysis produced differences significant at the .001 level. In all three cases (perceived street disorder, vandalism, and drug usage), respondents in the beats in which foot patrol was added perceived a much greater decline in the perceived severity of disorder than did respondents in either of the other two conditions. Furthermore, with respect to street disorder and vandalism, the perceived levels of problems were highest in the Drop condition and lowest in the Add condition, further suggesting a positive effect due to foot patrol. Perceived drug usage and prostitution, however, increased in the Retain beats and decreased in the Drop beats. Among nonresidential respondents, no effects supportive of the hypotheses being tested were discovered.

Perceived Crime Problems in the Area. Again, none of the three beat-level analyses produced differences among residential respondents that were statistically significant. However, two of the three analyses using individuals as units of analysis revealed differences significant at the .001 level. In both cases (perceived serious crime problems and perceived auto theft), respondents in the Add beats indicated a greater decline in the perceived severity of crime than did those in the other two conditions. Perceived problems in the Drop condition, however, were lower than in the Retain condition.

Among nonresidential respondents, although two of the items produced differences that were statistically significant, no consistent trends were suggested—with Add beat respondents perceiving the biggest deterioration in the rape problem but the Drop respondents perceiving the biggest deterioration in auto theft.

Perceived Likelihood of Victimization in the Area. None of the differences among means of any of the eight measures was statistically significant among residential respondents, using beats as the unit of analysis. At the individual level, however, the composite scale and five of the seven constituent items demonstrated differences significant at the .05 level. For the composite scale, respondents in the Add beats perceived the lowest likelihood of crime occurring. The highest likelihood, however, was perceived by those in the Retain beats. The same general pattern was displayed in most of the analyses of the individual items: Respondents in the Retain condition perceived the greatest likelihood of crime, and those in the Add condition the least.

None of the differences observed among nonresidential respondents was statistically significant, although it is noteworthy that the perceived likelihood of all types of crime increased in all three conditions.

Perceived Safety of the Area. Although the differences among means were not statistically significant among residential respondents using beats as the unit of analysis, they were significant at the .05 level using individuals as the analysis unit. Respondents in the Add condition perceived their areas to be the most safe; those in the Retain condition, however, perceived their areas to be the least safe. The differences observed among nonresidential respondents were not statistically significant.

Likelihood of Reporting Crimes to Police. None of the differences among means of the five measures analyzed among residential respondents was statistically significant using beats as the unit of analysis. Even if individuals are used as the unit of analysis, only one outcome measure—the likelihood of reporting a possible rape—showed differences in means that were statistically significant. In that case, respondents in the Drop beats were much more likely to say they would report an incident than were those in the other two conditions; those in the Retain beats were the least likely to say they would report an incident to the police. These items were not asked of nonresidential respondents.

Victimization. Only one statistically significant difference was found in the analysis among residential respondents when examining the one composite scale and the eight individual measures of victimization: Respondents in the Retain beats indicated a significantly greater reduction in the number of thefts that occurred in their neighborhood. This difference was so large that it was significant even if beats were used as the unit of analysis. Since no changes in the level of foot patrol were made in the Retain beats, no attribution of effects due to experimental conditions can be made. None of the differences among the means of nonresidential respondents was statistically significant.

Recorded Crime. Based on interrupted time-series analyses, no significant differences across experimental conditions were found between the changes in levels or trends in recorded crime for any of the eleven categories analyzed.

Evaluation of Police Service. At the individual level, respondents in the Add beats increased their evaluations of the job done by the police department more than those in the other two conditions; those in the Drop beats gave the lowest evaluations. The comparison of differences among the individual level means was significant at the .05 level.

Similarly, respondents in the Add beats were the least likely to perceive the problem of police protection to be a major one. Respondents in the Retain beats, however, were the most likely to perceive police protection to be a serious problem. None of the differences among means of nonresidential respondents was statistically significant.

SUMMARY AND CONCLUSIONS

In order to provide a better test of the value of foot patrol as a police tactic, the Police Foundation evaluated the effects of an experiment conducted by the Newark Police Department in which twelve small (8-16 block) strips of approximately 150-200 residential units and 35-50 nonresidential establishments were assigned to one of three experimental conditions:

(1) the Retain condition, in which foot patrol had existed for at least five years, and was to be continued;
(2) the Drop condition, in which foot patrol had existed for at least five years, and was to be eliminated; or
(3) the Add condition, in which foot patrol had not existed for at least five years, and was instituted.

Eight beats that had been patrolled consistently for some time were matched into four sets of two, based on several demographic characteristics. Based on a random selection process, one beat in each pair was to continue to receive foot patrol and the other such patrol was to be discontinued. In addition, foot patrol was begun in four areas similar to those previously patrolled on foot where it had not existed before. Despite internal opposition and significant layoffs of personnel, the Newark department implemented the experiment successfully from February 1978 through January 1979.

Interviews were conducted with residents and representatives of nonresidential establishments before and after the experimental period. Because the manipulation of foot patrol occurred from 5 p.m. to midnight on Monday through Friday evenings, it was expected that the experiment would have little or no effect on respondents from nonresidential establishments, most of which closed before the manipulations occurred. For residents, however, the presence of foot patrol was hypothesized to have the following effects:

(1) reduction in the level of perceived disorder problems in the area
(2) reduction in the level of perceived crime problems in the area
(3) reduction in the perceived likelihood of criminal victimization
(4) increase in the perceived safety of the neighborhood
(5) improved evaluations of police service
(6) increase in the likelihood of reporting crimes
(7) reduction in the precentage of residents victimized
(8) reduction in the number of recorded crimes

As expected, the results among nonresidential respondents indicate that they were not aware of the experimental manipulations and displayed no consistent patterns across experimental conditions.

Among residents of the experimental areas, however, perceptions of the experimental manipulation of foot patrol were quite accurate. In areas in which foot patrol was added, respondents saw a noticeable (and statistically significant) increase in such patrol; those in areas where foot patrol was eliminated indicated a sharp (and statistically significant) decline in the foot patrol they saw; respondents in areas where foot patrol was maintained said they saw somewhat less foot patrol, but the difference was not statistically significant.

It is not surprising that, because only twelve beats were involved in the study and statistical significance is highly dependent on sample size, such significance was rarely achieved when beats were used as units of analysis. Depending solely upon such analyses, however, biases the results toward the conclusion that no effect was produced. To counteract this bias, a second set of analyses, using individuals as the unit of analysis, were performed. These latter analyses yielded a number of significant findings, which will be discussed below.

With respect to perceived disorder problems, the addition of foot patrol produced reductions in all four measures analyzed. In three of those four analyses, the differences among the three experimental conditions were statistically significant; in all three cases, the perceived severity of the disorders declined more among those where foot patrol was added than in either of the other conditions. The results in areas where foot patrol was maintained, although generally positive, were not as consistently so as for residents of areas where foot patrol was added. For example, for two of the four measures examined, perceived disorder problems increased in the Retain beats, but the level declined in both the Add and Drop beats.

Adding foot patrol produced reductions in all three measures of perceived crime problems. In two of those three analyses, perceived severity of crime declined significantly more in the Add beats than in either of the other two conditions. For two out of the three measures examined, the changes in perceptions of crime among those in the Retain condition were less positive than among those in the Drop condition.

The results concerning the perceived likelihood of crime were similar to those for perceived disorder and crime problems. Six of the seven analyses produced differences that were statistically significant; in four of those cases, the change in perceived likelihood was most positive in the Add condition. In all six cases, however, the change was least positive in the Retain condition.

Similar results also were found with respect to the perceived safety of the area, which increased in the Add beats, declined somewhat in the Drop beats, and declined notably in the Retain beats. These differences were statistically significant.

Only one of the five analyses of measures of the likelihood of reporting crimes to police proved to be statistically significant. In that case, respondents in the Drop beats increased their likelihood of reporting a rape, but those in the other conditions decreased theirs.

Only one of the nine analyses produced differences in changes in victimization that were statistically significant. In that case, victimization decreased in all three conditions, albeit least in the Add condition and most in the Retain condition. No statistically significant differences were found among the changes in levels or trends of recorded crime across the three conditions.

Finally, evaluations of local police improved in the Add beats more than in either of the other two conditions on both measures analyzed; all of these analyses produced differences that were statistically significant. Again, the results were mixed with respect to the Retain condition. In one case, the change in evaluation of the job performed by the police declined less in the Retain condition than in the Drop condition, and it increased in the Add beats. With regard to the problem of police protection, however, residents of Retain beats demonstrated a considerably greater increase in concern about this problem than those in either of the other two conditions.

In summary, these results indicate that the *addition* of intensive foot patrol coverage to relatively short (8-16 block) commercial/residential strips during five evenings per week over a one-year period can have considerable effects on the perceptions of residents concerning disorder problems, crime problems, the likelihood of crime, safety, and police service. Such additional patrol, however, appears to have no significant effect on victimization, recorded crime, or the likelihood of reporting a crime.

The *elimination* of foot patrol after years of maintenance, however, appears to produce few notable negative effects. Similarly, the *retention* of foot patrol does not prove to have notable beneficial effects.

Two explanations for these findings appear plausible. First, the nature of the areas in which foot patrol was added may have differed notably from that of areas in which it had existed for several years. If these differences were great enough, findings comparing the Add beats to those in the other two conditions may be biased. Second, the effect of foot patrol may be strongest at its inception, then become minimal with its continuance. It is possible, of course, that both explanations may be valid and may even reinforce each other. For example, the kinds of people in the areas in which foot patrol was recently instituted may have been particularly attuned to, and affected by, such patrols and their novelty.

In any case, it would appear, based on these results, that the tactical use of foot patrol in areas that are not accustomed to it can have clearly positive effects. In addition, it appears that such patrol can be removed, at least temporarily, without incurring negative consequences. Perhaps the best use of scarce resources, then, would be to redeploy foot patrol officers to different areas periodically.

Finally, and perhaps most significantly, this study demonstrated that experiments involving police operations are not only possible—even under the most difficult of circumstances—but are rewarding and useful for scholars and practitioners alike.

REFERENCES

Adams, T. F. (1971). *Police patrol tactics and techniques*. Englewood Cliffs, NJ: Prentice Hall.

Bertram, D. K., & Vargo, A. (1976). Response time analysis study: Preliminary finding on robbery in Kansas City. *Police Chief, 43*(5), 74-77.

Blalock, W. M. (1960). *Social statistics*. New York: McGraw-Hill.

Bloch, P. B., & Ulberg, C. (1972). The beat commander concept. *Police Chief, 39*(9), 55-63

Bright, J. A. (1970). *Beat patrol experiment*. London: Home Office, Police Research and Development Branch.

Campbell, D. T., & Stanley, J. C. (1966). *Experimental and quasi-experimental design for research*. Chicago: Rand McNally.

Collins, E. (1979, November). *The New Jersey foot patrol program*. Paper presented at the annual meeting of the American Society of Criminology, Philadelphia.

Cook, T. C., & Campbell, D. T. (1979). *Quasi-experimental design and analysis issues for field settings*. Chicago: Rand McNally.

Fogelson, R. (1977). *Big-city police*. Cambridge, MA: Harvard University Press.

Gourley, G. D. (1974). *Patrol administration* (2nd ed.). Springfield, IL: Charles C Thomas.

Hogan, E. J., & Fagin, J. (1974). Integrating the policeman into the community. *Police Chief, 41*(12), 54-56.

Institute for Defense Analysis. (1966). *Part III: Analysis of response to police deterrence*. Unpublished manuscript.

International Association of Chiefs of Police. (1970). *The patrol operation*. Washington, DC: Author.

Kansas City, Missouri, Police Department. (1978). *Response time analysis: Vol. 2. Analysis*. Washington, DC: National Institute of Law Enforcement and Criminal Justice.

Kelling, G., Pate, T., Dieckman, D., & Brown, C. (1974). *The Kansas City Preventive Patrol Experiment: A technical report*. Washington, DC: Police Foundation.

Kinney, J. A. (1979, November). *Isla Vista foot patrol*. Paper presented at the annual meeting of the American Society of Criminology, Philadelphia.

Lane, R. (1975). *Policing the city: Boston, 1822-1885*. New York: Atheneum.

Pate, T., Ferrara, A., Bowers, R., & Lorence, J. (1976). *Police response time: Its determinants and effects*. Washington, DC: Police Foundation.

Pendland, M. B., & Gay, W. G. (1972). Foot patrols: The Fort Worth experience. *Police Chief 39*(4), 46-48.

Police Foundation. (1981). *The Newark Foot Patrol Experiment*. Washington, DC: Police Foundation.

Préfecture de Police, Paris. (1973). The beat system in Paris. *International Criminal Police Review, 271*, 248-258.

President's Commission on Law Enforcement and Administration of Justice. (1967). *Task force report: The police*. Washington, DC: Government Printing Office.

Press, J. S. (1971). *Some effects of an increase in police manpower in the 20th precinct of New York City* (Report R704-NYC). New York: New York City Rand Institute.

Reiss, A. (1971). The police and the public. New Haven, CT: Yale University Press.

Resource Planning Corporation. (1975). *A survey of households and business establishments in foot patrol, scooter patrol and control areas in Arlington County, VA*. Unpublished manuscript.

Richardson, J. F. (1970). *The New York police*. New York: Oxford University Press.

Schnelle, J. F., Kirchner, R. E., Casey, J. D., Useltor, P. H., Jr., & McNees, M. P. (1977). Patrol evaluation research: A multiple baseline analysis of police patrol during day and night hours. *Journal of Applied Behavior Analysis, 10*, 33-40.

Schnelle, J. F., Kirchner, R. E., McNees, M. P., & Lawler, J. M. (1975). Social evaluation research: The evaluation of two police patrolling strategies. *Journal of Applied Behavior Analysis, 4*, 353-365.

Chapter 8

EVALUATING A NEIGHBORHOOD FOOT PATROL PROGRAM
The Flint, Michigan, Project

ROBERT C. TROJANOWICZ

Public servants, including the police, often do not have intense interaction with the public and most of the problem-solving process is highly formalized, impersonal, and sterile. Informal communication is a rarity and motorized police officers can easily become isolated and aloof because of sporadic contacts with the public. This, in turn, gives the public an excuse to be apathetic.

Because of this lack of informal face-to-face contact, it is difficult for the motorized police officer to empathize with the community, understand the lifestyles of its members, and provide meaningful linkages between citizens and governmental services. In addition, information needed to prevent and control crime is often lacking. In order for the quantity and quality of information to be improved between citizens and the police there needs to be contact, communication, and trust.

Most people would trust a neighbor they have talked with and know something about more than one to whom they haven't even said hello. The same can be said for citizen perceptions of a police officer on foot compared with one cruising in a patrol car. A trust and rapport is built between citizens and foot patrol officers that would not normally occur with an officer shut in behind closed car windows. This face-to-face contact with the public also allows foot patrol officers to deter crime in a unique way. The information exchange increases the probability of solving crimes, apprehending offenders, and even preventing crimes before they occur.

AUTHOR'S NOTE: *Some of the material in this chapter is reprinted by permission of the* Journal of Police Science and Administration, *2(4), 410-419, copyright 1983 by the International Association of Chiefs of Police, Inc.*

Community policing can take many different forms, ranging from an officer who walks most of the tour, to an officer who rides a scooter, to a motorized officer who parks the squad car and walks a specified amount of time.

Community policing, of which foot patrol is a part, may be the necessary method of the future. Community residents will need to be more actively involved as the "eyes and ears" of their neighborhoods. Professional "paternalism" ("We know what is best for you") is no longer acceptable or cost-effective. Crime prevention is cheaper than reaction to crime once it occurs, and crime prevention necessitates cooperation between the police and the community.

Decreasing police budgets will dictate that more effective methods be developed. Police departments will need to find more efficient ways of utilizing police officers' "free patrol time." Estimates of the typical free patrol time in communities range between 40% and 60% of a motor officer's shift. Granted, the free patrol time does not occur in one block of time during the shift, but there are large segments of time that the patrol car can be parked and the officer walk and mingle with the public. Then, *contact* can be made, *communication* facilitated, and *trust* developed so that the exchange of information to prevent and solve crimes can take place.

Unfortunately, motor patrol officers are reluctant to leave their patrol cars for fear of not being able to respond quickly to emergencies. They also are uncomfortable in casual interactions with the public, fearing harassment, ridicule, and even danger. These reasons for officer reluctance to leave the patrol car are usually unfounded. Most responses to citizen requests are not of an emergency nature, and, if they are, an adjoining motor patrol officer can respond almost as quickly. Obviously, there needs to be coordination between adjoining motor beats so that both officers are not walking at the same time.

Fear of citizen harassment and ridicule of the officer when he or she is walking is usually unfounded and, in fact, most citizens welcome police officers in their businesses or in their neighborhoods. In addition, officer safety may even be increased by foot patrol (Trojanowicz & Banas, 1985). It is precisely via the natural, regular interaction between the officer and citizens that relevant information is exchanged—information that may encourage preventive citizen self-protection and may lead to the solution of crimes.

Because it is often difficult to persuade motor officers to leave their patrol cars, even for short periods of time, many communities have initiated community policing programs in which officers spend most of their time outside of their cars.

FOOT PATROL IN FLINT, MICHIGAN

The following is a discussion of the results of an experimental foot patrol program that was conducted in 14 neighborhoods of Flint, Michigan, between January 1979 and January 1982. The Neighborhood Foot Patrol Program (NFPP) was sponsored by a grant from the Charles Stewart Mott Foundation. A research team from Michigan State University,[1] under my direction, was asked by the Mott Foundation to conduct an evaluation of the program.

At the time that the Neighborhood Foot Patrol Program was initiated in 1979, Flint was experiencing many of the difficulties one would expect in a racially mixed industrial city heavily dependent upon the automobile industry. The unemployment rate was among the highest in the nation, and crime rates were rising. Two basic problems were believed to hinder effective crime prevention: the lack of neighborhood organization and citizen involvement in the crime prevention process and the lack of personal contact and interaction between police officers and community residents. It was generally agreed that a properly conceived and implemented foot patrol program could help organize the community for the purpose of crime prevention, and at the same time serve as a basis for improved communication between the police and the citizens of Flint.

The Flint Neighborhood Foot Patrol Program was an ambitious undertaking, and it experienced many of the difficulties that typically plague a new and innovative program. On balance, however, the Flint program was deemed a success, so much so that residents of Flint voted to increase their property taxes so that the entire city would be covered by foot patrol. Currently, there are 64 foot districts in Flint.

Foot patrol has been a widely accepted policing technique in some foreign lands, including England, Australia, Germany, and Japan. In this country, foot patrol was used extensively in the cities prior to World War II, and it has enjoyed something of a renaissance in the past decade. The most ambitious recent experiment in foot patrol took place in Newark, New Jersey, during the mid-1970s (see Police Foundation, 1981; Pate, this volume).

The Flint program, although similar to the above programs, had some unique characteristics. These unique aspects, as well as the most relevant findings, will be presented in this chapter.

GOALS OF THE PROGRAM

First, the Flint Neighborhood Foot Patrol Program, which covered about 20% of the population of Flint, was, from the very outset, an exercise in communication between the police officers and the citizens. Every effort was made to avoid imposing a program on the populace. While the Flint NFPP formally began in January of 1979, it had been in the planning stage for well over a year. Citywide meetings were held in Flint as far back as November 1977 for the purposes of keeping the citizens informed as to the exact nature of the program and of soliciting their views on how the program should function in the different neighborhoods. When, therefore, the program actually began, it had wide support among the citizens, who felt that it was, in a real sense, "their program." But more than this, it was a better program because it was based on a more complete understanding of the neighborhoods and their unique problems.

Second, the role an officer in the Flint NFPP was expected to play was developed out of very definite assumptions about the nature of police work. The Flint foot patrol officers were not expected to be just security officers, "shaking doors" and deterring criminal activity by their mere presence in uniform. It was assumed that it was better to prevent crime than to react to it, and it was further assumed that the various services the government provides can help to prevent crime if they are brought into play at an early enough stage. Consequently, officers in the Flint NFPP were expected to provide linkages to these governmental services. They were expected to be familiar with their neighborhoods, to recognize potential problems, and to make referrals to the appropriate social agencies when it was necessary to do so.

Third, the Flint program operated on the assumption that citizens themselves have an extremely important role to play in the prevention of crime and in the maintenance of public order. That is, they need to be the "eyes and ears" of their neighborhoods if crime is to be controlled. Therefore, the foot patrol officers in the Flint program were expected to function as catalytic agents of community organization. They were expected to encourage citizens to work together—in neighborhood associations, citizen watch groups, or some other form of organization—for their mutual support and protection.

Finally, it is difficult to overemphasize the importance of cooperation among the various groups involved. The Flint Neighborhood Foot Patrol Program was an excellent example of how a local police department can, with technical assistance from a university and practical guidance from the community, design and implement an effective program. The Flint Police Department, the Michigan State University research team, the citizens of the 14 experimental areas, and representatives of the Mott Foundation worked together on an ongoing basis to make the program a success. From its onset, the program was subjected to constructive criticism and change. Problem areas were identified quickly and alterations were made. Ideas that proved unworkable in practice were discarded, and new ideas were generated.

METHODOLOGY

The Mott Foundation grant for the Flint Neighborhood Foot Patrol Program established 10 basic goals:

(1) to decrease the amount of actual or perceived criminal activity
(2) to increase the citizen's perception of personal safety
(3) to deliver to Flint residents a type of law enforcement service consistent with the community needs and the ideals of modern police practice
(4) to create a community awareness of crime problems and of methods for increasing the ability of law enforcement agencies to deal effectively with actual or potential criminal activity
(5) to develop citizen volunteer action in support of, and under the direction of, the police department, aimed at various target crimes
(6) to eliminate citizen apathy about reporting crime to the police
(7) to increase protection for women, children, and the aged
(8) to monitor the activity of the foot patrol officers
(9) to measure the interface between the foot patrol officers and other units of the Flint Police Department and to measure as well the number of referrals to other agencies
(10) to evaluate the impact of training on the performance of foot patrol officers.

The research team evaluated and monitored the NFPP to see how well these goals were met. (The research team, however, did not have input into the construction of the goals.) Again, and for emphasis, this process of evaluation also provided technical assistance to the program. There was a constant interchange of information and ideas between the Flint Police Department and the research team. In addition, as director of the evaluation, I met a number of times with command officers from the Flint Police Department and staff of the Mott Foundation to discuss needed improvements. Also, there were yearly group community meetings. Residents could question police commanders, foot patrol officers, Mott Foundation representatives, and the director of evaluation about the program. These group meetings enabled citizens to understand better the problems in their neighborhoods and what they could do to prevent them. The evaluation process was not sterile, and it was understood from the beginning that because communities are dynamic, variables affecting them could not be held totally constant.

Because the members of the research team were in Flint and interacting with the citizens and the police officers on a regular basis, they developed a good deal of informal, as well as formal, information. Often the informal information served as a basis for technical assistance to the program, and it provided at all times a check on the formal research data. For the purposes of the formal evaluation, however, information was developed through five primary sources; these are discussed below.

(1) Personal Interviews. Numerous and extensive interviews were conducted with community residents, block club leaders, businesspeople, members of the local clergy, foot patrol officers, motor patrol officers, command officers, and representatives of various community agencies.

(2) Crime Statistics and Calls for Service. The crime statistics and calls for service from the 14 experimental foot patrol areas were gathered and analyzed. Comparisons were then made between the statistics gathered in 1978, the year before the NFPP began, and the years 1979, 1980, and 1981, when it was in full force. Early in the experiment an attempt was made to establish 14 comparable control areas to measure crime rates and calls for service and compare them with the 14 experimental areas. This became problematic, however, because as the popularity and expansion of foot patrol increased, many parts of the proposed control areas were provided with foot patrol services.

(3) Monitoring. The daily, weekly, and monthly reports of each foot patrol officer were sampled and examined for evidence of the extent and nature of his or her activities. The community newsletters that the foot patrol officers were encouraged to write were analyzed, and members of the research team were active in the community and the police department as participant observers.

(4) Media Content Analysis. Editorials, articles, and letters to the editor that appeared in the local media and dealt with the crime problem in Flint or with attitudes toward the NFPP were analyzed and coded.

(5) Intervening Variables. During the three-year experiment there were several intervening variables that could not be controlled. The city

had, at various times, the highest rate of unemployment in the nation; a drastically reduced tax base, necessitating the layoff of police officers, and causing a rotation of some of the foot officers in the 14 experimental areas; a court order closing the city jail and mandating the early release of offenders in the county jail to alleviate overcrowding; a change in the command structure of the foot patrol program; and the expansion of the 14 foot areas during the third year of the experiment due to the program's popularity and ultimate political pressure.

The comparison of crime statistics, calls for service, the monitoring, and the media content analysis are fairly self-explanatory. The conducting of interviews, however, was a more complicated process and requires further discussion. In general, the interview questions were designed to provide data on a wide range of variables, including experience with crime, crime reporting, police performance, recommendations for police improvements, awareness of the NFPP, and awareness of the kinds and numbers of police activities.

All of the officers assigned to the Flint Neighborhood Foot Patrol Program in the 14 experimental areas were interviewed during all three years of the project. In addition, a sample of motorized officers were also interviewed to serve as a control group.

For the purposes of evaluation, the research team treated businesspeople, block club leaders, and members of the clergy as a group apart from the community at large. It was believed that these groups of citizens, by virtue of their occupations and interests, were more likely to be well informed and active than citizens of the public at large. Table 8.1 illustrates the numbers and type of interviews.

In choosing subjects for interviews from the public at large, the research team adopted a twofold strategy. First, during the second and third years of the program, randomly selected community residents were interviewed. By doing this, the research team believed it could accurately assess community attitudes toward the NFPP. Yet, the research team also wished to have some sense of how community attitudes toward the NFPP had evolved over the course of three years. Consequently, a sample of residents was interviewed the first year and then reinterviewed in the second and third years.

FINDINGS

The following are many of the major findings of the evaluation. Space does not permit discussing all of the results. For a more detailed presentation of the results, see Trojanowicz (1983).

TABLE 8.1 Numbers of Interviews and Identifying Information

Sample Elements	Sample Period	Sample Size 1979	1980	1981
Questionnaire surveys				
Foot patrol officers in 14 foot patrol areas	police survey	6/1979-12/31/81	22	22	22
Motorized officers in 14 foot patrol areas	police survey	6/1979-12/31/81	45	24	16
Motorized officers in non-foot patrol areas	police survey	6/1979-12/31/81	23	0	0
Sergeants supervising foot patrol program[a]	police survey	1980-1981	3	4	4
Business personnel	business survey	6/1979-12/31/81	23	11	14
Clergy	clergy interview	6/1979-12/31/81	20	20	9
Social service agencies	social service agency survey	6/1979-12/31/81	19	21	19
Resident three-year panel in each of the 14 foot patrol areas[b]	community survey	12/31/81	84	48	44
Association leaders (block club) in each of the 14 foot patrol areas	community survey	12/31/81	23	18	17
Random resident sample	shortened survey	12/31/81	–	320	280
Association leaders non-foot area	community survey	12/31/81	14	13	13
Data analyses					
FPD crime complaint records for 14 foot patrol areas	daily entries	1/1/78-12/31/81			
Daily reports	daily reports	1/1/79-12/31/80			
Weekly reports	weekly reports	1/1/79-12/31/81			
Monthly reports	monthly reports	1/1/79-12/31/81			
Foot officer's flex hours		7/1/79-12/31/81			
FPD juvenile booking sheets	juvenile bureau daily booking sheets	9/1/80-12/31/81			
Content analysis of local area newspapers					
The Flint Journal	daily	1/1/79-12/31/81			
The Flint Voice	twice monthly	1/1/79-12/31/81			
East Village Reporter	every 2 weeks	1/1/79-12/31/81			

a. Includes three sergeants plus lieutenant in 1980 and deputy chief in 1981.
b. Panel sample for three years with attrition was 44.

Implementation Problems

It would have been surprising indeed if the evaluation had uncovered no shortcomings in the Flint Neighborhood Foot Patrol Program. The following were some of the major problem areas. Others will be presented in the section dealing with implications for policy.

There were the predictable difficulties between foot and motor patrol officers. Many of the motorized officers viewed the foot officers as not doing real "police work" and as having "choice" hours to work. Not only were some of the role expectations different for the foot officers, there was a misconception at the beginning of the program that foot officers should handle these occurrences. This, of course, created antagonism. The problem was rectified, however, and foot officers were expected to respond to all calls, including the serious ones, if they could get there first. The hostility between foot and motorized officers has subsided and is most evident in the large numbers of motorized officers who now desire to be a part of the citywide Neighborhood Foot Patrol Program.

During the third year of the program, because of its popularity and the ensuing political pressure in the city of Flint, it became necessary to expand the 14 foot patrol areas to an unwarranted extent, which quite naturally reduced the amount of contact officers had with residents. Likewise, there were problems with the performance of some officers, as well as a reluctance by others to make referrals to social agencies and work with juveniles. The training foot patrol officers received was also deficient, particularly in the areas of making referrals and helping officers develop strong communication and interpersonal skills. In addition, the supervision of the foot officers was uneven, and some officers were setting their own work hours, which usually meant working the daytime hours with weekends off. Other officers preferred to spend much of their time at their base stations or at "selected" businesses and residences. On balance, however, the evaluation showed that the Neighborhood Foot Patrol Program was well accepted by residents and beneficial for the city of Flint.

Citizen Perceptions

In regard to the data for the last year of the study (1981), the percentage of citizens who said they were satisfied (64%) with the NFPP, and who felt safer (68%) in their neighborhoods as a result of it, increased in each successive year of the evaluation. This finding is even more impressive inasmuch as it would have been reasonable to expect a decrease in citizen satisfaction with the program as a result of the expansion of the foot patrol areas during the third year.

Of the respondents in the last year, 30% knew of programs an officer was involved in; the majority said their neighbors liked the program; and 61% said that the program increased protection for women, children, and the aged. A total of 48% had suggestions for improving the program, such as the need for more officers, greater officer visibility and availability, smaller area size, and more night patrols.

There were 72% of the respondents who had either seen or had personal contact with a foot patrol officer, 36% knew the officer's name, and half of the remaining respondents provided an accurate physical description. In addition, 90% of the citizens were aware of the program; almost half knew the role of the foot officer; 62% said foot officers encouraged them to report crime and become involved in crime prevention; and 48% said the program had reduced crime (15% said it had not; the rest were undecided).

Even though some of the above findings are based upon perceptions, they nevertheless were consistent over the three years of the evaluation and the formal and informal data reinforced each other.

There is a tendency in some quarters to dismiss foot patrol programs as more cosmetic than substantive. This charge most often surfaces when, as happened in the Newark Foot Patrol Experiment, a program proves popular with the citizens but does not lead to a reduction in the crime. Yet, as Police Foundation (1981, p. 118) researchers point out in their analysis of the Newark experiment, such a charge not only ignores the known limitations of crime statistics, but unjustifiably trivializes the issue of citizen fear:

> If vulnerable and weak people feel safe as a result of specific police activity and if that feeling improves the quality of their life, that is terribly important.

Impact on Crime

The Flint Neighborhood Foot Patrol Program produced findings different from those of the Newark evaluation regarding the program's impact on crime. Crime rates were down, and down markedly, in Flint over the three-year evaluation period. As Table 8.2 illustrates, in 1978, the year before the NFPP began, there were 4,085 crimes reported in the 14 areas that were later to receive foot patrol. In

1981, there were 3,731 crimes reported in these 14 areas. Crime was down in all categories except for robbery and burglary, and these two crimes were up much higher for Flint in general. The foot patrol was less effective in reducing these serious crimes, because most of these offenses took place at night, when the officers on foot were not working. The total volume of reported crime across all 14 areas was down 8.7% over the life of the project—and at a time when crime rates in the rest of Flint had increased by 10% over this same three-year period.

Professionals in the field of criminal justice have long been aware that success or failure of a program cannot be determined through reference to crime statistics alone. Crime statistics are important, and ultimately the basis, for a great many important decisions. At the same time, however, they are susceptible to influence from a number of sources and judgments. The conclusions drawn for changes in the crime rates must be made cautiously.

Calls for service were down more than 40% over the period of the evaluation. There were 678 calls for service in 1978 and 384 in 1981—a decrease of 43.4%. The research team found that the less serious complaints, such as abandoned cars, neighborhood children, or barking dogs, were being handled informally by foot patrol officers. Citizens had an option other than relaying their complaints to central dispatch. As a result, many minor problems were handled more cheaply and efficiently, and the motorized patrols were more available to deal with the serious situations. Also, neighbors began to interact with each other as a result of involvement in neighborhood block clubs. They began to solve their problems with each other without involving the police, thus further reducing calls for service.

What is particularly persuasive is that changes in the crime statistics corresponded to changes in the NFPP in ways that were predictable. Although crime rates were down 8.7% over the life of the project, there were dramatic fluctuations in the data from year to year. During the first two years of the NFPP, crime rates were actually down in the vicinity of 20% in the 14 experimental areas. Then, in the third year, it was decided to expand the size of the patrol areas, in one instance up to 20 times the size of the original patrol area. The research team cautioned that this expansion would almost certainly diminish the effectiveness of the program. That, unfortunately, is precisely what happened. Crime rates, keeping the original boundary areas constant, were up sharply during 1981 though they still remained well below the 1978 level—the point being that with the expansion of the areas there was a direct, predictable increase in crime.

TABLE 8.2 Crime Statistics

Best Area Number	Total Number of Crimes		Increase or Decrease of Crime by Best Area	Burglary		Car Theft		Assault		Vandalism		Robbery		Criminal Sex Conduct		Larceny Home		Larceny Person		Larceny Vehicle	
	1978	1981		1978	1981	1978	1981	1978	1981	1978	1981	1978	1981	1978	1981	1978	1981	1978	1981	1978	1981
1	238	263	increase 10.5%	38 16%	101 38%	11 5%	7 3%	55 23%	44 17%	49 21%	25 10%	8 3%	7 3%	2 1%	2 1%	43 18%	56 21%	5 2%	3 1%	27 11%	18 7%
2	213	197	decrease 7.5%	39 18%	48 24%	8 4%	8 4%	51 24%	40 20%	40 19%	29 15%	6 3%	14 7%	2 1%	0 0%	36 17%	19 10%	5 2%	4 2%	26 12%	35 18%
3	159	172	increase 8.1%	24 15%	29 17%	11 7%	6 3%	31 19%	36 21%	37 23%	47 27%	3 2%	1 1%	2 1%	4 2%	29 18%	24 14%	0 0%	5 3%	22 14%	20 12%
4	138	138		30 22%	60 43%	7 5%	2 1%	33 24%	27 20%	19 14%	26 19%	3 2%	0 0%	1 1%	1 1%	24 17%	11 8%	6 4%	2 1%	15 11%	8 6%
5	379	342	decrease 9.7%	63 17%	111 32%	19 5%	9 3%	124 33%	70 20%	65 17%	36 11%	13 3%	4 1%	3 1%	4 1%	50 13%	71 21%	10 3%	11 3%	32 8%	26 8%
6	539	533	decrease 1.1%	121 22%	119 22%	10 2%	21 4%	163 30%	158 30%	67 12%	52 10%	22 4%	24 5%	8 1%	4 1%	89 17%	88 17%	18 3%	11 2%	41 8%	58 11%
7	298	243	decrease 18.5%	54 18%	72 30%	26 9%	6 2%	60 20%	22 9%	47 16%	50 21%	9 3%	10 4%	3 1%	4 1%	49 16%	50 21%	6 2%	9 4%	44 15%	20 8%
8	634	626	decrease 1.3%	123 19%	169 27%	14 2%	18 3%	175 28%	141 23%	84 13%	75 12%	16 3%	40 6%	15 4%	4 1%	154 24%	113 18%	12 2%	20 3%	41 6%	46 7%
9	289	97	decrease 66.4%	57 20%	16 16%	12 4%	7 7%	65 23%	20 21%	56 19%	16 16%	3 1%	1 1%	6 2%	0 0%	44 15%	20 21%	5 2%	1 1%	41 14%	16 16%
10	118	72	decrease 39.0%	27 23%	22 31%	6 5%	6 8%	19 16%	7 10%	16 14%	11 15%	1 1%	1 1%	1 1%	0 0%	31 26%	9 13%	4 3%	2 3%	13 11%	14 19%
11	249	319	decrease 12.0%	53 21%	66 30%	15 6%	14 6%	58 23%	47 21%	36 14%	19 9%	6 2%	8 4%	2 1%	2 1%	42 17%	26 12%	8 3%	7 3%	29 12%	30 14%
12	220	145	decrease 34.1%	34 15%	37 26%	6 3%	1 1%	62 28%	31 21%	49 22%	19 13%	4 2%	8 6%	4 2%	1 1%	26 12%	24 17%	5 2%	1 1%	30 14%	23 16%
13	216	166	decrease 23.1%	29 13%	41 25%	10 5%	3 2%	34 16%	26 16%	53 25%	36 22%	4 2%	1 1%	0 0%	1 1%	45 21%	32 19%	1 1%	3 2%	40 19%	23 14%
14	15[d]	175	increase 52.2%	14 12%	33 19%	2 2%	2 2%	19 17%	25 14%	30 26%	39 22%	3 3%	2 1%	1 1%	1 1%	22 19%	40 23%	4 3%	0 0%	20 17%	32 18%
Total	4,085[b]	3,731[c]	decrease[a] 8.7%	706	924	157	111	949	694	648	480	101	121	50	27	684	583	89	79	421	369
				increase[a] 31%		decrease[a] 29%		decrease[a] 27%		decrease[a] 26%		increase[a] 20%		decrease[a] 46%		decrease[a] 15%		decrease[a] 11%		decrease[a] 12%	

a. Percentage increase or decrease of crime from 1978 through 1981. When burglary and robbery are eliminated, the total decrease in crime from 1978 through 1981 is 21.8%.

b. Total includes 280 crimes from a general category.

c. Total includes 343 crimes from a general category.

d. Does not include the crimes from the general category.

168

Foot Versus Motor Patrol

Finally, there was evidence that suggested that foot patrol officers could perform certain important police functions more effectively than could motor patrol officers. In the 1981 data, for example, the 280 citizen respondents were asked to compare the effectiveness of foot and motorized patrol officers in the performance of six important police activities: (1) preventing crime, (2) encouraging citizen protection of themselves, (3) responding to complaints, (4) investigating the circumstances of crime, (5) working with juveniles, and (6) following up on complaints.

As Table 8.3 shows, in four of these six areas—namely, preventing crime, encouraging citizen self-protection, working with juveniles, and following-up on complaints—citizens rated foot patrol officers more effective by large margins.

Citizens in 8 of the 14 foot patrol areas rated foot patrol officers more effective in investigating the circumstances of crime. The percentages in this category were, however, much closer, and the citizens in the remaining 6 areas rated motor patrol as more effective. Many of the respondents felt the foot patrol officers had an advantage in this area because they knew their districts well and had gained the trust of the residents. Having that trust gave the officers, in turn, greater access to information vital to the solution of crime.

Only in the area of responding to complaints were the motorized patrols rated superior; citizens in 9 of the 14 areas rated motor patrol officers superior in the performance of this function. They discriminated quite sharply, however, between the kinds of complaints that were involved. The superior mobility of the motor patrol officers gave them an advantage, particularly in responding to emergencies. It was, however, their mobility, and not their training, that gave them this advantage. When foot patrol officers were available to respond to an emergency, they were judged equally effective. In responding to minor or chronic complaints (that is, complaints not requiring immediate and decisive action), the foot patrol officers were judged more effective. Businesspeople, block club leaders, and members of the clergy rated foot officers superior in all six categories.

In addition, foot patrol officers, far more than motorized officers, felt that knowing the community residents and teaching them to report crime were important law enforcement goals. The foot patrol officers also agreed strongly over the three years of the project that reassuring residents was an important aspect of the job—another point of departure from the opinions expressed by the motorized of-

TABLE 8.3 Responses (in percentages) to "On the Items Below, State Who Is More Effective, Motorized (MP) or Foot Patrol (FP) Officers"

Best Area Number	Number of Respondents	Preventing Crime		Encouraging Citizen Protection of Themselves		Responding to Complaints		Investigating the Circumstances of Crime		Working with Juveniles		Following Up on Complaints	
		FP	MP	FP	MP	FP	MP	FP	MP	FP	MP	FP	MP
901	15	40[a]	33	60[a]	13	13	73	20	53	67[a]	7	27	33
902	15	60[a]	20	73[a]	7	20	47	33	40	67[a]	20	33[a]	20
903	15	67[a]	27	73[a]	13	47[a]	40	53[a]	40	100[a]	0	33	33
904	15	33[a]	13	40[a]	7	27[a]	20	27[a]	20	40[a]	7	27[a]	7
905	14	43[a]	50	71[a]	21	28	43	36[a]	28	71[a]	14	57[a]	7
906	16	44[a]	25	37[a]	6	19	44	12	37	56[a]	6	19	19
907	15	67[a]	27	80[a]	13	20	73	40	47	93[a]	7	60[a]	40
908[b]	15	53[a]	33	88[a]	7	20	67	60[a]	13	73[a]	7	60[a]	20
909	15	60[a]	20	100[a]	0	27	60	47[a]	27	93[a]	0	80[a]	7
910	28	71[a]	11	79[a]	7	54[a]	36	57[a]	25	86[a]	4	61[a]	7
911	15	80[a]	20	93[a]	0	40	53	33	40	80[a]	20	67[a]	27
912	15	87[a]	13	100[a]	13	53[a]	47	80[a]	20	100[a]	0	100[a]	0
913	15	60[a]	40	80[a]	7	7	93	20	53	53[a]	33	53[a]	46
914	15	60[a]	40	93[a]	7	60[a]	40	73[a]	27	100[a]	0	80[a]	20
Businesses	14	100[a]	0	100[a]	0	64[a]	36	79[a]	7	100[a]	0	86[a]	0
Ministers	9	55[a]	0	78[a]	0	0	0	55[a]	0	89[a]	0	44[a]	0
Associations (Block Clubs)	14	71[a]	21	93[a]	7	50	50	57[a]	36	86[a]	14	71[a]	29
Total	260	62	23	79	7	32	48	46	30	80	8	56	19

NOTE: Rest of percentages are "both" or "don't know."
a. FP more favorable.
b. The 20 respondents included in all other data from Area 908 were not asked this question.

ficers. Foot patrol officers showed a willingness and desire to conduct special classes for residents and, in general, saw communication and community involvement as very important. Motorized officers placed more importance on aloofness or professional detachment. Over the three years of the study, the foot patrol officers consistently placed a greater importance on helping victims than did the motorized officers. They also placed a great importance on preventing crime in all three years.

None of this is meant to suggest that motorized patrol has outlived its usefulness and should be replaced by foot patrol. Nothing could be further from the truth. What is being stressed, however, is that both motorized patrol and foot patrol have their characteristic virtues and limitations. Motorized patrol is obviously the better choice in areas where the population is spread out and a foot patrol officer would be hampered by lack of mobility. Equally obvious is the fact that motorized patrols are superior in certain crisis situations in which speed of response time and the ability to carry specialized equipment are needed. Foot patrol, on the other hand, works best in more densely populated areas; and it can be superior in certain investigatory functions, in answering routine calls for service, and in obtaining information for the prevention of crime and the apprehending of offenders.

In this "age of limitations," police administrators will ask if foot patrol programs are cost-effective. Citizens will want to know if these programs are budgetarily sound. The evidence developed by the research team clearly indicates that foot patrol programs are cost-effective; they are an intelligent use of public funds. Not only do they appear to be effective in reducing crime, investigating the circumstances of crime, and involving citizens in the crime prevention, but they are by their very nature less expensive to maintain. Much of the work police officers do is not of an emergency nature, and motorized patrol can be an unnecessarily expensive way of dealing with routine calls. Quite simply, many situations do not require the use of such expensive technology.

The three-year study also revealed that citizens began reporting minor problems to the foot patrol officer, who often dealt with them informally. The savings potential here can be substantial. When problems are dealt with informally, a great burden is lifted from the criminal justice system as a whole. The result is that the police and the courts are then freer to deal with the more serious problems of the community. Not only is the foot patrol officer less expensive to deploy initially, but, inasmuch as a problem is dealt with at the lowest level possible, an additional savings is realized.

Above all, foot patrol programs can lead to a reduction in the crime rate mainly because of the partnership between the community and the police. When crime rates go down in an area, businesses are more likely to remain or relocate there, thus providing the kind of economic base cities need. However, one cannot, of course, think of benefits to the government alone. Crimes, do, after all, have victims, and any drop in the crime rate brings associate savings to the community at large. Through increased police contact with the public there was quite naturally increased communication. With the quantity and quality of communication improved, a greater trust developed between the police and the public, which often led to a greater exchange of information—information critical to the prevention and control of crime and the apprehension of criminal offenders.

IMPLICATIONS FOR POLICY

Community policing programs necessitate a critical analysis of traditional operations. The following are some of the areas that have implication for community and police department policy (Trojanowicz, 1984).

Politics

Community policing programs—that is, foot patrol—are not only a very popular policing style, but they are susceptible to pressures from community political leaders. Local politicians will find it tempting to try to use the foot patrol program. Foot patrol officers know the community well, are respected, and are in day-to-day contact with a lot of voters. Politicians may well try to have foot patrol officers do favors for selected individuals to help with election-year canvassing. Effective supervision can greatly reduce, or even prevent, negative political influence, and specific departmental policy related to this issue will help officers avoid unprofessional conduct.

Special Interest Groups

Demands made by individuals other than politicians will occasionally be a problem. Various residents will seek to monopolize the foot officer's time. In addition, businesspeople and school administrators may expect unwarranted foot officer presence in their businesses or schools.

The larger problem, however, is that in some communities special interest groups from the upper-middle and wealthy classes (or businesses) may either misuse a foot patrol program or react negatively to its implementation. In regard to foot patrol encountering a negative reaction, the thinking is that if there are only limited police resources in a community, spreading them out more evenly will reduce the special interest groups' chances of receiving "special treatment." Foot patrol can effectively neutralize community power and redistribute it throughout the entire community. The working-class and lower socioeconomic segments of the community are usually much more receptive to foot patrol than the upper-middle class or wealthy, who may have had their interests served ahead of others. In many communities, if not most, the impetus for foot patrol comes from the working-class, lower socioeconomic, or middle-class areas in the community. Foot patrol is viewed by these groups as a more personal, human response to community needs, as well as increased police service.

The policy implications are obvious. Innovative police programs need the support of community decision makers. If the decision makers are overly influenced by those groups that resist foot patrol, then the chance for the implementation and successful operation of a program are minimal.

Community Social Problems

Foot patrol is only one method of dealing with community social problems. The community needs to have a commitment to solving problems such as inadequate housing, unemployment, and racial tension. Foot patrol officers can affect social policy only in a limited way. If there are deep-seated racial problems in the community that go unresolved, a foot patrol program may be viewed as merely a public relations effort implemented to appease residents who are concerned about governmental services, including crime prevention. Effective community policing programs have the long-term commitment of community and departmental decision makers. They do not come and go depending on the social and racial climate of the community at any particular time.

Funding

The search for funds to support innovative police programs is not easy in this time of contracting city budgets. There are essentially three sources of public funding for community policing projects: the reallocation of existing resources, state or federal grants, and special taxes.

The Flint program was initially operated on an experimental basis with private funds and supplemented with public funding. To finance the present citywide foot patrol program, the citizens of Flint approved a special tax millage. The officers employed via this special tax millage were not supposed to replace existing human resources. Unfortunately, two years after the special millage of 1982, regular support for the police department was reduced to the point where the total sworn strength of the Flint Police Department was substantially the same as it was prior to the addition of the 76 foot personnel in 1982. The motor patrol division bore the brunt of the reductions because, by the special millage law, the foot patrol division had to be kept at full strength.

Motor officers felt they were overworked, and when they were delayed in responding to citizen requests, it was not uncommon for them to blame the situation on foot patrol because it was draining resources from the motor patrol. In reality, the funding for the two divisions was separate—regular funding supported motor patrol, and the *special* tax millage supported foot patrol. The reduction of the motor patrol irritated citizens because they felt the increased tax millage did not provide for increased officers as promised.

If the innovative program is merely viewed as a means of appeasing citizens or gaining increased tax dollars without increased services, then the program will ultimately fail because it will lose citizen support. Policymakers need to guard against negative, often unintentional, ramifications of a new program.

Role Specificity

Traditional police administrators may also view community policing programs as merely a *luxury* and not a real crime-fighting tool. Since foot patrol may involve "nontraditional" kinds of activities, with an emphasis on service and proactive measures, it is mandatory that the role of foot patrol officers be clearly identified, put down in writing, and reinforced through role call, training, and departmental policy.

The foot patrol program should not, however, emphasize only the "soft" or service functions. The law enforcement or "felony" aspects of "regular" police work should also be emphasized. For example, even though foot officers may have mobility problems, they often can be used as backup or support personnel in serious incidents. It is a critical mistake for department administrators to use foot patrol officers merely for service or "soft" activities. This creates antagonism between motorized and foot officers and reinforces the misconception that foot officers are social workers, not "real" police officers. Although foot officers act as *links* to social service agencies and *catalytic* agents for community organizations, they are *not social workers*. The delivery of non-law enforcement service is congruent with what police officers actually do when their daily activities are analyzed.

Organizational Structure

Sound management and supervision are important characteristics of a successful foot patrol program. Poor personnel selection and weak training are serious defects, but they can be overcome to some degree by strong leadership. The reverse, however, is rarely true. Even talented, well-trained officers will lose heart if management is complacent, disorganized or ineffective.

It is critical that the foot patrol program be placed under a strong and respected leader who either has command responsibilty for the motorized patrol or has positive rapport with the patrol division.

Although this was not the case in Flint, the most appropriate organizational placement for foot patrol is in the motor patrol division. Those foot patrol programs that are in an administrative services unit, or a special services division, often encounter severe problems, even to the point of open hostility between foot and motorized officers. Placement of the foot patrol operations in the motor patrol division facilities open communication extending to roll call and even to informal gatherings.

If the foot patrol officers are a part of the motor division, then there will be common supervision between foot and motor officers. It is generally more difficult to supervise foot patrol officers because they can "hide" in private residences and businesses, and ineffective foot patrol officers find many allies in the community to "cover up" for them or "back up" their stories explaining lack of productivity. Close supervision can begin at roll call and then be reinforced throughout the workday, with at least spot checks by supervisors. In addition, it is mandatory that policy dictate that there be a clear system of accountability and activity reporting with regular review by foot patrol supervisors.

Personnel Selection and Training

Personnel selection is important in any line of work, and it is especially critical in foot patrol. A foot patrol officer is out in the community every day interacting with the citizens. If he or she is lazy, bored, unhappy, unmotivated by the job, or otherwise ineffective, it will be obvious to the community residents. If poor personnel selection is a pervasive problem, the foot patrol program will rapidly deteriorate and lose public support. Department policy will need to reflect the differences in foot patrol and motor patrol styles of policing. Selection criteria should reflect those differences.

Even though foot officers should be expected and ready to perform all of the duties of a motor officer, additional training will be required. In most instanes, foot patrol officers will need supplemental training in communication skills, interpersonal skills, crisis-intervention skills, and knowledge of community resources and services. Departmental policy will need to address the different training needs of foot patrol officers.

Police Unions

Most union contracts are geared to conventional models of policing. Some of the most important foot patrol and community policing techniques may violate standard contract clauses. Some of the problem areas relate to job descriptions, shift preference clauses, shift changes, and compensation.

Another area of concern for many police unions is the issue of safety, because foot officers may walk alone, whereas their motorized counterparts may work in pairs. Research in Flint showed that foot patrol officers, although walking alone, felt safer than did motorized officers who were working in two-person cars (Trojanowicz, 1985).

If clauses in the contract do conflict with the goals of foot patrol, some negotiating will have to be done with the union. In Flint, for example, representatives from union and from management were able to work out a letter of agreement that satisfied both sides. This proved to be a workable solution. In the longer term, however, cities that are serious about foot patrol will want their negotiators to bargain for more initial flexibility.

CONCLUSION

The Flint Neighborhood Foot Patrol Program demonstrated that foot patrol officers can perform many traditional police functions more cheaply and efficiently than can other units of the police department; and because they have the potential for reducing crime, they can lead to additional savings for society. It is, however, difficult to quantify some of the most tangible benefits of the NFPP, such as the increased amount of information exchanged. The evaluation of the Flint program did show that citizens felt safer in their neighborhoods and were more active in preventing crime. There were signs, as well, of a growing mutual respect between the police and the community. These are important factors, yet it is difficult to evaluate them on a monetary level.

Because foot patrol officers make face-to-face contact with the public, they are able to act as *community organizers, dispute mediators, service brokers,* and *links* between the community and local social service agencies.

In addition, the foot patrol concept most closely accommodates the real job of the police that best suits community needs and department functions. Though most young officers think their job will involve the "gun-toting," "siren-wailing," "crook-chasing" portrait in the media and reinforced by their academy training, they find on the job that they spend most of their time mediating disputes, stopping neighborhood fights, or responding to complaints about barking dogs. The majority of their work involves delivering services to the community, not law enforcement activities. The most efficient method for accomplishing that work is through the use of neighborhood foot patrols.

An effective community policing program, that is, foot patrol, facilitates problem solving and acts as a natural vehicle for dealing with resident concerns. When problems are identified and solved by officers on a proactive basis, there is less opportunity for the "vigilante mentality" to permeate the community. In addition, citizens will not feel there is a need for a citywide review system, such as civilian review boards, because problems are being identified and solved on a regular basis and citizens have input into decision making via the normal processes of police-citizen interaction.

NOTE

1. Members of the research team were Robert Baldwin, Dennis Banas, David Dugger, Donna Hale, Hazel Harden, Philip Marcus, Stephen McGuire, John McNamara, Francisco Medrano, Catherine Smith, Paul Smyth, and Jesse Thompson.

REFERENCES

Police Foundation (1981). *The Newark Foot Patrol Experiment.* Washington, DC: Author.
Trojanowicz, R. (1983). An evaluation of a neighborhood foot patrol. *Journal of Police Science and Administration, 2,* 410-419.
Trojanowicz, R., & Banas, D. (1985). *Perceptions of safety: A comparison of foot and motor officers.* East Lansing: Michigan State University, National Neighborhood Foot Patrol Center.
Trojanowicz, R., & Smyth, P. (1984). *A manual for the establishment and operation of a foot patrol program.* East Lansing: Michigan State University, National Neighborhood Foot Patrol Center.
Trojanowicz, R., et al. (1983). *An evaluation of the neighborhood foot patrol program in Flint, Michigan.* East Lansing: Michigan State University, National Neighborhood Foot Patrol Center.

Chapter 9

STOREFRONT POLICE OFFICES
The Houston Field Test

WESLEY G. SKOGAN
MARY ANN WYCOFF

This chapter summarizes the results of a field test conducted by the Houston Police Department and evaluated by the Police Foundation. The project, carried out from the fall of 1983 through the summer of 1984, tested the hypothesis that the operation of a police community station in a neighborhood could reduce fear of crime and increase citizens' satisfaction with their neighborhood and with the police.

The evaluation found that the creation of the station had several statistically significant effects indicated by random sample surveys conducted before and after the program, and in the analysis of a subset panel of individuals who were interviewed at both times. The program, the evaluation methods, and the major findings are described in this chapter.

THE THREAT OF FEAR

Fear of crime can have corrosive effects on the social and economic fabric of cities. Although fear can have a reasonable basis in documented levels of crime, research has found that fear often exceeds what might be considered rational levels and is unrelated to the fearful individual's personal probability of victimization. There is

AUTHORS' NOTE: *Preparation of this report was supported in part by Grant 83-IJ-CX-0003, awarded to the Police Foundation by the National Institute of Justice, U.S. Department of Justice, under the Omnibus Crime Control and Safe Streets Act, as amended. Points of view or opinions stated in this report are those of the authors and do not necessarily represent the official position or policies of the U.S. Department of Justice or the Police Foundation. Other evaluators involved in this project were Tony Pate and Lawrence Sherman. Sampson Annan was director of surveys for the Police Foundation.*

some evidence that social disorder and physical deterioration in public areas are additional sources of fear. Although there is insufficient information about the causes of fear, there is a pressing need to try to assuage fear in order to short-circuit the cycle in which fear leads residents to abandon the streets or move away, either of which may lead to a decline of business, diminishing informal social control, more crime, more fear, and more flight.

THE HOUSTON PROGRAM

To promote the search for causes of, and cures for, fear of crime, the National Institute of Justice selected the Police Foundation to evaluate police-based fear-reduction strategies. Two cities were chosen in which to conduct the tests—Houston, Texas, a new city with low population density, rapid population growth, and an expanding economy; and Newark, New Jersey, an old, dense city with a declining population and a deteriorating revenue base. In each city, a Fear Reduction Task Force was created to consider possible strategies, select those most appropriate for the local conditions, and plan and implement the strategies over a one-year period.

The Houston Police Task Force hypothesized that one source of fear in their city might be a sense of physical, social, and psychological distance between ordinary citizens and police officers. When this process began in early 1983, Houston was a city of 1.8 million residents and 3,357 police officers distributed over 565 square miles. Almost all patrolling was done in vehicles. The average citizen had little opportunity to know police officers except in the stressful circumstances of receiving a ticket or talking to police following a victimization. Lack of interaction with "regular citizens" might cause officers assigned to a beat to have little understanding of the priorities and concerns of the people living there. Recognizing this, people might well feel that their police neither knew nor cared about them. The Task Force felt that such alienation could lead to public dissatisfaction with police services, to dissatisfaction with the neighborhood as one in which to live, and to fear of crime.

The Task Force concluded that the location of a small, storefront office in a neighborhood might provide one means of overcoming the feeling of distance between citizens and the police. Staffed by police personnel, the station would be open at times when it would be convenient for citizens to lodge complaints, give or receive information, or just stop by to chat with a local officer. The office would provide a base of operation for the area officers, whose job it would become to get acquainted with the neighborhood residents and businesspeople, identify and help solve neighborhood problems, seek ways of delivering better police service to the area, and develop programs to draw the police and community closer together. The effects of the station and its programs would be reinforced by a monthly police-produced newsletter that would be distributed by the community station staff.

Station and Staff

The Task Force located space in a small, one-story complex of glass-front offices. Good used furniture was provided by a large Houston firm, and the station sign was donated by another. The large one-room office was spacious, well-furnished, and comfortable. In addition to desks, chairs, and sofas, the office contained a photocopier and a soft drink machine that were available to the public.

One Task Force officer had primary responsibility for the new station. He consulted with the district captain in the selection of a second officer and the two, together with a civilian office coordinator, one community service officer and three police aides, constituted the original staff. Within four months of the opening the station was open from 10 a.m. to 9:30 p.m. weekdays and until 6 p.m. on Saturdays, and two more patrol officers were assigned to staff a second shift. The four station officers were freed from the responsibility of responding to calls for service in the area and from routine patrol; other officers maintained regular patrol assignments in the area. The station officers did patrol occasionally, however, and did respond to calls when they were patrolling and when residents called the station directly. It was the job of the station officers to design and implement the programs to be run out of the storefront and to be available when citizens came to the station seeking help and information.

The station was managed by the Task Force officer assigned to the station. Station officers did not report to regular roll calls and did not meet frequently with a lieutenant or sergeant. These supervisors were not expected to maintain close supervision of the station. This loose system of management and supervision worked well in this case because of the personal qualities of the station officers and because of their direct and frequent contacts with their district commander.

Programs Developed

The programs developed by the station officers included the following:

Monthly Meetings. Meetings were held on a monthly basis in a neighborhood church. The first attracted just over 100 residents; attendance in the seventh and eighth months averaged 250. Officers discussed crime and other items of interest to the neighborhood and then presented a guest speaker, who might be a department commander, judge, politician, banker, representative of a utility, or other person of interest to the local community.

School Program. Station officers met regularly with neighborhood school administrators to discuss school problems; as a result, officers began to work vigorously on the truancy problem. Truants were picked up and, unless involved in a crime, returned to school; older individuals who were with the truant children were advised to discuss the problem with the station officers, who might talk with the child and parents and refer them to a counseling agency.

Fingerprinting Program. Officers fingerprinted children whose parents brought them to the station. They later extended the program to a neighborhood hamburger shop in an effort to reach a larger segment of the community.

Blood Pressure Program. Area residents were invited to have their blood pressure taken at the station on one day each month when a nurse or paramedic would be available to take the readings.

Ride-Along Program. Area churches and civic clubs were invited to select one of their members to ride with an officer patrolling in the neighborhood.

Park Program. A park in the center of the neighborhood had been taken over by rowdy persons who caused other residents to be reluctant to use it. Officers began to patrol the park regularly and made several arrests. During the summer months they instituted monthly athletic "contests" (softball, football, volleyball, and horseshoes) in which residents played against police officers. Residents returned to the park and a soft drink company that had removed a vending machine due to repeated vandalism installed another one at the park swimming pool.

Newsletters. On five occasions between November 1983 and June 1984, the station staff distributed approximately 450 newsletters to the neighborhood. An additional 50-100 newsletters were picked up each month by visitors to the station.

Table 9.1 presents administrative data indicating the frequency of various storefront activities, the number of hours the station was open by month, and the number of persons participating in various programs.

EVALUATION DESIGN AND METHODOLOGY

Five areas, closely matched in terms of size, demographic characteristics, land use, level of crime, and other characteristics, were selected to be included in the overall Houston Fear Reduction Program. One of those areas was selected to be the program area in which the police community station would be located. Another of the five neighborhoods was designated the comparison area, in which no new police programs would be introduced. Any changes discerned in this area would be interpreted as representative of prevailing trends in the city during the time of the study.

Personal interviews were conducted with large samples of randomly selected residents of the program and comparison areas three months before, and nine months after, program implementation began. Sample households were chosen randomly from a list of all residential addresses in each area. Then, a random (Kish) selection was made of an individual adult respondent. At least five callbacks were made before a sample respondent was classed as a noncompletion. Table 9.2 presents a basic description of the evaluation surveys. These surveys had area response rates ranging from 75% to 78%. Attempts to conduct interviews with a set of respondents both before and after the program began were less effective, producing completion rates of approximately 62% and 53% in the program and comparison areas, respectively. This was expected, given the mobile populations of these areas and the large number of apartment dwellers and renters living there. Interviews also were conducted with owners and managers of businesses and other establishments (such as churches). The response rates for these surveys were all higher than 80%.

Tests for possible effects of the police community station were designed to measure program effects on both the area and on individual residents.

TABLE 9.1 Numbers of Station Hours, Activities, and Participants by Month

Month	Hours Open	Citizen Walk-In	Phone Calls	Reports Taken	Children Fingerprinted	Blood Pressures Taken	Attendance at Monthly Meetings	Total Arrests by Officers
November	184	135[a]	3	2	_[d]	_[d]	_[d]	0
December	168	49	32	4	_[d]	_[d]	_[d]	4
January	168	47	39	11	_[d]	_[d]	_[d]	3
February	185[b]	124	78	6	18	_[d]	110	40
March	282	183	112	6	16	_[d]	122	33
April	_[c]	270	238	4	87	73	140	73
May	263	200	253	29	108	9	127	25
June	224	234	254	20	21	19	134	36
July	224	235	225	16	11	23	157	37
August	291	210	308	32	9	31	230	40

a. Includes 125 persons attending grand opening.
b. Hours expanded on February 20.
c. Not recorded.
d. Program not yet in operation.

TABLE 9.2 Evaluation Survey Description

	Residential Survey		Residential	Nonresidential Survey	
	Wave 1	Wave 2	Panel Subset	Wave 1	Wave 2
Program Area					
Completed interviews	406	460	239	45	41
Response rate[a] (%)	77	81	62	88	82
Comparison Area					
Completed interviews	389	403	183	39	44
Response rate[a] (%)	75	78	53	81	88

a. Response rate subtracts vacancies and ineligible respondents.

Wave 1-Wave 2 Change

Possible program effects were examined by pooling the results of surveys conducted with random samples of residents interviewed before and after the introduction of the program, both in the program area and in the comparison area.

The pooled data were analyzed, controlling for area of residence, wave of interview, and numerous other control factors (age, sex, race, and so forth). Program effect was judged by the significance of the coefficient associated with an indicator for respondents who lived in the program area *and* were interviewed after the program was inaugurated. A disadvantage of such an approach is that the various control factors cannot account for all of the nonprogram differences between residents of the two areas, so we cannot be sure that differences in outcome measures can be attributed to it.

Panel Change

Possible program effects also were examined by comparing the results of surveys conducted with a panel of the same persons before and after the program was implemented, both in the program area and in the comparison area. Interviewing the same people twice yielded a *pretest* score for each respondent on the outcome measures. The panel data were analyzed to isolate the effect of living in the program area as opposed to the comparison area, controlling for the pretest scores and many other factors ("covariates" such as victimization and age) that might also differentially affect the outcomes. As with the pooled data, if the coefficient associated with living in the program area was significant at the probability level of .05, controlling for the pretest and the covariates, it was taken as evidence of program effect. One disadvantage of a panel survey spaced over 12 months is that inevitably only certain types of people can be found and interviewed the second time, making it potentially inappropriate to generalize any findings to the population of the area as a whole. The pooled cross sections were much more representative, albeit without the advantage of a pretest.

To further explore possible program impacts among panel members, we examined responses to questions that asked whether or not respondents *recalled* being exposed to particular components of the program. Measures of a number of program outcomes were compared for panel respondents living in the program area who recalled being exposed and respondents who said they did not. This approach attempts to identify respondents who actually encountered the program, and presumably provides the most favorable evaluation of program impact. A major disadvantage of this approach is that people may choose to be or not to be exposed to the program; those who choose exposure may differ in statistically uncontrollable ways from those who do not choose exposure. What may appear to be program effects resulting from exposure may actually be the results of differences among people. Further, respondents do not always accurately report their exposure to program activity, thereby causing these data to contain unmeasurable errors.

Finally, possible subgroup-specific effects, suggesting differential program impacts upon members of particular age, sex, racial, or other subgroups, were examined using tests for statistical interaction. This analysis was designed to determine whether or not the community station program might have had an effect on certain types of area residents and had no effect at all—or a different type of effect—on other kinds of people. As with the recalled program-exposure analysis, these tests were made using the panel sample so that pretest scores on the outcome measures could be controlled. As a result, this test has the same general advantages and disadvantages of the panel data analysis discussed above.

Questions were included in the survey to measure each of the following outcomes:

  (1) recalled program exposure
  (2) fear of personal victimization in the area
  (3) perceived area personal crime problems
  (4) worry about area property crime victimization
  (5) perceived area property crime problems
  (6) perceived area social disorder problems
  (7) satisfaction with area

(8) evaluation of police services
(9) defensive behaviors to avoid personal victimization
(10) victimization

FINDINGS

Wave 1-Wave 2 Analysis

Recalled Exposure. In both the program and comparison areas there were significant increases in the percentage of respondents who indicated they were aware of the community station, perhaps because of stories about it and other community stations in a local newspaper that was distributed in both test areas. However, the percentage of increase in the program area (from 2% to 65%) was much larger than the increase in the comparison area (from 3% to 11%). Only in the program area was there a significant increase in the percentage of respondents who had attended a monthly meeting at which a police officer was present (0 to 8%). In the posttest survey, 13% of those in the program area, but only 4% in the comparison area, said they were aware of the distribution of a monthly police newsletter in the community.

The evaluation survey conducted in the program area after the office was in operation revealed that recognition of and contact with the community station was very differentially distributed. Some people living in the area "got the word" in large numbers, but others did not. Table 9.3 documents some of those differences. It examines the demographic correlates of two program exposure measures. One measure involved showing respondents an area map and asking if there was "a small community police office located here where you can get information from the police and talk to them about neighborhood problems?" If they knew of an office, respondents were then asked if they had called or visited it. The second measure in Table 9.3 combines those two forms of program contact.

As Table 9.3 indicates, blacks, low-income residents, those with less education, renters, younger people, and short-term area residents all were significantly less likely than their counterparts either to know about or have direct contact with the community station. These differences in program exposure often were very large, and indicate that the storefront—for all of its outreach activities—was touching only part of the community. As discussed below, this may explain in part why some area residents appear to have been more affected than

TABLE 9.3   Demographic Correlates of Recalled Program Exposure
(program area Wave 2 respondents)

| | Percentage Recalling Program Contact and Significance of Subgroup Differences (p <) | | |
	Know a Small Police Office in Area	Called or Visited Office	N
Sex			
Males	61	17	242
Females	69	21	218
	(.12)	(.37)	
Race			
Blacks	43	2	123
Whites	77	12	261
Hispanics	57	3	68
	(.001)	(.002)	
Income			
Under $15,000	47	9	146
Over $15,000	72	24	302
	(.001)	(.001)	
Education			
Not high school graduate	59	11	148
High school graduate	67	23	312
	(.14)	(.01)	
Housing			
Owners	80	26	247
Renters	46	12	213
	(.001)	(.001)	
Age			
15-24	53	14	76
25-49	61	16	272
50+	81	30	111
	(.001)	(.005)	
Number of adults in household			
1	55	11	115
2	68	21	299
3+	64	24	46
	(.07)	(.04)	
Length of residence (years)			
0-2	46	10	218
3-5	71	18	73
6-9	83	22	37
10+	86	35	132
	(.001)	(.001)	

NOTE: Number of cases is for "visited or called storefront." N is approximately the same for both measures. Chi-square test of significance.

TABLE 9.4   Program Effects on Pooled Wave 1 and Wave 2 Respondents

Outcome Measures	Relation to Living in Program Area	Statistically Significant? (p<)	
Fear of personal victimization in area	down	yes	(.001)
Perceived area personal crime problems	down	yes	(.001)
Worry about property crime victimization in area	down	no	(.33)
Perceived area property crime problems	down	yes	(.001)
Perceived area social disorder problems	down	yes	(.03)
Satisfaction with area	up	no	(.29)
Evaluations of police service	up	no	(.38)
Defensive behaviors to avoid personal victimization	down	yes	(.001)
Victimization by personal crime	down	no	(.16)
Victimization by property crime	down	no	(.42)

NOTE: Controls for 13 covariates. The number of cases is about 1657 for all analyses.

others by the community station. It is our suspicion that a "passive" storefront office would have been even more differentially visible and consequential.

Impact. Across the two surveys, residents of the program area, compared to those in the comparison area, reported a statistically significant (p < .05) decrease between the pretest and posttest surveys in the following:

(1) fear of personal victimization in the area
(2) perceived area personal crime problems
(3) perceived area property crime problems
(4) perceived area social disorder problems
(5) defensive behaviors to avoid personal victimization

Respondents in both the program and comparison areas showed significant increases in evaluations of police service, suggesting there may have been a citywide phenomenon causing an improvement in attitudes toward the police in Houston. This was the only significant change registered in the comparison area. There were no changes in victimization by personal or property crime, or in assessments of police aggressiveness. Table 9.4 summarizes many of these differences.

Respondents from nonresidential establishments in the program area, relative to those in the comparison area, were more likely, at a statistically significant level, to register decreases in fear of personal victimization in area. There were no significant changes on any other outcome measures in either area (see Table 9.5).

Panel Analysis

Recalled Exposure. Panel respondents in both areas also indicated significant increases in awareness of the community station. However, there was a 73% increase in awareness in the program area (from 1% to 74%) and only a 12% increase (from 2% to 14%) in the comparison area.

Impact. Panel respondents in the program area, relative to those in the comparison area, were more likely, at a statistically significant level (p < .05), to have lower scores on fear of personal victimization in area and perceived area personal crime problems. These findings are summarized in Table 9.6.

The *effects of recalled exposure* to various program components were assessed by regressing the posttest outcome measures on the program awareness measures, controlling for the pretest outcome score, and 16 measures of the demographic background and crime experiences of residents of the program area. The following conclusions were reached:

(1) Respondents who reported being aware of the community station had higher scores on evaluation of police service after program implementation.

(2) Persons who remembered calling and visiting the station had higher scores on perceived area social disorder problems. (Further analysis found that people who contacted the station were more likely to have experienced victimization than those who reported no contact. The higher perception of area problems may be a function of the victimization.)

(3) Persons who recalled having seen a police officer in the area in the previous 24 hours scored lower on fear of personal victimization in area, perceived area personal crime problems, and perceived area social disorder problems. They had higher scores on satisfaction with the area and evaluation of police service.

Assessments of possible *differential program effects on subgroups* of panel respondents were made through an analysis of "treatment-

TABLE 9.5 Changes in Outcome Measures by Area Location for Nonresidential Samples

Outcome Measures	Program Area		Comparison Area	
	Direction of Area Change	Statistically Significant? (p <)	Direction of Area Change	Statistically Significant? (p <)
Fear of personal victimization in area	down	yes (.01)	down	no (.025)
Worry about property crime victimization in area	up	no (.50)	down	no (.10)
Perceived area property crime problems	down	no (.10)	down	no (.25)
Perceived area social disorder problems	down	no (.25)	down	no (.25)
Employee and patron concern about crime	down	no (.025)	down	no (.05)
Favorable change in business conditions	up	no (.50)	up	no (.25)
Satisfaction with area	up	no (.40)	up	no (.25)
Evaluations of police service	up	yes (.001)	up	no (.10)
Victimization by robbery	down	no (.50)	down	no (.90)
Victimization by burglary	up	no (.95)	up	no (.70)
Victimization by vandalism	down	no (.70)	up	no (.70)
N	45-41		39-44	

NOTE: One-tailed t-tests of significance.

TABLE 9.6 Program Effects on Panel Respondents

Outcome Measures	Relation to Living in Program Area	Statistically Significant? (p <)	
Fear of personal victimization in area	down	yes	(.03)
Perceived area personal crime problems	down	yes	(.04)
Worry about property crime victimization in area	up	no	(.36)
Perceived area property crime problems	up	no	(.56)
Perceived area social disorder problems	down	no	(.39)
Satisfaction with area	up	no	(.32)
Evaluations of police service	up	no	(.08)
Defensive behaviors to avoid personal victimization	no change	no	(.88)
Victimization by personal crime	up	no	(.14)
Victimization by property crime	down	no	(.31)

NOTE: Direction of effect of area of residence and significance level controls for the pretest score and 16 covariates (age, race, victimization, housing, and so on). The number of cases is about 415 for all analyses.

covariate interaction'' effects. This consisted of creating special analytic measures that were assigned a value of 1 for respondents who lived in the program area *and* belonged to a subgroup of interest (such as blacks, renters, the poor), and assigned a 0 otherwise. Then, likely outcome measures were regressed against the "main effects" in this analysis model (that is, area of residence and group membership) and the interaction term, controlling as well for pretest scores on the outcome measures. Table 9.7 presents the sign and significance of the coefficient associated with "being in the group and living in the area" when those other factors have been statistically controlled.

Among the twelve outcome measures examined, blacks appeared to do worse relative to other groups on six of them; renters were significantly differently affected on three measures. Table 9.8 provides a more detailed examination of these seven outcomes by presenting average pretest and posttest scores for various racial and housing tenure groups.

Table 9.8 makes it clear that in no case were renters living in the program area significantly worse off after the community station was in operation. Rather, on one measure their view of the area showed an

TABLE 9.7 Regression Analysis of Impact of Program Area of Residence Upon Subgroups Program and Comparison Areas (all panel respondents)

Outcome Measures	Blacks		Hispanics		Female		Victims		Age		Live Alone		High School Graduates		Renters	
	Sign	(p <)	Sign	(p <)	Sign	(p <)	Sign	(p <)	Sign	(p <)	Sign	(p <)	Sign	(p <)	Sign	(p <)
Fear of area personal victimization	+	(.08)	−	(.56)	−	(.70)	−	(.04)*	+	(.10)	+	(.12)	−	(.34)	−	(.83)
Perceived area personal crime problems	+	(.01)*	−	(.07)	−	(.82)	−	(.58)	−	(.53)	+	(.21)	−	(.17)	+	(.09)
Worry about area property crime victimization	+	(.01)*	−	(.42)	−	(.99)	−	(.20)	−	(.06)	+	(.67)	−	(.51)	+	(.05)*
Perceived area property crime problems	+	(.001)*	−	(.06)	−	(.91)	+	(.83)	−	(.16)	+	(.50)	−	(.64)	+	(.18)
Perceived area social disorder problems	+	(.001)*	−	(.03)*	+	(.48)	−	(.96)	−	(.30)	+	(.05)*	+	(.44)	+	(.02)*
Satisfaction with area	−	(.001)*	+	(.37)	−	(.73)	−	(.69)	+	(.06)	−	(.01)*	+	(.52)	−	(.001)*
Evaluations of police service	−	(.01)*	+	(.64)	−	(.19)	+	(.36)	−	(.75)	−	(.24)	+	(.27)	−	(.17)
Defensive behaviors to avoid personal crime	−	(.65)	−	(.36)	+	(.96)	−	(.51)	+	(.01)	+	(.10)	+	(.19)	+	(.30)
Total victimization	+	(.15)	−	(.04)*	+	(.35)	−	(.18)	+	(.87)	+	(.60)	−	(.58)	+	(.91)
Personal victimization	+	(.71)	−	(.24)	+	(.48)	−	(.13)	−	(.50)	+	(.94)	−	(.29)	−	(.68)
Property victimization	+	(.06)	−	(.05)*	+	(.90)	+	(.15)	+	(.88)	+	(.65)	−	(.57)	+	(.51)

NOTE: Number of cases is approximately 420 for all analyses. Victimization is a dichotomy—victim or nonvictim. Regression analysis includes pretest, area of residence, subgroup membership, and an area-subgroup interaction term. This table reports the sign associated with the interaction term and its significance.
*p < .05.

TABLE 9.8 Indicators of Program Effects for Subgroups (panel respondents only)

	Mean Scores and Significance for Subgroups					
	Program Area			Comparison Area		
	Wave 1	Wave 2	(p <)	Wave 1	Wave 2	(p <)
Perceived personal crime problems						
Owners	1.62	1.24	(.01)	1.29	1.33	(.25)
Renters	1.59	1.35	(.01)	1.53	1.33	(.01)
Blacks	1.63	1.36	(.01)	1.32	1.13	(.01)
Whites	1.60	1.26	(.01)	1.42	1.37	(.24)
Hispanics	1.63	1.22	(.01)	1.46	1.48	(.44)
Worry about property crime						
Owners	2.20	2.00	(.001)	1.98	1.91	(.17)
Renters	2.14	2.19	(.27)	1.84	1.82	(.39)
Blacks	2.21	2.30	(.27)	1.88	1.74	(.13)
Whites	2.18	2.03	(.01)	1.94	1.90	(.29)
Hispanics	2.13	1.94	(.06)	1.89	1.88	(.46)
Perceived property crime problems						
Owners	1.95	1.60	(.001)	1.97	1.91	(.17)
Renters	1.94	1.83	(.12)	1.55	1.47	(.13)
Blacks	2.00	1.98	(.44)	1.53	1.41	(.14)
Whites	1.97	1.63	(.001)	1.62	1.54	(.11)
Hispanics	1.81	1.46	(.01)	1.42	1.48	(.31)
Perceived disorder problems						
Owners	1.50	1.35	(.001)	1.36	1.38	(.30)
Renters	1.67	1.58	(.09)	1.39	1.38	(.42)
Blacks	1.64	1.67	(.37)	1.34	1.29	(.25)
Whites	1.54	1.36	(.001)	1.39	1.38	(.43)
Hispanics	1.48	1.33	(.04)	1.37	1.49	(.11)

Satisfaction with area				
Owners	2.42	2.66 (.001)	2.43	2.48 (.22)
Renters	2.42	2.32 (.19)	2.54	2.60 (.24)
Blacks	2.35	2.24 (.22)	2.63	2.70 (.28)
Whites	2.39	2.64 (.01)	2.42	2.50 (.15)
Hispanics	2.53	2.62 (.25)	2.43	2.43 (.99)
Evaluations of police service				
Owners	3.28	3.52 (.01)	3.35	3.40 (.25)
Renters	3.09	3.32 (.01)	3.22	3.40 (.025)
Blacks	3.15	3.11 (.36)	3.52	3.52 (.48)
Whites	3.23	3.59 (.001)	3.30	3.42 (.04)
Hispanics	3.29	3.36 (.31)	2.97	3.17 (.09)
Numbers of cases				
Owners	162		90	
Renters	67		79	
Blacks	42		43	
Whites	160		98	
Hispanics	34		37	

NOTE: One-tailed paired t-tests of significance. Number of cases varies slightly from scale to scale.

improvement that was not significant although among homeowners it was significant; on two other measures renters were *very slightly*—and not significantly—less sanguine than owners in the posttest survey. There was no treatment-renter interaction effect on nine other outcome measures.

Table 9.8 also presents similar breakdowns by race. There it can be seen, for example, that whites showed significant improvement in their views of neighborhood problems, although blacks and Hispanics simply were unaffected, and that the same was true for their evaluations of police service.

We find, then, that blacks and renters did not suffer *negative* consequences of the program as one might erroneously conclude from the treatment-covariate analysis in Table 9.7. Table 9.8 demonstrates that the negative coefficients resulted primarily from the fact that the perceptions of blacks and renters did not shift for the better over time, as they did for other racial groups and owners. Although living in the program area does not appear to be related to a deterioration of conditions for blacks and renters, it is clear that these groups experienced very few of the apparent program benefits measured for other subgroups.

DISCUSSION

The Houston police community station appears to have been successful in reducing citizens' levels of fear and in improving their perceptions of their neighborhood and their attitudes toward the police. These findings are supported most strongly by the analysis of two waves of residential surveys. To the extent to which measured program *awareness* was responsible for these effects, it is important to note the significant increase in "awareness" of the community station among respondents in the comparison area as well as in the program area. Although the test station was physically removed from the comparison area, the test station and two other community stations in Houston had been publicized by local newspapers and television stations. This vicarious knowledge about the station may have cast a "shadow program effect" across the comparison area that served to blur the distinction between program and comparison area respondents.

The fact that there was only one significant effect for respondents from businesses and other nonresidential establishments is not surprising, as these respondents are more likely to have had routine contacts with the police prior to the implementation of the station. Also, the small number of such establishments in these surveys decreased the likelihood of detecting statistically significant change. Furthermore, there was no reason to believe that commercial sections of the neighborhoods were suffering adverse financial consequences from fear of crime. That they did not report improvement in business to an extent that corresponded with the more positive attitudes of program area respondents may indicate that fear was not yet a problem that was harming business in the area.

The lack of positive program effects for blacks and renters may be a function of their lower levels of awareness of the program. The community station program relied, in part, on established civic organizations to attract residents to station programs. To the extent that blacks and renters are less likely to be members of these organizations, the program needs to utilize other means of reaching these people.

RECOMMENDATIONS

Based on our interpretation of the data, we would recommend that other police departments that perceive a need to help citizens feel more secure in their neighborhoods consider establishing community police stations similar to the one described and evaluated here. Based on observations of the program, we offer the following additional recommendations concerning the operation of a community station program.

(1) Personnel. The creativeness and willingness to work on the part of the community station officers and their staff were perhaps the most critical elements of the operation. Much of the success of this station seems attributable to the skills of the station officers. Given the nature of their work, we believe that station staff members must be highly self-motivating and capable of working effectively without close supervision. Some commanders might be tempted to "bury" a lazy officer in a storefront operation, but such an assignment would bury the station as well.

(2) Personnel Involvement. The station described here was created by the two officers who ran it. They found the space, moved the furniture, hung the pictures, advertised themselves to the community, and designed and implemented the programs. As a result of their efforts and the community's enthusiastic response to the opening of the station, they felt proudly proprietary of it. We have no experience

with turnover of key personnel in such an operation, but suspect it would be important to devise ways of giving new station personnel a sense of ownership of already-established programs.

   (3) Supervision. This station worked well with a minimum of supervision. Such a loose structure would not work well in all situations; in this case, it probably succeeded because of the strong relationship between the district commander and the officer in charge of the station. However, if the station officer needed more supervision, or if the commander had several stations to attend to, more consideration would have to be given to the development of a formal supervisory structure for the stations. (The Detroit Police Department appears to have worked out a satisfactory arrangement for the management and supervision of its storefront stations.) Substantial management *support* also is needed, especially in the start-up phase, as space and furnishings must be found, contracts negotiated, work schedules devised, and programs developed.

   (4) Programs. There is no way of knowing which of the many Houston programs was most effective in producing the positive outcomes we have attributed to the station. Indeed, it may well be the mix of programs that was effective. In any case, it seems unlikely that there is a "package" of programs that could be transferred to another station. All of the programs implemented in Houston may be worth consideration for use elsewhere, but the success of community station programs likely depends on their match with the needs of the community.

   (5) Familiarity with the Community. Getting to know the area and the people who live there appears to have been an important factor in the success of the Houston station. To get the program started, the officers who opened the station had to make a lot of community contacts. Officers assigned to the station later will not have the same motivation to learn the community and will have to be encouraged to do so, perhaps through assignment to programs that will necessitate meeting people.

   (6) Station Atmosphere. It is important that the station give the impression that it is a place intended to accommodate citizens rather than police officers. The Houston station accomplished this with its open front, comfortable furnishings, and ready welcome for visitors. The only time a citizen was observed by our on-site process monitor to hesitate about entering was when three officers were talking together. Citizens must not be given the feeling, common to traditional police stations, that they are intruding upon "police business." Any effort to

combine a police substation with a storefront operation should reserve a front room of the office and a front parking lot for use solely by citizen visitors.

(7) Publicity. The community station cannot be effective unless residents know about it, and every means should be made to publicize the existence of the station and its programs. The repeated use of large numbers of fliers distributed by the community station staff probably was effective as a means of publicizing the station's opening and later programs. Good coverage in the local community paper also was useful.

(8) Community Involvement. The station staff made good use of existing community institutions as a means of drawing the community into the station program. A local church was used for the monthly meetings, which drew crowds too large for the station to accommodate. Neighborhood civic groups were used as "organizing agents" for the monthly meetings. This approach appears to have worked well for members of these groups, but other approaches will have to be developed for groups of residents who are not already affiliated with existing neighborhood organizations. The differential visibility of the station and the socially skewed distribution of contacts with it was noted by the staff of this program, and, since the evaluation, they have developed special new programs to extend their "coverage" to the entire neighborhood.

(9) Selling the Program. The officers had to sell the program to individuals and groups whose support they needed. They did this, in part, through publicity and their own enthusiasm. But they also appear to have done it by offering others the chance to be involved in an adventure. The patrol officer who managed the station rarely asked businesses or organizations for help; rather, he deliberately gave them the "opportunity to do something for the neighborhood." The skills of a good salesperson were in evidence.

Finally, any department considering the development of a community station program should take a firsthand look at one already in successful operation. Exemplary storefront stations can be observed in Houston, Texas; Newark, New Jersey; Santa Ana, California; Detroit, Michigan; and perhaps in other cities.

IV

PREVENTING CRIME IN AND AROUND COMMERCIAL ESTABLISHMENTS

Chapter 10

EVALUATING CRIME PREVENTION THROUGH ENVIRONMENTAL DESIGN
The Portland
Commercial Demonstration Project

PAUL J. LAVRAKAS
JAMES W. KUSHMUK

This chapter discusses our respective evaluations of the Crime Prevention Through Environmental Design (CPTED) Commercial Demonstration Project, which was implemented in a commercial strip in Portland, Oregon, from 1974 through 1979. The first effort to evaluate this project was conducted in 1977 (Lavrakas, Normoyle, & Wagener, 1978), with a follow-up evaluation in 1979-1980 (Kushmuk & Whittemore, 1981). Both evaluations were funded by the National Institute of Justice (NIJ), and each was planned and conducted "post hoc"; that is, there was no opportunity to gather a broad range of pretest data prior to the implementation of the CPTED Demonstration Project. Furthermore implementation of CPTED strategies was "uncontrolled"; that is, the "treatment" was a *naturalistic process* depending in large part on the local political environment in Portland. As such, a "theory-based evaluation" (see Lavrakas, 1978) was conducted to maximize our ability to determine whether or not CPTED effort (input variables) led to the attainment of CPTED proximate goals (intervening variables), and, if so, whether or not this led to the attainment of CPTED ultimate goals (impact variables).

AUTHORS' NOTE: *The 1977 evaluation reported here was supported by Contract J-LEAA-022-74, awarded to the Westinghouse Electric Corporation by the National Institute of Law Enforcement and Criminal Justice, U.S. Department of Justice. The reevaluation was supported by Grant 79-NI-AX-0061, awarded to the Office of Justice Planning and Evaluation, City of Portland, by the National Institute of Justice, U.S. Department of Justice. Both awards were made under the Omnibus Safe Streets Act of 1968, as amended. Points of view or opinions stated in this chapter are those of the authors, and do not necessarily represent the official position or policies of the U.S. Department of Justice or the authors' agencies of employment.*

goals (intervening variables), and, if so, whether or not this led to the attainment of CPTED ultimate goals (impact variables).

CPTED THEORY AND PROJECT PLANNING

In 1974, a consortium of firms headed by the Westinghouse Electric Corporation received a contract from NIJ (then named the National Institute of Law Enforcement and Criminal Justice) to begin planning demonstration projects that would further develop and test the evolving theory of CPTED. This theory was based on earlier work (such as Jacobs, 1961; and Newman's, 1972, work on "defensible space") linking the design of the physical environment to the behavior of the users of that environment (including both the offender and non-offender populations). Westinghouse planned tests of CPTED in three different environments: a residential neighborhood, a public high school, and a commercial strip. The commercial demonstration project was implemented in the Union Avenue Corridor (UAC), a 3.5-mile long urban arterial commercial strip located in the northeast section of Portland, Oregon.

A commercial strip (UAC) was selected as one of the CPTED demonstration project sites because of its particular susceptibility to crime problems, due in part to its configuration, the types of enterprises located there, and the general changes in shopping trends that have had a negative impact upon the vitality of these commercial areas (Kaplan, O'Kane, Lavrakas, & Hoover, 1978). These strips include those business areas that have traditionally developed along major streets and highways and that provide services to the users of those thoroughfares as well as to nearby residents. In the UAC, portions of the streets that connected the strip with other shopping districts and with surrounding residential areas were also considered as part of the target area.

The UAC strip runs from Portland's central business district to near the city's northern boundary (the Columbia River). This strip was once a thriving business area along one of the city's four major north-south routes. By the early 1960s, however, UAC had passed its business "boom" period, and became marred by many vacant lots, boarded-over windows, derelict structures, and night spots of dubious repute. Potential investors were often reluctant to invest in the area due to the specter of crime and fear. This downturn in the viability of the UAC business community was exacerbated by Portland's civil (racial) disturbances in the late 1960s.

The CPTED funding that Westinghouse received from NIJ did not include the funding needed for project implementation at the demonstration sites. Rather, Westinghouse assistance to the city of Portland included grant development and other "funds-leveraging activities" to help the city secure implementation funding for UAC. At the time the idea of launching a CPTED demonstration project was presented to Portland officials (1974), there was no model to present as an example of what might be expected. CPTED was a new program based largely upon theories and narrowly focused case studies advanced by criminologists, behaviorists, and environmental specialists. The aim was to create a planning model that would take into account local problems, priorities, and resources, as well as to provide opportunities to evaluate the implementation of CPTED strategies. The overall approach received a favorable response from Portland officials, and the mayor authorized the Westinghouse consortium to develop a preliminary CPTED plan for local review.

Building upon the previous work (Jeffery, 1971; Newman, 1972; Scarr, 1973; Reppetto, 1974) the Westinghouse consortium developed a CPTED Commercial Demonstration Plan for Portland (Bell, Day, Tien, & Hanes, 1976). The primary emphasis of this plan was on strategies that were designed to reinforce desirable existing activities, eliminate undesirable ones, create new positive activities, and otherwise support desirable use patterns so that crime prevention theoretically would become an integral part of the UAC environment. There were four operating hypotheses that provided the underlying rationale for all CPTED implementation strategies: access control, surveillance, activity support, and motivation reinforcement (see Kaplan et al., 1978).

Access Control. These strategies focused on decreasing opportunity for crime by keeping potential offenders out of particular areas. In its physical form, access control is manifested through the deployment of target-hardening anticrime devices, such as locks, bars, and alarms. Access control can also be created by the deployment of psychological barriers to the would-be offender: for example, use of timers on indoor lighting at night, and "territorial markers" (signs, hedges, and parkways).

Surveillance. Surveillance strategies are meant to increase the ability of nonoffenders to view (notice) a suspicious person/event or the commission of a crime. In turn, this increased capacity for surveillance is assumed to increase the "risk" perceived by potential offenders, thus creating a deterrence effect. A distinction can be made between formal and natural (informal) surveillance strategies. Formal surveillance is an organized effort carried out by police or citizen patrols to convey to potential offenders the impression that surveillance is routinely occurring and highly likely at any given location. Formal surveillance is also manifested through mechanical devices, such as closed-circuit television. Natural surveillance is theoretically achieved through design strategies, such as channeling the flow of pedestrian activity to put more observers near potential crime areas, or by creating a greater capacity for observation by, for example, installing more windows along the street sides of buildings, using bus shelters with see-through plastic walls, and trimming trees and shrubs around residential structures.

Activity Support. These strategies are aimed at reinforcing existing and new behavior patterns that make effective use of the built environment. This follows the reasoning that in every community there are resources and activities capable of sustaining constructive community crime prevention. Support of these activities is hypothesized to bring a vital and coalescing improvement to a given community and to result in a reduction of the vulnerable social and physical elements that permit criminal activity.

Motivation Reinforcement. In contrast to those anticrime strategies that aim to make offenders' operations more difficult, motivation reinforcement strategies strive to affect offender motivation and, hence, behavior relative to the designed environment by increasing the perceived risk of apprehension and by reducing the criminal payoff. These strategies also seek to positively reinforce the motivation of citizens in general to play a more active prevention role by enhancing the community's image and identity.

These four key operating hypotheses are not mutually exclusive; together they formed the basis upon which the Westinghouse consortium laid out a set of project objectives for the CPTED commercial demonstration in Portland (see Figure 10.1). In turn, these theory-based objectives provided the foundation upon which to build the interrelated anticrime strategies that were hypothesized to lead to a reduction of crime and fear, and a general improvement of the quality of life in UAC.

CPTED Commercial Demonstration: 1974-1977

After a year of working with Portland officials, the Westinghouse consortium developed a demonstration plan for UAC (Bell et al., 1976) that recommended seven CPTED strategies, with no assurances

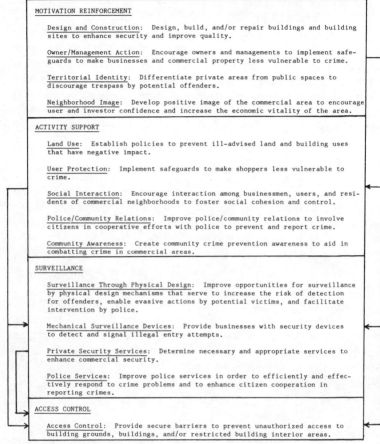

MOTIVATION REINFORCEMENT

Design and Construction: Design, build, and/or repair buildings and building sites to enhance security and improve quality.

Owner/Management Action: Encourage owners and managements to implement safeguards to make businesses and commercial property less vulnerable to crime.

Territorial Identity: Differentiate private areas from public spaces to discourage trespass by potential offenders.

Neighborhood Image: Develop positive image of the commercial area to encourage user and investor confidence and increase the economic vitality of the area.

ACTIVITY SUPPORT

Land Use: Establish policies to prevent ill-advised land and building uses that have negative impact.

User Protection: Implement safeguards to make shoppers less vulnerable to crime.

Social Interaction: Encourage interaction among businessmen, users, and residents of commercial neighborhoods to foster social cohesion and control.

Police/Community Relations: Improve police/community relations to involve citizens in cooperative efforts with police to prevent and report crime.

Community Awareness: Create community crime prevention awareness to aid in combatting crime in commercial areas.

SURVEILLANCE

Surveillance Through Physical Design: Improve opportunities for surveillance by physical design mechanisms that serve to increase the risk of detection for offenders, enable evasive actions by potential victims, and facilitate intervention by police.

Mechanical Surveillance Devices: Provide businesses with security devices to detect and signal illegal entry attempts.

Private Security Services: Determine necessary and appropriate services to enhance commercial security.

Police Services: Improve police services in order to efficiently and effectively respond to crime problems and to enhance citizen cooperation in reporting crimes.

ACCESS CONTROL

Access Control: Provide secure barriers to prevent unauthorized access to building grounds, buildings, and/or restricted building interior areas.

SOURCE: Kaplan et al. (1978).
NOTE: The four key hypotheses are not mutually exclusive. Surveillance objectives also serve to control access; activity support involves surveillance; and motivation reinforcement provides support for the other three hypotheses.

Figure 10.1 Relationship of Commercial Environment Objectives to CPTED Operating Hypotheses

that all (or any) would be implemented or that the final demonstration would be limited to these activities alone. These seven strategies were as follows:

(1) creation of a "Safe Streets for People" component
(2) creation of a Residential Activity Center and miniplazas along Union Avenue

(3) general promotion of UAC
(4) improved transportation both into and out of UAC
(5) security services provided by a UAC security adviser
(6) increased law enforcement support throughout UAC
(7) development of a "Cash Off the Streets" program

The first two strategies involved physical redesign of certain streets and intersections, improved street lighting, massive road improvements on Union Avenue, and social strategies intended to increase constructive use of the built environment. These changes were reasoned to improve UAC safety, make it more attractive, and provide activity nodes for residents and shoppers. Corridor promotion was concerned with planned community events (for example, ethnic market days), organization and support of the business and residential communities, and general economic development. In order to improve transportation services, plans were made to upgrade waiting areas at bus stops and provide special services for elderly and handicapped residents. A full-time security adviser was to be responsible for conducting security surveys of UAC business establishments and residences. This individual would also make crime prevention presentations throughout the target area, and would provide technical assistance to the city's redevelopment plan for Union Avenue. As a means of increasing law enforcement support, improved police patrols, revision of patrol districts, and creation of a UAC storefront police precinct were proposed. The final strategy was "Cash Off the Streets," which was intended to motivate citizens (especially older residents) not to carry any substantial amount of currency in UAC, while simultaneously advertising the program so that the all residents, including the local offender population, could not help but be aware of it.

The successful implementation of these strategies depended on a number of city agencies working together toward common goals. As it came to be implemented, the UAC CPTED demonstration was closely tied in with the Portland Planning Bureau's decision to deploy a Union Avenue Redevelopment Program (along the entire thoroughfare, not just in the target area), and the Portland Police Department's decision to create an active Crime Prevention Bureau serving the entire city. A Westinghouse on-site coordinator was hired in March 1975 to facilitate the interworkings of the various local agencies in UAC. A new coordinator was hired in mid-1976 and worked through 1977, which marked the end of the Westinghouse consortium's assistance to the UAC CPTED demonstration.

In early 1978, the first evaluation study was completed (Lavrakas et al., 1978). As of that date, the following anticrime strategies had been implemented, and constituted the CPTED "treatment" received by UAC:

(1) The Crime Prevention Bureau of the Portland Police performed security surveys of all UAC business establishments (approximately 210) and of approximately 160 target area residences, with a sergeant serving informally as UAC's security adviser.

(2) The city had received a $440,000 LEAA grant to install high-intensity lights along Union Avenue and in-fill lighting along residential side streets, with the work completed in early 1977.

(3) A "Safe Street for People" was constructed along a cross street that was to link a planned senior citizens' housing complex with Union Avenue. The existing street was repaved, curbs were redesigned to necessitate slow vehicular speeds, sidewalks were repaved with walk-up ramps at curbs, and physical amenities and landscaping were provided. A second "Safe Street" was constructed along another cross street that linked Union Avenue with Woodlawn Park, and recreational facilities at the park were improved, including increased lighting.

(4) New bus shelters, designed to enhance natural surveillance, were installed throughout UAC.

(5) A business proprietors' organization, the Northeast Business Boosters, was organized and nurtured through the efforts of the various local CPTED actors.

(6) A "Clean-Up Day" and "Sunday Market" were organized to improve the physical appearance of UAC and to promote community spirit.

In addition, technical assistance was provided by the consortium's on-site coordinator and the police sergeant in developing other planned improvements that had not been implemented as of early 1978. These included an 80-unit housing project for the elderly, a $4.5 million road improvement program, and efforts to attract new businesses to locate in the target area.

CPTED Commercial Demonstration: 1978-1981

The reevaluation of the commercial CPTED demonstration (Kushmuk & Whittemore, 1981) documented significant activities and changes occurring on Union Avenue for a three-year period following the facilitative support of the Westinghouse consortium. This study focuses on the progress of activities initiated during the Westinghouse phase, the maintenance of favorable environmental changes reported in the first evaluation, and new and spin-off activities.

The most significant and visible change that occurred during this follow-up period was the start of the UAC street redesign at an increased cost of $9.5 million in state highway funds. Construction was nearly completed by the end of 1981. The physical appearance of the corridor was improved by way of this renovation, which included landscaped median strips, left-turn-only lanes, and the prohibition of on-street parking on Union Avenue, a change that was meant to increase traffic flow.

The new street was an important symbol of resurgence for Union Avenue, yet it stood in contrast to the strip itself, which was still marred by abandoned businesses and many vacant lots, most certainly signs of economic hard times for small businesses in general. One design criticism of the new street configuration was raised. The median strip and faster traffic tended to create a psychological barrier, if not a physical one, between the east and west sides of Union Avenue, rather than emphasizing the natural "territorial" boundaries of the distinct neighborhoods which ran north to south. For example, there were no physical markers installed to set off the ethnically rich middle section of the corridor from the north and south ends. Furthermore, the miniplazas, residential activity nodes, or other design features recommended by the Westinghouse consortium to increase pedestrian traffic, identification, and feelings of safety, were not realized in the final reconstruction of Union Avenue.

The reevaluation in tracking the maintenance of other CPTED activities and environmental changes found a general pattern of stabilization after the Westinghouse presence ended. Business proprietors and residents judged by the appearance of Union Avenue to have stayed the same or improved slightly, but almost half of the businesspeople believed that the somewhat derelict appearance of Union Avenue was still a factor negatively affecting their businesses. Some small, but important, businesses were convinced to locate on Union Avenue as economic development efforts continued by the city's Portland Development Commission.

Two large concerns, a Veterans Administration hospital and a senior citizens' housing project, that had been courted by Westinghouse failed to materialize. Instead, site selection for the V.A. hospital was made in another, more prominent, area of the city. And unfortunately, the "Safe Street for People" that had been constructed to link Union Avenue to these proposed facilities now led to nothing more than vacant lots. This well-lighted but infrequently used "Safe Street" stood as a reminder of how difficult it was to maneuver the large-scale CPTED physical design strategies fully into place; that is, those that required interagency cooperation and considerable long-term political support.

There were no new promotional events aside from the two that occurred in 1977. The new street lights and bus shelters were well maintained during the follow-up. Some new businesses opened, but others closed. In general, those with knowledge of Union Avenue's past and present judged the commercial area to be in a stabilization phase, trying to hold its own. There were still some concerns about crime and safety, but now of equal or greater concern was the poor state of the economy in general. There were, too, some feelings of disillusionment—a belief that more had been promised than delivered by Westinghouse and the city government. Some business proprietors and leaders perceived the city's energies to be shifted away from Union Avenue and toward a newly gentrified area closer to downtown.

In contrast, there was some evidence of new activities and program spin-offs. A lower-income housing project was built near UAC that employed the CPTED concepts of target hardening, lighting, natural surveillance, and outdoor activity nodes for residents within the bounds of a high open-bar iron fence. The design appeared to be secure against crime, yet without an overly fortified look. A condominium project was built near Woodlawn Park, which was connected to Union Avenue by the second "Safe Street." Although attractive in appearance and a positive influence on the neighborhood, this project seemingly did not employ CPTED design features.

THE 1977 EVALUATION

Evaluation Planning

The first evaluation of the UAC CPTED demonstration was conducted by Lavrakas et al. (1978), at a time when the demonstration strategies were mostly implemented, and thus by necessity required "post hoc" evaluative techniques. The methods chosen were designed to determine (a) the extent to which the Commercial Demonstration was a valid implementation of CPTED theory, and (b) the extent to which any measurable attainment of CPTED's ultimate goals could be linked to the UAC demonstration.

In the absence of control over "when" and "where" CPTED strategies were implemented, the use of one overall quasi-experimental evaluation design was not possible. Rather, a "theory-based" evaluation plan was developed. To develop this type of evaluation plan, it was first necessary to identify clearly the "hypothesized CPTED process" for UAC in an evaluation framework (see Figure 10.2). This framework delineated the *measurement points* associated with CPTED theory. These measurement points are the constructs/variables related to (a) the effort that was expended, (b) the proximate goals the effort tried to bring about, and (c) the ultimate goals that were eventually to be attained.

Effort Measurement Points included a description (number, type, quality) of project activities, a documentation of the costs associated with these activities, and an assessment of the quantity and quality of the immediate changes in UAC's environment. As shown in Figure 10.2, Proximate Goal Measurement Points are manifestations of the four CPTED operating hypotheses: access control, surveillance, activity support, and motivation reinforcement. An assessment of these measurement points is central to the evaluation of the CPTED process, because proximate goals are the bridges that link CPTED effort (that is, demonstration activity) to ultimate goals. Unless it can be shown that CPTED proximate goals were attained, it would not be possible with this type of an evaluation to attribute any attainment of ultimate goals to the CPTED demonstration. This reasoning follows from Weiss's (1972) distinction between *program* failure or success and *theory* failure or success: that is, unless it was found that the UAC demonstration was a valid implementation of CPTED theory, there could be no valid test of the theory.

Once the measurement points for the evaluation were identified, the approach of "multiple operationalization" (see Crano & Brewer, 1973) was taken in determining the specific types of data to gather. In this way, the findings of the evaluation would not rest on any one method of data collection. Instead, a number of data collection techniques were employed to gather data elements for each of the measurement points.[1]

Data Collection Methodology

Retrieval of UAC Crime Reports. Crime reports from the crime analysis files of the police department were retrieved, by month, for

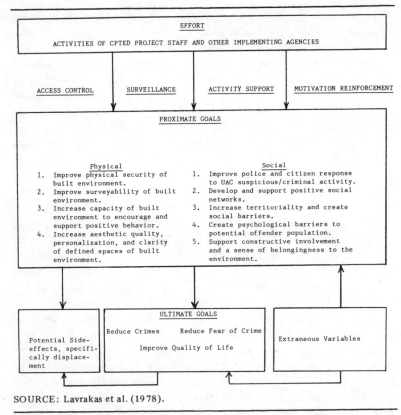

SOURCE: Lavrakas et al. (1978).

Figure 10.2 CPTED Evaluation Framework

the period October 1974 through September 1977. This had to be done by hand screening all reported crimes in northeast Portland to find those that occurred within the target area boundaries. This was done for commercial burglary, commercial robbery, purse-snatching, street robbery, street assault, rape, and residential burglary.

Interviews with UAC Business Proprietors. Three independent samples of randomly chosen UAC business proprietors were interviewed in person, in the spring ($n = 49$), summer ($n = 37$), and fall ($n = 48$) of 1977, to determine their crime-related experiences, perceptions, and reactions. The questionnaire took approximately 30 minutes to complete.

Interviews with UAC Residents. Two randomly chosen independent samples of residents of the UAC target areas (that is, living within three blocks of Union Avenue) were interviewed via telephone in the spring ($n = 97$) and fall ($n = 80$) of 1977. Residents were asked similar, though fewer, questions as those asked of the business proprietors. The questionnaire took about 15 minutes to complete.

Interviews with Key Persons. In December 1977, in-person interviews were conducted with 16 individuals with special knowledge about UAC, including business and community leaders, and patrol officers from the Northeast Police District. The interviews lasted 30-60 minutes and these key persons were asked to make a number of "expert" judgments about UAC's past, present, and future conditions.

UAC Observations. A series of evening observations (lasting about 30 minutes each) were conducted in UAC to record the pedestrian activity level from April 1977 through November 1977. For each evening observation, the same fixed route was traveled by an observer who was a passenger in an automobile. Throughout the observation run, most of which traveled along Union Avenue, the observer recorded (via tape recorder) the gender, race, age grouping, and activity of all visible pedestrians. A total of 73 evening observations were peformed, with time of observation randomly scheduled between 6:00 p.m. and 12:00 a.m. Temperature and precipitation data for each evening were later merged with the recorded data for each observation run.

Retrieval of Economic Data. Access was granted to tax files in Portland's Business License Division, to allow for the retrieval of data about net and gross annual sales of UAC businesses. Files for 350 existing or once-existing UAC businesses were reviewed.

Results and Conclusions

Proximate Goals. Based on a synthesis of the various data that were gathered to measure the attainment of the proximate goals (see Figure 10.2), the authors of the first evaluation report assessed the extent to which each of the goals were attained as a direct result of the CPTED project activities. These judgments are shown in Table. 10.1.

Due primarily to the comprehensive security surveys and follow-up surveys performed by the Portland Police at all UAC businesses, it was concluded that the levels of physical security reported by the business proprietors who were interviewed represented a very significant increase in the physical security of the UAC business community. On the other hand, findings indicated that despite the 160 security surveys provided to residences in the UAC target area, the overall physical security of residential structures did not improve significantly.

With the addition of high-intensity street lighting along Union Avenue and the addition of in-fill lighting on residential streets, and

TABLE 10.1   Degree of Attainment of CPTED Proximate Goals

Proximate Goals	Degree of Attainment
Physical environment	
increased physical security	high (business); low (residential)
increased surveillability	moderate
increased potential for usability	low
Improvement in psychological dimensions	low
Social environment	
improved crime prevention behavior	moderate (business); low (residential)
improved law enforcement response	no change necessary
increased community cohesiveness and social networks	high (business); low (residential)
increased psychological barriers	low-moderate
increased usage of built environment	low
increased identification with UAC	low-moderate

SOURCE: Lavrakas et al. (1978).

based on the results of the various interviews, the evaluators concluded that there was a moderately significant improvement in the
surveillability of the UAC built environment.

Despite the intentions of the original demonstration plan (Bell
et al., 1976), little was accomplished to make the overall physical environment more usable by the nonoffender population. There were
some locations in which improvements were made (for example, the
two Safe Streets for People), but considering the target area in its en-
tirety, one could, at best, conclude that a low level of increased potential usability of the built environment had been achieved. Similarly,
there was little evidence that psychological dimensions of the physical
environment (such as aesthetics, personalization, and clarity of defined
spaces) had changed in any measurable way. Findings from the
various interviews and from the observational data supported this
conclusion.

Similar to the findings regarding a meaningful increase in the
physical security of the UAC environment, survey results indicated
that at businesses a significant increase in crime prevention measures
was realized. In contrast, interviews with residents did not indicate
much change related to any CPTED project activities. In terms of the
Portland police, and despite the recommendations in the demonstration plan, the authors concluded that no change was necessary, that is,
law enforcement response in UAC was well organized and as effective
as could be expected within the inherent limits of policing.

One of the most significant proximate goal attainments was the
greatly increased level of "social cohesiveness" in the UAC business

community, as manifested by the revitalization of the Northeast Business Boosters. On the other hand, there was little evidence of any notable increase in "cohesion" within the residential community. In fact, there was some suggestive evidence that the black and white communities were becoming more polarized—an issue that none of the CPTED strategies addressed.

Some evidence was found to suggest possible improvement in the sociopsychological dimensions, such as increased identification with the area as reflected by greater feelings of territoriality. But the observational data did not indicate any overall increase in the actual usage of the UAC environment by pedestrians. There was evidence, though, that blacks were a greater proportion of pedestrians compared to whites, even though the percentage of UAC residents who were black remained basically unchanged.

Based on this assessment of proximate goal attainment, the authors of the first evaluation concluded that the implementation of CPTED design strategies in UAC should be regarded as a moderate program success in the business environment and a lesser success in the residential environment. They went on to say:

> It is beyond the scope and resources of this evaluation to carefully document whether more should have been accomplished, [but] there are many reasons to state that a good start has been made to implement the CPTED concept in UAC. (Lavrakas et al., 1978, p. 55)

Ultimate Goals. Given that the demonstration was judged to be a moderate "program success," it was reasoned that there was enough attainment of proximate goals to justify an investigation of the attainment of CPTED ultimate goals (that is, a test for success or failure of CPTED theory). Data gathered via the various methods provided multiple ways of testing for CPTED's effects on UAC's crime rates, levels of fear of crime, the business community's viability, and the general quality of life in UAC.

Using the 36 months of reported crime data retrieved from the police department files, a set of time-series analyses (Bower, Padia, & Glass, 1974) were performed to determine whether or not there was any change in reported crime rates. Linked to the security surveys of businesses, there was a significant 48% decrease in commercial burglaries following the start of the security surveys. For this same time period, there were far smaller decreases in residential burglary (14% drop) and commercial robbery (17% drop). Similarly, the citywide rate for burglary dropped slightly (about 10%). Because the security surveys of UAC businesses should have shown an impact primarily on commercial burglary, it was concluded that this pattern of results showed a significant reduction in crime (commercial burglary) directly related to CPTED activities. Interviews with businesspersons, key persons, and residents supported this conclusion.

The observational data that were collected showed no significant change (increase or decrease) in pedestrian usage of the UAC environment. Since usage of the environment is so closely linked to fear of crime (see Lavrakas, 1982), these observational data did not suggest any decrease in fear levels. Results from the various surveys, however, suggested that there had been a small decrease in fear of crime throughout UAC since the early 1970s, but one that had not been large enough to rid the community of its reputation as a "high-crime" area.

Information that was retrieved from the Business License Division files suggested possible improvements in the general viability of UAC's business community, but there was no certainty after adjusting for the effects of inflation that there was any "real" growth. In contrast, through survey data there was a consistent finding that businesspersons and key persons believed the viability of UAC had improved significantly since the early 1970s and at least some of this improvement was attributable to the CPTED demonstration. Similarly, data from the various types of interviews led to the conclusion that the overall quality of life in UAC had improved in the past few years compared to before 1974, and that at least some of this improvement, especially a renewed confidence in community, should be claimed as a CPTED success.

In sum, the first evaluation judged the CPTED Commercial Demonstration (1974-1977) a qualified "theory success." From a criminal justice research standpoint, it was suggested that the CPTED concept merited further testing, and from the standpoint of the city of Portland, it was suggested that the UAC CPTED program be continued.

THE 1980 REEVALUATION

The second evaluation of the CPTED Commercial Demonstration (Kushmuk & Whittemore, 1981) was performed by Portland's criminal justice planning office with funds provided by the National Institute of Justice. The federal government's renewed interest in

CPTED stemmed from a major review of "urban reactions to crime" programs (R. Rau, personal communication, 1979).[2] Given the focus of CPTED theory on enduring and institutional changes, a follow-up study was a welcomed and rare opportunity to study the longer-term effects of anticrime strategies.

The evaluation design and methods of the earlier Lavrakas et al. (1978) study were essentially replicated, that is, the focus of the reevaluation was on the CPTED proximate and ultimate goals at the levels of "program" and "theory" success. A major theme of the reevaluation was the "institutionalization" of CPTED, a hypothesized long-term outcome of the Westinghouse CPTED effort (Kaplan et al., 1978). CPTED goals were studied as enduring environmental conditions by looking at the sustained effects beyond the facilitative efforts of the Westinghouse consortium. Given the opportunity for a retrospective study, the investigators were also highly interested in judging which commercial strategies and combinations of strategies were the most successful in the long run, and in drawing some lessons from the Portland experience for future programs and policies.

DATA COLLECTION METHODOLOGY

Monthly reported crime rates were collected by hand for a full 60 months (1975-1979) from the Records Division of the Portland Police Department. This covered a period before, during, and after the major CPTED initiatives. Using standard UCR crime definitions, data were collected for commercial and residential burglary, commercial robbery, and "street" crimes (noncommercial robbery, assault, purse-snatching, and rape).[3] Crime figures for UAC (the commercial strip plus adjacent residential neighborhoods) and citywide minus UAC were collected, the latter serving as a "control group."

The reevaluation also replicated the 1977 surveys of business proprietors ($n = 78$, interviewed in person in late 1979) and residents ($n = 101$, interviewed via telephone in mid-1980). These more recent attitudes and perceptions were compared to the 1977 results in the areas of environmental conditions, social cohesion, fear of crime, and quality of life. Unfortunately, the business proprietors and residents surveyed in 1977 could not be identified and reinterviewed, thereby employing a panel survey design; instead, new random samples of business proprietors and residents were selected. Information on business openings and closings and commercial property values was also collected.

The final types of information used in the reevaluation included the Westinghouse source documents previously cited in this chapter, and, more important, interviews with city officials, police officials, community and business leaders, those who implemented CPTED strategies, and others with knowledge of or involvement in Union Avenue's recent past and present. These perceptions were very important in understanding the mechanisms of CPTED as a major commercial redevelopment effort. Of particular interest was the type of leadership and sustained effort required to actualize CPTED improvements fully.

Results

The physical improvements that followed the years of the Westinghouse consortium's efforts have been discussed above. Discussion here is limited to the nature of the enduring attainment of one CPTED proximate goal, social cohesion, and the three ultimate goals of reduced crime, reduced fear of crime, and improved quality of life.

Social Cohesion. Social cohesion as it was manifested within the UAC business community took the form of two highly successful CPTED strategies: organization of concerned UAC business proprietors into a group called the Northeast Business Boosters (NEBB) in 1976, and Union Avenue security adviser services. These two strategies were highly interrelated; that is, the police sergeant serving as security adviser was, in fact, the same individual who brought NEBB to life. These two strategies coalesced the business community around the common concerns of safety and business vitality. During the follow-up period, it was found that both of these activities had become highly institutionalized. NEBB continued to meet monthly, with attendance averaging 20-25 UAC and other northeast Portland businesspersons. Their primary focus had shifted somewhat from crime concerns to economic development. The security adviser position, abolished in 1977 because of a lack of federal funds, was not renewed, but the police department continued to provide the same services through its Community Crime Prevention Division. This sustained the positive and cooperative relationship that had been established between businesspeople and the police.

Reinforcing this conclusion was the finding from the 1979 survey of UAC business proprietors that they had maintained their target-hardening anticrime behaviors since 1977. The commercial environment was judged to be as secure as it was following the 1976-1977 security survey and street lighting programs. Furthermore, the business community's general attitudes toward the police were still quite favorable in 1979.

As stated before, the CPTED Commercial Demonstration was not primarily intended to bring about major changes in residential neighborhoods, yet the adjacent neighborhoods were defined as part of UAC. Thus, included in the original planning were strategies such as activity centers, "Safe Streets," and ethnic pride events: Residents were not only potential users of UAC businesses but also an important part of the "eyes on the street" of a community mobilized against crime. As was found by the 1977 evaluation, the reevaluation found little evidence of any attainment of increased residential cohesiveness. No further efforts were made to organize existing neighborhood groups against crime in a way that was accomplished through NEBB for the business community. The 1980 residential survey also documented racial polarization in attitudes toward the police. In 1977, similar proportions of white and black UAC residents expressed unfavorable attitudes toward the way the police were doing their job (about one in five). In 1980, however, perceptions had changed along racial lines, with unfavorable attitudes held by merely 7% of whites compared to 36% of blacks. Both during and after the reevaluation some significant events occurred regarding complaints of police harassment and excessive use of force that confirmed that blacks' dissatisfaction with the police was dividing the community.

In sum, coalescing the UAC residential community was a far more difficult task than for the business community, given the historical events that were unfolding in northeast Portland. The importance of accommodating racial differences and defusing racial tensions while trying to mobilize a community against crime has also been noted in other community anticrime evaluations (see Lavrakas & Maier, 1984). Unlike a business community that often shares a common, and thus a unifying, interest in "profits" regardless of the racial makeup of its members, racial differences among residents seem to constitute a major obstacle that anticrime programs must overcome in an effort to attain the CPTED proximate goal of community cohesion.

Level of Crime. Two of the CPTED strategies implemented in 1976-1977 were amenable to a test of CPTED's potential to reduce crime. Unfortunately, the two interventions, commercial security surveys and UAC street lighting, had occurred during overlapping time periods, and thus for the purposes of the reevaluation it was concluded that their relative effects could not be effectively partialed out.

Using a broader set of monthly crime statistics than had been available to the 1977 evaluation, time-series analyses (Box & Jenkins, 1976) were performed testing for the joint effects of these interventions (Griswold, Eagle, & Schneider, 1980).

Traditional ordinary least squares (OLS) regression was performed, testing for each intervention month at a time, but the more conclusive test was ARIMA modeling for the 60-month time series. For commercial robbery, an abrupt intervention effect of the initial security surveys was hypothesized and tested. For both commercial and residential burglary, it was hypothesized that crime reductions would result from both the security surveys and street lighting (implemented over a 14-month period) so that a gradual effect through completion of the street lighting project was tested. Since no information was available on the schedule of street light installation, a linear effect was assumed. UAC street crime reductions were also tested as a gradual effect beginning the first month of street light installation through completion. Time-series analyses were performed for UAC crime, non-UAC crime (citywide minus UAC), the ratio of UAC/non-UAC crime, and, in the case of street crimes, additional analyses for central UAC (the busy street life area), north-south UAC, and nighttime UAC. The most parsimonious ARIMA models were selected and tested for, using procedures recommended by McCleary and Hay (1979).

The most important finding from the analyses was a reduction in commercial burglaries attributable to the combined commercial security survey and street lighting interventions, a conclusion supported by both the OLS regression and the 60-month time-series analyses. Commercial burglaries in UAC were reduced (ARIMA [0, 1, 1]; $t = 3.35, p < .01$) and commercial burglaries in the rest of the city showed a nonsignificant change (see Figure 10.3). The test on the ratio of UAC/non-UAC commercial burglaries also indicated a significant reduction (ARIMA [2, 1, 1]; $t = 2.23, p < .05$), providing further evidence that the commercial burglary reduction was unique to UAC businesses. The comparative monthly percentages of UAC/non-UAC crime were 3.9% for the preintervention data compared to 2.5% for the remaining months (see Figure 10.4)

The analyses for street crimes did not yield a UAC crime-reduction effect attritutable to the street lighting. A significant reduction for central UAC street cimes was found (ARIMA [0, 0, 0]; $t = 2.29$, $p < .05$), along with marginal effects for nighttime UAC and total UAC. However, the most important test of a UAC/non-UAC reduction did not yield a significant effect.

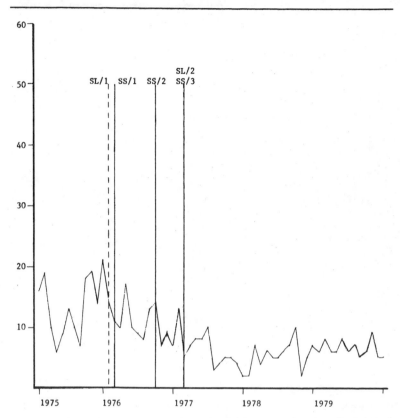

NOTE: SL/1 = beginning of street lighting installation; SL/2 = completion of street lighting installation; SS/1 = first security surveys (initial survey); SS/2 = second security surveys (first follow-up); SS/3 = third security surveys (second follow-up).

Figure 10.3 Monthly UAC Commercial Burglaries

For the remaining two crimes, residential burglary and commercial robbery, no significant changes were found, which could be attributed to the lack of CPTED interventions specifically targeted to have an impact on these crimes. Furthermore, there was no evidence of a displacement effect (increased residential burglary) or a diffusion effect (decreased residential burglary), unlike the suggestive findings of the 1977 evaluation. Finally, there was no effect of the security survey program on commercial robbery.

Fear of Crime. Fear of crime was studied through the data gathered in interviews with business proprietors and residents that reflected self-reported fear in UAC during the daytime and nighttime, and

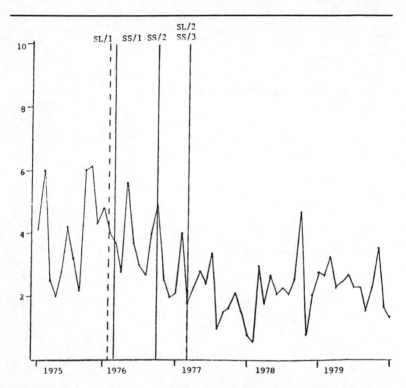

NOTE: SL/1 = beginning of street lighting installation; SL/2 = completion of street lighting installation; SS/1 = first security surveys (initial survey); SS/2 = second security surveys (first follow-up); SS63 = third security surveys (second follow-up).

Figure 10.4   Monthly UAC/Portland Percentages of Commercial Burglaries

whether or not any concerns or fears of being victimized affected use of the Union Avenue area. In general, there was little change between these fear measures and those found in the 1977 evaluation. Residents and business proprietors were still somewhat fearful, especially during the night hours. (The reader is reminded that both the evaluations gathered business and residential interviews *after* the security survey and street lighting interventions were completed.) The only group to show a change in fear of crime was the elderly, who expressed increased levels of fear in 1980 compared with 1977.

Quality of Life. The CPTED goal of improving the UAC quality of life was most directly addressed in the reevaluation via measures of the UAC's economic vitality. Although new businesses opened and others closed, the net effect since the early 1970s was a slow, but steady, increase and stabilization in the number of operating retail and commercial establishments in UAC. Supporting this trend of economic stabilization were the findings of an independent market and economic analysis of the Union Avenue commercial district performed in 1980 (Pacific Economica, 1980). It was found that recent land prices for Union Avenue commercial property were comparable to other commercial areas of Portland, areas that traditionally had more positive reputations than the UAC. Union Avenue appeared to be catching up in its commercial real estate values.

Conclusions

Based on their reevaluation, Kushmuk and Whittemore (1981) concluded that the most successful CPTED strategies were (a) security services (including the security survey programs), (b) organization and support of the business community (Northeast Business Boosters), and (c) the street lighting program. These strategies were well implemented, became institutionalized, and had demonstrated long-term effects on reducing commercial burglaries. Of moderate success were the economic development activities. Large-scale and comprehensive improvements in the physical environment (with the exception of the redesign of Union Avenue, itself, which was accomplished independent of CPTED), promotional events, and residential social cohesion were judged to have achieved, at best, low levels of success.

Several important lessons were learned from the Portland CPTED experience. First, a realistic time line and strong political support are essential for ensuring the implementation of a design program as comprehensive in nature as CPTED tried to be. The experience in UAC suggests that at least five years of strong, consistent leadership from the inception of a CPTED program is a realistic timetable for large-scale environmental changes to be achieved. Westinghouse, as a facilitator and advocate for CPTED concepts in Union Avenue's redevelopment, and despite some disillusionment due to unfulfilled expectations, was judged to be an important catalyst for what did actually happen—this was the almost unanimous perception of UAC community leaders and local people involved in the redevelopment efforts.

Linked to this basic conclusion was the observation of the potential danger in underestimating the time and effort needed to implement large-scale CPTED-type improvements when "selling" such a program to a city. Unrealistic expectations not realized can turn into disillusionment among business leaders and jeopardize redevelopment, which is likely to escalate the crime/fear/urban decay process further.

A second major lesson was that anticrime strategies involving complicated and concerted efforts among various government, community, and private agencies are extremely difficult to maneuver into place, regardless of the effort and leadership provided by a coordinating organization. By contrast, those that involved only a few groups with harmonious interests, and that grafted onto what was naturally present in the community (for example, the security adviser building on the Northeast Business Boosters) experienced more success within a short period of time.

A third important lesson was that changes in the social environment, in particular the residential sector, are often more difficult to accomplish than visible changes in the physical environment. In UAC, business proprietors were more easily coalesced around common crime and economic concerns than was the residential community, which was diverse and, in a racially heterogeneous area with underlying tensions, far more difficult to bring together.

THE PORTLAND CPTED EXPERIENCE
IN PERSPECTIVE

More than a decade after the beginning of the Westinghouse work in Portland, we can look back on our respective evaluations of the UAC CPTED Commercial Demonstration and make some additional observations, beyond the conclusions from our 1978 and 1981 evaluation reports. As with many comprehensive anticrime programs, the UAC CPTED effort was difficult to evaluate for two basic reasons. First, the target area, the Union Avenue Corridor, had a unique combination of crime patterns, economic conditions and racial composition that precluded collecting comparable data in an "equivalent" comparison area elsewhere in Portland. Thus, the use of a traditional quasi-experimental evaluation design (see Cook & Campbell, 1976), with "treatment" and "control" commercial strips, was not a realistic option. Furthermore, had such a comparison site existed in Portland, there is little reason to believe that it could have been kept from implementing its own redevelopment efforts, perhaps even ones that employed CPTED-like concepts.

A second problem for the evaluations was the diffuse nature of the many CPTED strategies, which often had hard-to-define starting points and ending dates. In addition to the obvious problem this caused for analyses such as the time series, it contributed to a different type of threat to the *internal validity* (see Campbell & Stanley, 1963) of the conclusions: Were the observed changes in UAC due primarily to the Westinghouse/CPTED effort, or would they have happened in due course anyway, as part of the city's urban renewal efforts?

These methodological limitations were addresses as thoroughly as possible, through the use of a comprehensive "theory-based" evaluation. This evaluation framework tried to gather the best available information to document effects at various stages of the hypothesized CPTED model (as shown in Figure 10.2). For example, the time-series tests of changes in UAC crime rates related to CPTED interventions represented the most powerful (that is, methodologically rigorous) set of data that the evaluations were able to employ. In contrast, the question of the importance of a "facilitator" (in this case Westinghouse) could be answered only with very soft data gathered from key-person interviews. In sum, however, and considering the validity of the various types of data that were available, we still are confident that the evaluations reached basically accurate (that is, internally valid) conclusions.

In addition to these considerations, the issue of the external validity of the findings is important to consider. Is the UAC CPTED experience, which occurred within a specific political and social context, generalizable to other cities, other commercial sites, and/or other climates of government support? The Union Avenue Corridor was selected as "theoretically" representative of other urban cities with pockets of decline. Since there are many such areas within other cities, the UAC experience in one sense might hold up in other settings. On the other hand, the Portland demonstration occurred at a time when there was available rather generous federal spending on anticrime programming (that is, the 1970s).

Could such a comprehensive anticrime effort succeed in these days of reduced federal support? Possibly not, but some of the Portland findings suggest that much can be accomplished by nurturing and building upon existing community resources. Businesspersons have a stake in creating an environment that is economically viable *and* free of high levels of crime and fear of crime. In Portland, the successful combination of the security adviser services (already included in the Portland Police Department's annual budget) and the Northeast Business Boosters (supported via the *voluntary* efforts of the business community) demonstrated that police agencies can work effectively with citizens in addressing common concerns *without* large additional public expenditures. Business proprietors were more willing, and probably more able, than residents to incur the cost of target-hardening measures (for example, better locks and alarms). Although the cost savings to the UAC businesses associated with the reduction in commercial burglaries were not documented by our evaluations, there seems little doubt that the business community received a considerable payoff from investment in crime prevention measures.

Joint local public/private sector initiatives stressing the interrelationships among crime, fear of crime, and economic viability appear feasible, and are probably preferable to reliance on extensive outside (federal) funding. Such ventures are being tried in other cities since the Portland experience (see Curtis, 1985), not always under the rubric of "CPTED," but with a CPTED-like approach. We will await an assessment of these programs before further judging the validity and feasibility of CPTED in other contexts.

NOTES

1. A listing of all the data elements used in this evaluation is presented in Lavrakas et al. (1978), but is much too lengthy for presentation here.

2. Dr. Richard Rau was project monitor of the reevaluation grant for the National Institute of Justice.

3. Regarding "street" crimes, it was not possible to distinguish between stranger-to-stranger and nonstranger assaults, nor between assaults that occurred indoors versus outdoors. Hence, this category as a measure of the amount of stranger-to-stranger crime that occurred on the street in UAC is a somewhat imprecise measure.

REFERENCES

Bell, L., Day, D., Tien, J., & Hanes, L. (1976). *CPTED Commercial Demonstration Plan* (mimeo). Arlington, VA: Westinghouse Electric Corporation.

Bower, C. P., Padia, W. L., & Glass, G. V. (1974). *TMS: Two Fortran IV programs for analysis of time-series experiments* (mimeo). Boulder: University of Colorado.

Box, G. & Jenkins, G. (1976). *Time series analysis: Forecasting and control.* San Francisco: Holden-Day.

Campbell, D., & Stanley, J. (1963). *Experimental and quasi-experimental designs for research.* Chicago: Rand McNally.

Cook, T., & Campbell, D. (1976). *Quasi-experimentation: Design and analysis issues for field settings.* Chicago: Rand McNally.

Crano, W., & Brewer, M. (1973). *Principles of research in social psychology.* New York: McGraw-Hill.

Curtis, L. (1985). *American violence and public policy.* New Haven, CT: Yale University Press.

Griswold, D., Eagle, J., & Schneider, A. (1980). *CPTED time series analysis of the impact of street lighting and commercial security surveys on Union Avenue crime* (mimeo). Eugene, OR: Institute for Policy Analysis.

Jacobs, J. (1961). *The death and life of great American cities.* New York: Random House.

Jeffery, C. R. (1971). *Crime prevention through environmental design.* Beverly Hills, CA: Sage.

Kaplan, H., O'Kane, K., Lavrakas, P. J., & Hoover, S. (1978). *CPTED final report on commercial demonstration in Portland, Oregon* (mimeo). Arlington, VA: Westinghouse Electric Corporation.

Kushmuk, J., & Whittemore, S. (1981). *A re-evaluation of crime prevention through environmental design in Portland, Oregon: Executive summary.* Washington, DC: Government Printing Office.

Lavrakas, P. J. (1978) Theory-based evaluation planning: A CPTED example. *Bellringer: A Periodic Review of Criminal Justice Evaluation, 9/10,* 15-18.

Lavrakas, P. J. (1982). Fear of crime and behavioral restrictions in urban and suburban neighborhoods. *Population and Environment, 5(4), 242-264.*

Lavrakas, P. J., & Maier, R. A., Jr. (1984) Racial differences as barriers to effective community crime prevention. Paper presented at the meeting of the American Psychological Association, Toronto.

Lavrakas, P. J., Normoyle, J., & Wagener, J. (1978). *CPTED commercial demonstration evaluation report* (mimeo). Evanston, IL: Westinghouse Electric Corporation.

McCleary, R., & Hay, R. (1979). *Applied time series for social sciences.* Beverly Hills, CA: Sage.

Newman, O. (1972). *Defensible space.* New York: Macmillan.

Pacific Economica. (1980). *Inner northeast Portland: An income and market analysis.* Portland: Author.

Reppetto, T. (1974). *Residential crime.* Cambridge, MA: Ballinger.

Scarr, H. A. (1973). *Patterns of burglary.* Washington, DC: Government Printing Office.

Weiss, C. (1972). *Evaluation research.* Englewood Cliffs, NJ: Prentice-Hall.

Chapter 11

THE COMMERCIAL SECURITY FIELD TEST PROGRAM
A Systemic Evaluation of Security Surveys in Denver, St. Louis, and Long Beach

JAMES M. TIEN
MICHAEL F. CAHN

Given the millions of dollars spent annually in the conduct of security surveys and in the subsequent compliance with survey recommendations, it is reasonable to ask: Is the crime prevention approach of security surveys effective against commercial crimes? For several reasons, previous studies or evaluations of security survey programs have been unable to provide an answer to this important question. The Commercial Security Field Test (CSFT) program, funded by the National Institute of Justice (NIJ), was developed specifically to address the above-stated question, especially in regard to the commercial crime of burglary. This chapter describes the evaluation of the CSFT program. In the first section, some pertinent issues are addressed and background information is provided. In the second section, the critical evaluation findings are detailed. Finally, we present two important recommendations.

AUTHORS' NOTE: *This chapter is based on work undertaken in connection with Grant 79-NI-AX-0105, awarded to Public Systems Evaluation, Inc., by the National Institute of Justice, U. S. Department of Justice, under the Omnibus Crime Control and Safe Streets Act of 1968, as amended. Points of view on opinions stated in this document are those of the authors and do not necessarily represent the official position or policies of the U.S. Department of Justice. The authors would, however, like to acknowledge the guidance, understanding, and support of Dr. Richard L. Rau, the NIJ project monitor.*

BACKGROUND

Prevalence and Economic Impact of
Crimes Against Commercial Establishments

Although the economic well-being of a business is affected primarily by market conditions, it is also affected by crime. The U.S. Department of Commerce (1975) estimated that crime cost the business community $9.3 billion in 1975. Small commercial establishments are affected adversely by crime; for some small businesses, the cost of crime could mean the difference between survival and failure (Small Business Administration, 1969; U.S. Congress, 1977). Typically, small businesses operate on a thin profit margin, leaving no room for losses due to crime.

Of all the commercial crimes, it is conjectured that larceny—including shoplifting and employee theft—causes the greatest dollar loss to businesses (American Management Association, 1977; Chelimsky, 1979). Although no data are available, it is generally agreed that larceny is the overwhelming reason for inventory shrinkage, which is becoming a severe problem for most businesses. During 1982, some 0.80 million cases of shoplifting and 1.02 million larcenies from buildings were reported to the Federal Bureau of Investigation (1983). However, as demonstrated by the National Crime Panel Surveys (1977), it should be noted that larceny is an extremely underreported crime. After larceny, burglary—the unlawful entry of a structure to commit a felony or theft—is the most costly commercial crime. Some 1.06 million commercial burglaries were reported to the FBI (1983) in 1982; as in the case of larceny, and because of underreporting, this figure should be considered an underestimate of the actual number of commercial burglaries in 1982. Although less frequent and costly than either larceny or burglary, robbery—the unlawful threat or use of force to commit a felony or theft—is actually a more serious crime because it could lead to a violent confrontation between victim and offender. Some 0.17 million commercial robberies were reported in 1982 (FBI, 1983); again, this figure should be considered an underestimate. In sum, although larceny, burglary, and robbery are the most costly and widespread of all the commercial crimes, there are, of course, other commercial crimes, including arson and vandalism.

Inasmuch as many of the offenses committed against commercial establishments are crimes of opportunity (that is, largely unplanned acts committed by amateurs in situations where merchandise, money, or equipment is readily accessible and the risk of detection is relatively low), the law enforcement focus has been primarily in the area of crime prevention or opportunity reduction. In particular, nearly every law enforcement agency in the country is conducting crime prevention or security surveys, which typically involves first the inspection of a commercial premise from a crime opportunity perspective and then the recommendation of physical, procedural, and/or behavioral changes that are directed at reducing the identified opportunities. Security surveys are usually conducted following the occurrence of a crime (in most instances, a burglary) or by request of the owner or manager of the business.

Given the millions of dollars spent annually in the conduct of security surveys and in the subsequent compliance with survey recommendations, it is reasonable to ask: Is the crime prevention approach of security surveys effective against commercial crimes? In reviewing the literature, we found that although several studies focus on the general aspects of security surveys and commercial crimes (Small Business Administration, 1969; Kingsbury, 1973; White et al., 1975; International Training, Research, and Evaluation Council, 1977; Gunn et al., 1978; Bickman & Rosenbaum, 1980), only a handful (Touche Ross and Company, 1976; Minnesota Governor's Commission on Crime Prevention and Control, 1976; Lavrakas, Maxfield, & Henig, 1978; Eversen, 1979; Pearson, 1980) deal with the results of an actual implemented security survey program.

Several conclusions can be drawn from the research on prior security survey programs. First, the programs were all parts of larger, more complex, crime prevention efforts, so that the resultant impacts could not have been attributed solely to the intervention of security surveys. Second, data regarding compliance with survey recommendations were conspicuously lacking; whatever evidence was presented suggested a low level of compliance—thus bringing into question whether or not the conduct of security surveys resulted in an actual "treatment" of the surveyed establishments. Third, the programs' research designs or selection schemes usually called for (a) a dispersed (that is, city-, county-, or statewide) focus for the conduct of security surveys, and (b) a poorly controlled before-and-after (that is, pretreatment and posttreatment) analysis of the crime impact measures. Fourth, the reported crime impacts were almost exclusively about burglary, largely because data on larceny were unavailable and data on robbery were too few.

Given the above described problems of program complexity, low compliance, inadequate research design, and inadequate crime data, it is not surprising that the prior evaluations of security survey programs resulted in findings that are statistically inconclusive. The Commercial Security Field Test (National Institute of Justice, 1979) sought to overcome these problems.

The Commercial Security Field Test: An Assessment of Security Surveys

In particular, the program complexity problem was to be mitigated by the somewhat singular, security survey-oriented focus of the CSFT; the low compliance problem was explicitly dealt with by the CSFT, which called for the carrying out of compliance-enhancing activities; and the inadequate research design problem was also addressed by the CSFT's strong emphasis on evaluation. However, the inadequate crime data problem pervading previous studies could not be overcome by the CSFT; again, extreme underreporting of larcenies and low robbery rates, together with the fact that the resultant security survey recommendations were minimally focused on reducing the opportunities for larcenies and robberies, resulted in a CSFT program that was almost exclusively directed at the commercial crime of burglary.

Although the CSFT program grants were awarded officially by the National Institute of Justice to the Denver Anti-Crime Council, the Long Beach Police Department, and the St. Louis Commission on Crime and Law Enforcement in April 1980, program-related activities had been ongoing for more than a year. In particular, and as is the custom in all NIJ-sponsored field tests, a CSFT Program Coordinating Team (PCT) was formed in the latter part of 1978. While identifying candidate cities in which to conduct the CSFT program, the PCT completed the *Test Design* (NIJ, 1979) for the program in May 1979. This design document reviewed pertinent background material; articulated a set of program purposes, goals, and objectives; defined an experimental selection scheme or research design; discussed a number of evaluation-related concerns; and suggested criteria for city selection as well as strategies for program implementation. By the time the evaluation grant was awarded to Public Systems Evaluation, Inc. (PSE) in October 1979, the list of candidate cities had, for all intents and purposes, been reduced to the final three candidates—Denver, Long Beach, and St. Louis.

Following the grant awards to the three cities in April 1980, the three grantees endeavored to meet the requirements of the *Test Design* (NIJ, 1979) by identifying candidate pairs of commercial test (that is, experimental and control) areas that had relatively high commercial crime rates as well as other specified characteristics. By October 1980 and following PSE's review of the submitted site information, the PCT had randomly—by coin tosses—assigned them to experimental and control groups. Subsequently, security surveys were conducted in the experimental areas and several follow-up visits were made both to encourage compliance with survey recommendations and to determine the level of compliance. Finally, on April 1, 1981, it was decided that the formal one-year test or evaluation period could begin. A year later, a final set of compliance checks was made in the experimental areas.

Because of evaluation considerations, the CSFT program that was eventually implemented in the three cities reflected a revised version of the program stipulated in the *Test Design*. First, while the *Test Design* called for 20-60 business establishments per test area, the grantees were encouraged to select test areas with a larger number of establishments for evaluation purposes. Second, the emphasis in the *Test Design* on establishing a close cooperative relationship between business and police could have resulted in a more complex program in which other crime prevention activities (for example, special police patrols assigned to the experimental areas) might have occured—and, therefore, confounded the evaluation findings. Instead, the grantees were advised to cooperate with the businesspeople only to the extent of facilitating the conduct of the security surveys and enhancing compliance with survey recommendations. Third, pairwise matching of commercial areas on the basis of multiple criteria (that is, crime rates, social demographics, traffic patterns, police community relations)—as originally envisioned in the *Test Design*—could not be accomplished. In fact, it was not possible to find even one matched pair among the ten pairs proposed by the grantees. In response to this design difficulty, we, as evaluators, were able to develop and implement an alternative ("split-area") research design in which the surveyed (experimental) areas were split into two groups according to whether the CSFT crime prevention staff categorized them as "treated" or "untreated." Identifying an establishment as treated meant that it was judged to be less prone to burglary victimization as a result of compliance with the survey recommendations. This conceptual split was undertaken toward the end of the one-year test period by the same police officers and CSFT staff who were initially involved in the conduct of the security surveys; they categorized each surveyed establishment by reviewing from a risk-to-burglary perspective the establishment's compliance with the survey recommendations. Overall, 194 of the surveyed establishments were considered treated, and 236 were considered untreated. Actually, as expected, compliance—as defined by the percentage of recommended changes complied with—was a determining factor in whether or not an establishment was considered treated; the treated establishments had an average compliance level of 77.3%, as opposed to a 42.4% figure for the untreated establishments. Further, the sets of treated and untreated establishments were determined to be equivalent in terms of the types of businesses contained in each. In evaluation terms, this was implemented retrospectively, the split-area research design can be considered to be a quasi-experimental design for the purpose of this study. In sum, the above-indicated modifications to the original *Test Design* reflected the CSFT's emphasis on evaluation.

Using a Purposeful and Systematic Evaluation Approach

It is recognized that a major reason for the failure of program evaluations is the inadequacy of the evaluation designs. One of the prevalent factors contributing to this inadequacy is that the design does not occur in conjunction with the development of the program itself. As evaluators, we were fortunate in the case of the CSFT program to have been able to specify the evaluation design in parallel with the final development of the program's initial *Test Design* (NIJ. 1979)—prior to program implementation. Our attendance at the major program planning sessions, as well as at NIJ's Program Coordinating Team meetings, was critical in two respects. On the one hand, the planning effort benefited from our presence because all planning decisions were continuously assessed relative to their potential impact on the evaluation effort; as discussed earlier, several program components were modified because they threatened to invalidate the anticipated evaluation findings. On the other hand, the fact that the PCT's decision-making process in regard to the program's rationale, objectives, and components was fully exposed to us resulted in the development of a sound, systemic evaluation design, characterized by pertinent test hypotheses, a quasi-experimental selection scheme, an appropriate measures framework, relevant measurement methods, and valid analytic techniques. As identified by Tien (1979), a systemic evaluation views a program from a systems perspective and includes input, process, outcome, and systemic measures and issues, including those of transferability and generalizability. Alternatively, a systemic evaluation is at once an audit, formative, and summative evaluation.

The evaluation design for this CSFT effort was based on an explicit application of the "dynamic rollback" approach advanced by Tien (1979). The "rollback" aspect of the approach is reflected in the ordered sequence of interrogatories or steps that must be considered before an evaluation design can be developed: The sequence rolls back in time from (a) a projected look at the range of program characteristics (that is, from its rationale through its operation and anticipated findings); to (b) a prospective consideration of the threats (problems and pitfalls) to the validity of the final evaluation; to (c) a more immediate identification of the evaluation design elements. Thus, the anticipated program characteristics identify the possible threats to validity, which in turn point to the design elements that are necessary to mitigate, if not to eliminate, these threats. The "dynamic" aspect of the approach refers to its nonstationary character; that is, the components of the process must be constantly updated, throughout the entire development and implementation phases of the evaluation design. In this manner, the design elements can be adaptively refined, if necessary, to account for any new threats to validity that may be caused by previously unidentified program characteristics. In sum, the dynamic rollback approach is an adaptive process for developing purposeful and systematic evaluation designs.

It was the application of this dynamic rollback approach that prompted us to recommend larger test areas, to advise against establishing a closer cooperation between the police and the businesspeople beyond facilitating the conduct of security surveys and enhancing compliance with survey recommendations, and to develop an alternative split-area research design. Additionally, we undertook several activities that contributed to the validity of our evaluation findings. First, we were particularly careful about monitoring compliance with survey recommendations, because with low compliance it would have been questionable whether or not there was indeed a sufficient program treatment.

Second, we undertook extensive on-site monitoring; in addition to periodic site visits from our Cambridge, Massachusetts, office, we had an on-site person in Long Beach and in St. Louis during the entire period of evaluation. (Because of staff turnover, our on-site presence in Denver was not continuous.) Further, we developed and administered several data collection instruments and questionnaires; all of this contributed to a multi-measurement approach to data collection and analysis. Conclusions based on a range of measurements are likely to be more reliable because they go beyond the limits of any one measure; they help to prevent wrong conclusions that arise from misleading—single-sourced—data.

Third, perhaps one of the major contributions of this evaluation effort has been the highlighting of the importance of risk as a measure within the context of crime prevention. Although the concept of risk is not new, the development and application of a risk model—as briefly outlined in the final section—is ground-breaking. Although the modeling process explicitly contributed to this evaluation (that is, in defining "treated" and "untreated" establishments), we feel that the model could provide a much-needed framework for arriving at rational (that is, purposeful and consistent) survey recommendations.

Fourth, although the split-area research design provided a very good control for neighborhood and other environmental factors (because of the co-location of both treated and untreated establishments in a test area), the retrospective implementation of the design raised a potentially severe regression artifact problem, as recognized by Campbell and Erlebacher (1975). More specifically, because the selection of treated and untreated establishments did not take into account the key measure of crime, the two groups of establishments would most likely not be equivalent in terms of this measure; as a result, a selection-regression artifact interaction could occur and threaten the validity of the observed impact on crime. Fortunately, we were able to develop a statistically based model that was able to correct for this threat; further, the model was able to correct for another problem—the selection-intervention interaction threat to validity—that is typically also a consequence of a retrospectively configured research design. In sum, although the difficulties associated with a retrospectively implemented design would usually preclude it from being an effective design, we feel that, in this case, because we have comparability among the test units, as well as a model that corrects for the two most important statistically related difficulties, it is justified to say that we have an effective design that would yield valid findings concerning the impact of security surveys on crime (for a detailed discussion of the model, see Tien, 1980).

It should be noted that the split-area model can be applied to many situations in which there are two—including experimental and control—groups, one deemed treated and the other not. Further, the one-selection measure model can be straightforward extended to the case of several selection measures.

FINDINGS

The CSFT program shed light on three critical subject matters: the impact of security surveys on commercial burglary, the impact of security surveys on fear, and the impact of business/police relations on the conduct of security surveys and the compliance with survey recommendations.

Burglary Reduction

A common—but not scientifically sound—approach to considering the impact of a treatment is to compare the before (pretreatment) values or statistics of each impact measure with its after (posttreatment) statistics. In Table 11.1, we provide the burglary rate (that is, number of burglaries per establishment per year) statistics in terms of "treated" and "untreated" establishments, which, as indicated earlier, were categorized from a risk-to-burglary perspective that was based on which survey recommendations had been complied with. In reviewing Table 11.1, we note that although there are some impressive changes in burglary rates on a pretreatment-posttreatment basis, the changes are not statistically significant, as per a one-sided z-test of the difference between two sample means at a 0.05 level of significance. The reason for this apparent contradiction is, of course, the dispersed nature of the distribution of the burglary rate (as reflected in the relatively large standard deviation figures); in fact, if one were to compute the coefficient of variation (that is, ratio of standard deviation to the average rate) for each set of rate and standard deviation entries in Table 11.1, one would find quite large coefficient of variation values ranging between 2.37 and 4.13.

Careful scrutiny of Table 11.1 reveals two interesting trends: The treated establishments experienced a decrease in burglary (except in the case of St. Louis), while at the same time the untreated establishments experienced an increase. Again, although encouraging, these trends are not credible because they are based on a nonexperimental or weak pretreatment-posttreatment research design that cannot control for a number of environmental factors that might have changed from the pretreatment period to the posttreatment period. In particular, it is important not only to consider the burglary statistics of the treated and untreated establishments separately, on a pretreatment-posttreatment basis, but also to compare both sets of statistics in a single statistical test, as is done in our split-area analysis. In this manner, any environmental changes affecting the treated establishments—except for the treatment (that is, security surveys with compliance)—would be controlled for by considering their effect on the untreated establishments (which are located in the same areas as the treated establishments).

TABLE 11.1 Commercial Burglary Statistics: Pretreatment-Posttreatment Design Analysis

City	Number of Establishments	Pretreatment Period (10/1/79-9/30/80)		Posttreatment Period (4/1/81-3/31/82)		Percentage Change in Rate	z-Statistic[a]
		Rate	Standard Deviation	Rate	Standard Deviation		
Denver							
Treated	70	0.257	0.652	0.114	0.363	−55.6	−1.60
Untreated	76	0.184	0.687	0.237	0.709	+28.8	0.47
Total	146	0.219	0.670	0.178	0.572	−18.7	−0.56
Long Beach							
Treated	62	0.323	1.113	0.226	0.525	−30.0	−0.62
Untreated	63	0.079	0.326	0.095	0.390	+20.3	0.25
Total	125	0.200	0.823	0.160	0.465	−20.0	−0.47
St. Louis							
Treated	62	0.210	0.792	0.290	0.687	+38.1	0.60
Untreated	97	0.247	0.693	0.278	0.800	+12.6	0.29
Total	159	0.233	0.731	0.283	0.756	+21.5	0.60
All cities							
Treated	194	0.263	0.863	0.206	0.538	−21.7	−0.78
Untreated	236	0.182	0.616	0.216	0.684	+18.7	0.57
Total	430	0.219	0.738	0.212	0.622	−3.2	−0.15

a. At a 0.05 level of significance, the z-statistic must be less than −1.64 for the change to be statistically significant. Using this criterion, none of the reductions in commercial burglary rates listed above is statistically significant.

TABLE 11.2　Commercial Burglary Statistics:
　　　　　　　　Split-Area Design Analysis

Burglary Statistics	12-Month Evaluation Periods				21-Month Evaluation Periods in Denver
	Denver	Long Beach	St. Louis	Total	
Net impact (in percentages)	−64.8	+63.0	+9.9	−11.9	−74.2
z-Statistics[a]	−1.65	1.55	0.20	−0.46	−1.82

a. At a 0.05 level of significance, the z-statistic must be less than −1.64 for the change to be statistically significant. Using this criterion, only the reductions in Denver's commercial burglary as listed above are statistically significant.

Table 11.2 contains the results of applying the split-area model to the burglary statistics in Table 11.1 Overall, the net impact of security surveys (with a high level of compliance) was determined to be an 11.9% decrease in the burglary rate. Although not statistically significant, this result is still quite impressive and somewhat credible (in that it is based on a quasi-experimental split-area design that, although retrospectively implemented, can control for many environmental changes). Of critical interest are the Denver results. On a 12-month basis, the net impact of the CSFT program in Denver was a *statistically significant* 64.8% reduction in burglary rate, and on an extended 21-month basis, the corresponding figure was an even more significant 74.2% reduction. (Inasmuch as Denver maintained its crime statistics on a readily accessible computer, we decided in the interest of research to obtain additional data from Denver.) These statistically significant and credible results constitute strong evidence of the effectiveness of commercial security surveys—given that survey recommendations are complied with—as a strategy for reducing the incidence of commercial burglary. Further, because the 21-month results represent an improvement over the 12-month results, there is some evidence that the effectiveness is lasting.

Several other comments should be made regarding Table 11.2. First, given Long Beach's quite favorable results when employing the pretreatment-posttreatment design (see Table 11.1), it is surprising to see in Table 11.2 that the net CSFT impact under the split-area design was a 63.0% increase. Actually, it should be noted that it was *inappropriate* to have applied the split-area design to the Long Beach burglary statistics; the reason is that the corresponding pretreatment burglary rates of the two groups (treated and untreated) of establishments were very different, as indicated in Table 11.1. This significant difference, in turn, implied that the two groups of establishments were not even closely comparable or equivalent with respect to burglary, so that no statistical model—including the split-area model—could have corrected for the difference. In sum, the net impact statistic for Long Beach in Table 11.2 is *not* valid. Second, as might have been expected (given the results in Table 11.1), the net impact of a 9.9% increase in burglary rate for St. Louis is not surprising; however, interestingly enough, this figure seems less dramatic than the comparable pretreat-ment-posttreatment figures in Table 11.1. Third, despite integrating the invalid but large increase for Long Beach and the slight increase for St. Louis, the net overall impact for the three cities is still a significant—though not statistically significant—reduction in the burglary rate of 11.9%; this result highlights the fact that the split-area model is not a simple additive model but a sophisticated statistical model. Fourth, if Long Beach were to be excluded from the split-area analysis, then the overall findings in Table 11.2 would be correspondingly and signifi-cantly improved.

In addition to the above-cited statistical reasons for the different findings in the three cities, there are other reasons. Most important through our on-site monitoring and subsequent analysis of the survey recommendations, the Denver staff members were able to make their survey recommendations in a more rational manner than their counterparts in Long Beach and St. Louis. For example, before con-ducting a security survey of a business establishment, the Denver staff reviewed the reports of any prior burglaries at that establishment. Prior burglary reports were not available in Long Beach at the time security surveys were conducted, and only partially available in St. Louis. Additionally, in analyzing the survey recommenda-tions, we noted that Denver had a wide range of recommendations, Long Beach had similar recommendations for each establishment, and St. Louis tended to make only inexpensive recommenda-tions that stood a better chance of being implemented. Consequently, the lack of rationality in arriving at survey recommendations may cast doubt on whether or not adequate treatments were implemented in Long Beach and St. Louis. Another possible reason for the poor find-ings in St. Louis is that the surveyed establishments were located in areas that were so depressed they could not be "turned around"; in-deed, the burglary rate in each of St.Louis's commercial test areas in-creased significantly during the period of evaluation.

In sum, in response to the question of whether or not security surveys are effective against commercial burglary, the answer is yes only if the treatment is adequate—that is, the survey recommendations are (a) rationally identified and (b) complied with. Interestingly, this important finding suggests that the traditional manner of conducting security surveys—in which neither the rationality of the survey recommendations nor their compliance is emphasized—is totally inadequate.

Finally, although the split-area design was able to control for the environmental factors and the underlying model was able to correct for several statistical threats to validity, one threat or problem that remains bothersome is the issue of crime displacement. Since the treated and untreated establishments in the split-area design are obviously physically close to each other, there is naturally a potential for crime displacement. Further, as Reppetto (1975) indicates, geographical displacement is only one possibility; there could also be temporal, tactical, target, and functional displacements of crime. Perhaps the only way to ascertain crime displacement is to undertake an extensive offender interview study, which remains a costly and controversial method of research. Another issue that we would have liked to address—if the data were available—was the impact of the CSFT on attempted burglary. In particular, to what extent were security surveys—and compliance with survey recommendations—a factor in a burglary being only an attempt? Unfortunately, such detailed data are not available; even a conscientiously written crime report seldom addresses *why* a burglary attempt was unsuccessful. A third issue of interest is which, if any, of an establishment's characteristics are correlated with its crime or victimization rate. Although we looked at several characteristics (such as type of business, years in business) for which we had some reasonably reliable data (from the Security Survey Instrument), we found that only the type of business seemed to correlate with its crime rate; as might be expected, food and drink establishments were burglarized most often, and professional businesses were victimized the least.

Fear Reduction

An obvious corollary to the question of crime reduction is whether or not there was a commensurate fear reduction. Being a highly subjective and emotional measure, fear is difficult to gauge. Nevertheless, if it were defined to be fear of being burglarized, then part a of Table 11.3 indicates a definite reduction in the level of such fear—some 61.8% of the surveyed proprietors stated that they felt less vulnerable to burglary as a result of the CSFT program. On the other hand, if it were defined to be fear of personal safety, then part b of Table 11.3 indicates no change in the level of such fear— some 54.4% of the surveyed proprietors stated that they felt no change in their personal safety as a result of the CSFT program.

The above-stated results are not surprising given the burglary-oriented focus of the CSFT program. Certainly, we would have hoped that the program would lower the proprietors' fear of being burglarized, although we would not have expected any effect on their fear of personal safety (inasmuch as burglary is a crime against property, not against a person).

Business/Police Relations

Lowering the proprietors' fear of being burglarized was just one aspect of improved relations between the business establishments and the police, as a result of the CSFT program. In fact, 88.5% of the proprietors felt that the program constituted an effective means of responding to the problem of commercial crimes against small businesses. When asked whether or not the CSFT program should continue and be funded locally, 77.1% of the proprietors responded in the affirmative.

The enhanced business/police relations were due, primarily, to the proprietor-surveyor relationships established as a result of the follow-up compliance checks, and, secondarily, to the area-specific crime prevention newsletters that were circulated periodically to the surveyed establishments. In Long Beach, these relations helped to establish a new business organization, which in time got involved in activities other than crime prevention. Again, as has been found in other studies, the long-term vitality of any organization depends on its involvement in a range of issues, even though it may have been initiated by a single issue such as crime prevention.

What did the enhanced business/police relations do for the CSFT program? They facilitated survey conduct and encouraged compliance with survey recommendations. Although it could possibly have done more (for example, encouraged special police patrols), it was limited to these two aspects in order, as explained earlier, not to confound the resultant evaluation findings. In regard to the first aspect, it should be noted that survey team members in police uniform were more credible and readily acceptable to the business proprietors than were those in civilian clothes, especially on their first visit. Although this might suggest that the conduct of security surveys should be solely a police

TABLE 11.3   Business Proprietors' Perceptions of Program Impact on Burglary and Personal Safety

a. Impact on Burglary:
"Compare how *vulnerable* to the following crimes you feel your business is *now* (since April 1981) as compared to *before* the CSFT (before 1980)." (responses in percentages)

City	Much Less Vulnerable	Less Vulnerable	No Change	More Vulnerable	Much More Vulnerable	Don't Know
Denver (N = 112)	33.0	38.4	25.9	0.0	0.0	2.7
Long Beach (N = 74)	13.5	26.0	50.7	0.0	0.0	13.7
St. Louis (N = 55)	21.8	38.2	29.1	1.8	0.0	9.1
Total (N = 241)	24.5	37.3	30.3	0.4	0.0	7.5

b. Impact on Personal Safety:
"How would you compare your personal safety *now* (since April 1981) with that *before* the CSFT (before October 1980)?" (responses in percentages)

City	Increased Substantially	Increased Somewhat	No Change	Decreased Somewhat	Decreased Substantially	Don't Know
Denver (N = 108)	4.6	17.6	57.4	4.6	5.6	10.2
Long Beach (N = 78)	1.3	14.1	47.4	16.7	1.3	19.2
St. Louis (N = 51)	2.0	11.8	58.8	7.8	2.0	17.6
Total (N = 237)	3.0	15.2	54.4	9.3	3.4	14.8

function, it should be noted that a private security firm could also conduct security surveys, provided it receives the backing of the local business organization (which in fact might formally recommend the firm to its members).

Compliance

In regard to compliance with survey recommendations, several remarks should be made. First, as detailed in Table 11.4, the business establishments complied much less with the recommended physical changes than with the recommended procedural changes. As might be expected, recommendations involving physical improvements—and, therefore, expenditures of money and labor—received less attention than recommendations involving procedural changes that typically were cost free to implement. Overall, a significant 59.1% compliance rate was achieved by the CSFT program.

Second, although several different compliance strategies (such as low interest loans, hardware discounts, and insurance discounts) were envisioned by each city in August 1980, in reality the five follow-up visits became the strategy of choice in all three cities; in fact, it would be safe to say that most of the others were never seriously explored. For example, the effectiveness of seminars on crime prevention techniques and procedures was limited by their low attendance. In order to determine the impact of follow-up visits on compliance, one test area in Denver received security surveys only, with no follow-up visits except for the final compliance check at the end of the test period. This test area achieved a 31.5% compliance rate—almost precisely equal to the 31.7% rate achieved in Multnomah County (Pearson, 1980) under very similar treatment conditions. Consequently, it can be stated that follow-up visits resulted in nearly a doubling (from 31.5% to 59.1%) of the CSFT's measured compliance level.

Third, as for the question of the general effect of prior victimization on compliance, part a of Table 11.5 indicates a definite, though not pronounced, trend. The 372 unvictimized (by prior burglary) establishments evidenced a lower compliance rate than either the 33 establishments that had been burglarized once during the 12-month pretreatment period or the 12 establishments that had been burglarized twice during the same period.

Fourth, as summarized in part b of Table 11.5, compliance is a reasonable proxy measure for risk reduction or degree of treatment; the treated establishments had a 77.3% compliance level, and the un-

TABLE 11.4 Survey Compliance by Type of Recommendation (in percentages)

Recommendation Category	Denver Recommended Changes (N = 1808)	Denver Final Compliance	Long Beach Recommended Changes (N = 712)	Long Beach Final Compliance	St. Louis Recommended Changes (N = 1591)	St. Louis Final Compliance	Overall Changes in Category (N = 4111)	Overall Final Compliance
Exterior	6.2	51.9	7.2	57.4	8.7	47.1	7.3	52.0
Doors	27.2	39.2	27.9	40.6	28.1	43.2	27.7	40.9
Windows	14.1	30.8	8.7	55.3	15.2	42.0	13.6	38.3
Skylights, vents float hatches	3.2	20.4	3.8	33.6	1.1	11.7	2.5	22.6
Alarms	4.1	43.6	9.4	58.7	6.7	61.2	6.0	55.7
Miscellaneous	0.7	62.7	0.6	50.4	0.8	40.7	0.7	51.0
Safes	1.5	59.8	0.4	33.6	0.4	52.9	0.8	55.7
Interior sight lines	2.3	83.9	5.9	79.3	1.0	72.7	2.4	81.1
Special security	11.6	49.4	23.5	67.1	4.4	54.3	10.8	57.5
Inventory controls	3.0	93.6	0.3	100.0	0.8	89.4	1.7	91.8
Access control	1.9	60.2	1.1	37.8	2.0	76.0	1.8	64.2
Procedures	24.3	94.4	11.2	76.9	30.7	98.3	24.5	94.3
Total	100.0	56.5	100.0	57.2	100.0	63.0	100.0	59.1

TABLE 11.5   Compliance by Prior Burglary and Burglary
              Treatment Status

a. Compliance by Prior Burglary

Number of Burglaries in Pretreatment Period		Average Compliance (percentage)
0	(N = 372)	57.5
1	(N = 33)	65.9
2	(N = 12)	73.3
3	(N = 4)	33.8
4	(N = 3)	46.7
5	(N = 1)	58.0
8	(N = 1)	0.0

b. Compliance by Burglary Treatment Status

	Number of Establishments	Final Compliance (percentage)
Denver		
Treated	69	73.6
Untreated	76	38.5
Total	145	55.2
Long Beach		
Treated	62	85.9
Untreated	63	30.5
Total	125	58.0
St. Louis		
Treated	61	72.8
Untreated	95	53.3
Total	156	60.9
All cities		
Treated	192	77.3
Untreated	234	42.4
Total	426	59.1

treated establishments had a 42.4% compliance rate. Part b of Table
11.5 highlights another interesting point; it says—according to the
subjective assessment of the program staff—that a 42.4% compliance
level implies that the establishments are untreated. Given that the
available information from other security survey programs—including the Multnomah County program—suggests that their compliance levels, however measured, were less than 40%, one can question
whether or not those programs were actually "treated."

Fifth, in terms of generalizing the CSFT program findings, it was
obvious that the costly compliance-enhancing activity of follow-up

visits rendered the program somewhat atypical. However, at issue was whether or not security surveys *with* compliance can result in a decrease in commercial crime, because we already knew from previous studies that security surveys with limited compliance did not seem to affect crime. Thus, if the CSFT program could demonstrate the former result, then it could have been generalized that security surveys do constitute an effective crime prevention approach, *provided* there is compliance with the survey recommendations. Indeed, this is exactly what the CSFT program has been able to demonstrate, together with the observation that the survey recommendations must be arrived at in a rational manner.

RECOMMENDATIONS

Based on the findings highlighted in the previous section and the current state of knowledge regarding commercial crime prevention and security surveys, two recommendations are outlined herein.

Development of a Risk-Based
Security Survey Instrument that
Would Enhance the Rational Development
of Survey Recommendations

As noted earlier, our review of the security survey recommendations pointed to the fact that they were somewhat inconsistent; further, they seemed to lack a rational basis. Although it is usually assumed that a security surveyor first assesses the potential crime problem of an establishment before making recommendations, we observed at times that certain recommendations were made irrespective of what could have been the crime problem. Additionally, available security survey instruments do not provide a process by which rational (that is, purposeful and consistent) recommendations can be developed; they simply list the possible recommendations that could be made. In sum, we strongly recommend the development of a security survey instrument that would enhance the rational development of survey recommendations. Such an instrument must, we believe, recognize the explicit "risk" that an establishment faces with respect to say, burglary. The instrument should incorporate an explicit risk-to-burglary assessment step that could, for example, be based on a simple—yet intuitively satisfying—risk model that we developed as part of a self-imposed task to consider risk within the context of commercial crime prevention (Cahn & Tien, 1983).

Our risk model recognizes that a crime (in this case, burglary) can be prevented or mitigated at three possible points during its commission. First, a burglary attempt may not even be made if, for example, the would-be burglar realizes that his or her chances for being detected and apprehended outweigh potential gain from the burglary. Thus, good indoor/outdoor lighting or a guard dog might serve to deter a burglary attempt. Second, even if a burglary attempt is made, it is still possible to have, for example, chicken-wired windows and metal doors that might discourage the would-be burglar or at least slow his or her progress so that he or she would stand a greater chance of being detected and apprehended. Third, even if a burglary attempt is successful, it is yet possible to have the valuable items in a strong safe so that the loss would be minimal, apart from the damage-related cost.

The above three steps of a burglary commission can be measured by the following three variables, respectively.

(a) *Likelihood* [L(n)]: probability that n burglary attempts will be made in, say, a one-year period.
(b) *Vulnerability* [V]: probability that, given a burglary attempt, the attempt will be successful.
(c) *Cost* [C]: average cost or loss, given that a burglary attempt is successful.

Mathematically, it can be shown that the expected number of *attempted* burglaries per year is equal to

$$E \text{ [Attempted Burglaries]} = \sum_{n=0}^{\infty} nL(n) \qquad [1]$$

Similarly, the expected number of *successful* burglary attempts per year is equal to

$$E \text{ [Successful Burglaries]} = \sum_{n=0}^{\infty} nL(n)V \qquad [2]$$

The risk-to-burglary—R—can then be defined as the expected cost or loss due to all successful burglaries per year; that is, it can be shown to be equal to

$$R = E \text{ [Burglary-Related Cost]} = \sum_{n=0}^{\infty} nL(n)VC \qquad [3]$$

Thus, a crime prevention effort would attempt to minimize the risk to burglary by implementing strategies that would decrease L, V, C, or any combination of the three; for example, an intrusion alarm might have an impact on all three risk components.

Although intuitively satisfying, the model represented by equation 3 is actually a simple version of perhaps a more complex—and, we hope, more realistic—model. For example, the model assumes that the vulnerability of an establishment to any burglary attempt is the same. However, it might be more realistic to assume that there is a "learning process" so that the establishment becomes less vulnerable with each attempted burglary; in such a case, V would be a function of n, the number of burglary attempts per year. Similarly, C could also be a function of n. Another level of complexity might be the potential interaction among the variables L, V, and C. In sum, the preliminary risk model should be further developed, evaluated, and incorporated into an appropriate security survey instrument, together with a "how-to" manual.

Conduct of Additional Evaluations of Security Survey Programs

A parallel and, indeed, complementary recommendation to the above recommendation of developing a risk-based security survey instrument is to conduct additional evaluations of security survey programs in which such an instrument is employed. We would suggest using the split-area design in a prospective manner; that is, the "treated" business establishments are randomly selected in each test area prior to program implementation. The treated establishments might be subjected to a risk-based security survey with a heavy emphasis on compliance, and the untreated establishments might either receive no security surveys or be subjected to a traditional survey (in which neither the rational development of survey recommendations nor the compliance with survey recommendations is emphasized). Our recommendation that several evaluations be undertaken is based on the recognition that each evaluation yields but one data point; a number of data points are required before a sound judgment can be made. In this vein, we would also recommend that additional data be collected from the three CSFT program cities to see if the longer-term impacts sustain our earlier findings; again, this would be an important exercise, given our findings in Denver for the extended 21-month period.

REFERENCES

American Management Associations. (1977). *Crimes against business projects: Draft report*. New York: Author.

Barlow, S. R., & Kaufman, E. (1977, March). *Crime prevention unit evaluation*. Seattle, WA: Executive Department, Law and Justice Planning Division.

Bickman, L., & Rosenbaum, D. P. (1980, July). *National Evaluation Program Phase I: Assessment of shoplifting and employee theft programs*. Evanston, IL: Westinghouse Evaluation Institute.

Cahn, M. F., & Tien, J. M. (1980, August). *Systemic evaluation of the Commercial Security Field Test*. Cambridge, MA: Public Systems Evaluation.

Campbell, D. T., & Erlebacher, A. (1975). How regression artifacts in quasi-experimental evaluation can mistakenly make compensatory education look harmful. In E. L. Struening & M. Guttentag (Eds.), *Handbook of evaluation research* (Vol. 1, pp. 597-617). Beverly Hills, CA: Sage.

Chelimsky, E. (1979, February). *Security and the small business retailer*. McLean, VA: Mitre Corporation.

Everson, T. G. (1979, January). *Greendale Crime Prevention Project*. Madison: Wisconsin Council of Criminal Justice.

Federal Bureau of Investigation. (1983). *Uniform crime reports: Crime in the United States, 1982*. Washington, DC: U.S. Department of Justice.

Gunn, L. G., et al. (1978, January). *Evaluation report: City of Seattle Hidden Cameras Project*. Seattle, WA: Office of Policy Planning, Law and Justice Planning Office.

International Training, Research, and Evaluation Council. (1977). *Crime prevention security surveys*. Washington, DC: Law Enforcement Assistance Administration, National Institute of Law Enforcement and Criminal Justice.

Kingsbury, A. M. (1973). *Introduction to security and crime prevention surveys*. Springfield, IL: Charles C Thomas.

Lavrakas, P. J., Maxfield, M. G., & Henig, J. (1979, June). *Crime prevention and fear reduction in the commercial environment*. Evanston, IL: Northwestern University, Community Crime Prevention Workshop.

Minnesota Governor's Commission on Crime Prevention and Control. (1976, May). *Minnesota crime watch*. Minneapolis: Author.

National Crime Panel Surveys. (1977). *Criminal victimization in the U.S., 1975*. Washington, DC: Law Enforcement Assistance Administration.

National Institute of Justice. (1979, May). *Commercial security test design*. Washington, DC: Law Enforcement Assistance Administration.

Pearson, D. A. (1980, March). *Evaluation of Multnomah County's Commercial Burglary Prevention Program*. Salem: Oregon Law Enforcement Council Evaluation and Research Unit.

Rasmussen, M., Muggli, W., & Crabill, C. M. (1978, December). *Evaluation of the Minneapolis Community Crime Prevention Demonstration*. St. Paul, MN: Crime Control Planning Board.

Reppetto, T. A. (1975, April). Crime prevention and the displacement phenomenon. *Crime & Delinquency*.

Skogan, W. (1979, June). Measurement issues in the Evaluation of Community Crime Prevention Program. In *Review of criminal justice evaluation, 1978*. Washington, DC: Law Enforcement Assistance Administration, National Institute of Law Enforcement and Criminal Justice.

Small Business Administration (1969, April). *Crime against small business: A report to the Select Committee on Small Business* (Senate Document No. 91-14). Washington, DC: U.S. Senate.

Tien, J. M. (1979, September). Toward a systematic approach to program evaluation design. *IEEE Transactions on Systems, Man and Cybernetics, 9*, 494-515.

Tien, J. M. (1980). *A split-area research design for the Commercial Security Field Test* (Internal report). Cambridge, MA: Public Systems Evaluation, Inc.

Touche Ross and Company (1976). *Target Hardening Opportunity Reduction (THOR) project evaluation component*. Atlanta: Author.

U.S. Congress. (1977). *Crime and its effects on small business: Hearing before the Subcommittee on Special Small Business Problems* (95th Congress, 1st Session). Washington, DC: Government Printing Office.

U.S. Department of Commerce. (1975). *Crime in retailing*. Washington, DC: Government Printing Office.

White, T. W., et al. (1975, September). *Police burglary prevention programs*. Washington, DC: Law Enforcement Assistance Administration, National Institute of Law Enforcement and Criminal Justice.

V

THE MEDIA AND CRIME PREVENTION: PUBLIC EDUCATION AND PERSUASION

Chapter 12

THE "McGRUFF" NATIONAL MEDIA CAMPAIGN
Its Public Impact and Future Implications

GARRETT J. O'KEEFE

Citizen involvement in crime prevention activities has emerged as a critical issue in recent years as it has become more clear that such actions can play a key role in controlling the level of crime. As such, numerous efforts have been aimed at encouraging citizen participation in activities directed at reducing their own risk of victimization and that of others. One highly prominent effort has been the six-year-old "Take a Bite Out of Crime" national public information campaign, featuring "McGruff"—the crime dog—and produced under the sponsorship of the Crime Prevention Coalition, with the cooperation of the Advertising Council.

This chapter addresses the following points: (1) the impact of the Take a Bite Out of Crime national media campaign on citizen peceptions, attitudes, and behaviors regarding crime prevention; and (2) the application of the findings of that evaluation toward strategies for subsequent communication efforts aimed at increasing citizen participation in crime prevention activities. Specifically, this chapter will focus on the impact of the first two years of the campaign, from late 1979 to November 1981. I begin with an overview of the campaign and its strategies, and then discuss the problems and methodologies in-

AUTHOR'S NOTE: *This research was supported under a grant from the National Institute of Justice, U.S. Department of Justice (Grant 81IJCX0050). I would like to thank Professor Harold Mendelsohn, Professor Kathaleen Reid-Nash, Elise Henry, and Beth Rosenzweig for their assistance on various phases of the project.*

volved in its evaluation. A summary of findings of the evaluation will
then be presented, followed by policy recommendations for subsequent crime prevention media campaigns.

THE "McGRUFF" CAMPAIGN

The "McGruff" or "Take a Bite Out of Crime" campaign was
produced under the sponsorship of the Crime Prevention Coalition,
with the major media portions of it directed by the Advertising Council. Since its debut in October 1979, it has aimed at promoting citizen
involvement in crime prevention efforts, mainly through increased
self-protection against burglary and street crime, and, most notably,
through neighborhood cooperative efforts among citizens. In 1984,
the campaign's perspective was broadened to include victimization of
children as well.

The Crime Prevention Coalition initially specified four major objectives for the campaign:

(1) to change unwarranted citizen feelings about crime and the
    criminal justice system, particularly feelings of frustration and
    hopelessness;
(2) to generate an individual sense of responsibility for reducing
    crime among citizens;
(3) to encourage citizens, working within their communities and
    with local law enforcement agencies, to take collective crime
    prevention action; and
(4) to enhance existing crime prevention programs at the local,
    state, and national levels.

The federal Office of Justice Assistance, Research and Statistics
worked with the Crime Prevention Coalition as the general coordinator of the campaign and as its main funding source. In 1978, the
Advertising Council agreed to direct a major national media campaign
on crime prevention. The council developed campaign themes, objectives, and materials in cooperation with the Crime Prevention Coalition. Dancer Fitzgerald Sample served as the volunteer advertising
agency responsible for implementing the campaign. Although the
media portion of the campaign served as its centerpiece, a full range of
other activities were organized to complement it, with heavy emphasis
on the support of community, business, and law enforcement
organizations to urge citizens to act on the information provided
through the mass media.

The final design for the media campaign focused upon a trench-coated, animated dog character named McGruff. McGruff's role was to educate people about what they could do to prevent crime, from simple steps, such as locking their doors and windows, to joining with their neighbors in crime watch efforts. The keynote slogan was McGruff's admonishment to citizens to "take a bite out of crime." Public service advertisements (PSAs) featuring McGruff providing various kinds of preventive information were designed for television, radio, newspapers, magazines, billboards, and posters. The eventual goal was for McGruff to become regarded by the public as a symbol for crime prevention in much the same way as Smokey the Bear is recognized for forest fire prevention.

Additional activities supporting the media campaign included use of McGruff for numerous statewide and community crime prevention efforts, as well as by major businesses, including the Southland Corporation (7-11 stores). An in-depth booklet detailing citizen crime prevention steps was published in English and Spanish, as were 10 others dealing with such specific topics as rural crime, sexual assault, street crime, and crimes against senior citizens.

By mid-1981, media response to the campaign had been exceptionally strong in comparison with other public service advertising efforts. Over $100 million in documented broadcast time and print space had been donated by national and local media companies, making McGruff one of the most popular of all Advertising Council efforts. About a million of the booklets had been distributed free of charge in response to the ads, and another 250,000 were sold through the Government Printing Office. More than 100 requests had been received for negatives to use in reprinting the booklets locally. The Department of the Army printed 300,000 McGruff booklets for use in its programs.

Our evaluation focused almost exclusively upon citizen reactions to the media portion of the campaign, and was conducted in concert with its first three phases. The first phase focused on offering audiences information about how to protect their homes and property, and is best exemplified by the televised "Stop a Crime" PSA featuring McGruff touring a home and pointing out ways to avoid burglary. The second and third phases, both under way in 1980, emphasized the importance of observing and reporting suspected criminal activity, and of organizing community and neighborhood groups to help reduce crime. These phases were typified respectively by the "Gilstraps" television PSA, which showed neighbors alerting police about a suspicious moving van at a house, and the "Mimi Marth" PSA, which depicted an elderly woman's successful efforts at neighborhood crime patrol in Hartford.

EVALUATION BACKGROUND AND DESIGN

There have been only a few and somewhat inconclusive efforts in recent years to study the impact of public information campaigns. Considering the enormous financial and time commitments given PSAs by both their producers and exhibitors, surprisingly little is known about who attends to them and even less about their possible influences. Those PSAs warranting free media placement ordinarily are relegated to status behind regular paid ads and are apt to appear only as space or time becomes available. Most televised PSAs, for example, run during the least watched viewing periods, and newspaper PSAs are rarely seen on more heavily read pages. Competition between PSA sponsors for media placement is heavy, and many of the ads fail to be disseminated at all.

A previous study of PSA audiences in general (O'Keefe, Mendelsohn, & Lui, 1980) indicated that PSAs have an attentive audience, including good numbers of persons who believe them, find them helpful, and take certain kinds of actions as a result of having seen them. Well-planned and -executed public information campaigns including PSAs as a main component often seem capable of triggering responses from at least some members of their target audiences. Two traditional indicators of such responses have been the volume of requests received for more information concerning an issue and the increase in financial contributions to sponsoring groups. Several successful national campaigns over the years based largely upon television PSAs have generated information requests numbering in the thousands per week over the short run, and even local campaign efforts can result in hundreds of such requests weekly (see Rice & Paisley, 1981). Of course, whether or not the recipients of that information are making use of it in any meaningful way is a largely unanswered question.

The few rigorous empirical evaluations that have been conducted of the more consequential effects of such campaigns generally suggest at best ambiguous influences due to media components by themselves. It appears particularly difficult to effect change in such deep-rooted behavioral patterns as alcohol and drug abuse and cigarette smoking (Hanneman & McEwen, 1973; Schmeling & Wotring, 1976, 1980; O'Keefe, 1971; Atkin, 1979), although such attempts are not always fruitless (McAlister, et al., 1980). Campaigns may enjoy more success in terms of increasing knowledge about some topics (Salcedo, Read, Evans, & Kong, 1974) and attitude change may result under some conditions (Mendelsohn, 1973), particularly if nonmedia supports, such as interpersonal communication channels, are operative (Douglas, Westley, & Chaffee, 1970). However, Maccoby and Solomon (1981) present rather striking data illustrating the impact of PSAs combined with other media contents on knowledge of and behavioral change concerning heart disease risk factors.

In sum, the evidence on the effects of public information campaigns in general and of PSAs specifically is quite mixed. The opportunity afforded by the National Institute of Justice to evaluate independently the impact of the McGruff campaign allowed an examination not only of crime prevention campaigns, but of the fuller implications of other types of media campaigns as well.

More specifically, the research aimed to (a) examine citizen exposure and reaction patterns to the first two years of the campaign; (b) investigate cognitive, attitudinal, and behavioral changes related to crime and crime prevention among citizens exposed to the campaign; (c) generate and clarify hypotheses concerning the effects of broad-based long-term crime prevention campaigns on citizens; and (d) recommend policies and strategies for the development of more effective prevention campaigns.

The diversified nature of the campaign, as well as its rather generally stated objectives, led us to pose our own more narrow criteria for judging McGruff's effectiveness. The organizing construct developed was citizen crime prevention *competence,* which includes several key psychological orientations and behaviors that citizens may demonstrate in varying degrees. The campaign can be regarded as being effective to the extent that persons exposed to it (a) became more fully *aware* of the publicized crime prevention techniques; (b) held more positive *attitudes* concerning their own reponsibilities for helping reduce crime, and the effectiveness of citizen-based preventive actions; (c) felt more *capable* of carrying out preventive actions to reduce victimization risks to themselves and others; and (d) became likelier to engage in *behaviors* aimed at reducing crime.

Research Design

The nature of the campaign's dissemination precluded the use of such optimal field experiment designs as comparing campaign-exposed and -nonexposed communities on a randomly selected basis. Not only were the PSAs released nationally to all pertinent media channels, but there was no ability to control or predict when or where individual media organizations would air or publish the materials. A "next-best" two-phase evaluation design option was chosen in which, first, a national probability sample of citizens was interviewed two years after the campaign's onset to determine the penetration of McGruff over the nation and within various subgroups, and to examine exposed individuals' self-perceptions of the campaign's effectiveness. The second phase entailed a panel sample survey in which respondents in three representative cities were interviewed prior to the campaign and then reinterviewed two years later in order to examine more objectively the changes in their crime prevention competence levels as a function of their exposure to McGruff.

The national sample survey included 45-minute personal interviews with a standard multistage area sample of 1,200 adults during November 1981. The instrument included aided and unaided recall measures of exposure to the Take a Bite Out of Crime PSAs, extensive self-report measures of the campaign's perceived impact on the competence variables, and an array of items dealing with respondents' orientations and behaviors concerning crime and its prevention. The first wave of the panel sample survey consisted of personal interviews with a probability sample of 1,049 adult residents of Buffalo, Denver, and Milwaukee. Items focused upon background information concerning prevention competence, orientations toward crime, and media uses. In November 1981, 426 of the original respondents were successfully recontacted and interviewed by telephone. Exposure to the PSAs was ascertained by respondent self-reports, and key items from the first wave were repeated to allow for change score analysis. Change score comparisons between the exposed and unexposed groups were carried out by simple group comparison tests as well as by regressed change score techniques incorporating multivariate control procedures. (For a full description of the methodology, see O'Keefe & Mendelsohn, 1984.)

KEY FINDINGS

The key findings of the McGruff evaluation are summarized below. Detailed results appear in O'Keefe and Mendelsohn (1984) and O'Keefe (1985).

Campaign Exposure

The campaign had quite widespread penetration among the American public. Just over half of the U.S. adults interviewed recalled having seen or heard the McGruff PSAs within two years of the campaign's start. Given the catch-as-catch-can dissemination of PSAs, this suggests a rather heavy commitment on the part of media channels to use them, and that the ads were salient enough to make at least a minimal impression on substantial numbers of people.

Television was clearly the medium of choice by which the most people saw the most PSAs. It is not clear whether that was because more of them were shown over television or because the television ads were more memorable to people; I suspect that both reasons were operative, and perhaps others as well. It does appear, however, that the ads were quite heavily repeated across the media: A third of the respondents said they had seen or heard from them more than 10 times.

The campaign's penetration was extensive enough to reach a highly diversified audience demographically, and no economic or social class appeared beyond the campaign's reach. Although McGruff was decidedly likelier to reach younger adults, a third of the people over age 64 could recall the ads.

Persons who regularly either watched more television or listened more to the radio were likelier to have come across the PSAs, having greater opportunity to do so. Exposure to the campaign was also somewhat greater among persons who saw themselves as initially less knowledgeable about crime prevention, and among those who saw citizen crime prevention efforts as potentially effective in controlling crime. Just why this occurred is somewhat unclear, but, for whatever reasons, McGruff appeared to be reaching an audience, at least in part, rather ideally targeted to the campaign's themes. However, it should be added that across the board the PSAs reached substantial numbers of citizens with widely varied perceptions, attitudes, and behaviors regarding crime and its prevention.

Among those exposed to the campaign, a greater amount of attention was paid by persons who saw themselves as more knowledgeable about prevention and those more confident about being able to protect themselves from crime. More attention was paid also by individuals already engaged in a range of prevention activities, as well as those who felt that getting more information about prevention would be useful to them. This pattern is in keeping with the "selective attention" hypothesis: People tend to pay more attention to message content that they are already interested in and/or in agreement with. However, as we have seen above, there was less evidence of selective *exposure* to the campaign.

Campaign Effectiveness

The format and content of the PSAs elicited favorable reactions from the vast majority of the audience. Most said they thought the ads were effective in conveying the message, that they liked the McGruff character, and that they felt the information in the ads was worth passing on to other people. These reactions were consistently favorable across the sample, although younger persons tended to rate the ads most highly. From a perspective of long-term impact, that is quite encouraging.

The campaign appeared to have a sizable impact on what people knew about crime prevention techniques. Nearly a quarter of the national sample exposed to the campaign said they had learned something new about prevention from the PSAs, and nearly half said they had been reminded of things they had known before but had forgotten. Campaign-exposed persons in the panel sample were significantly likelier than those unexposed to show increases in how much they thought they knew about crime prevention.

Similarly, the McGruff PSAs appeared to have a positive influence on citizens' attitudes about crime prevention. Nearly half of the national sample respondents who recalled the ads said they made them feel more confident in their ability to protect themselves from victimization, and that citizen prevention efforts were an effective means of preventing crime. Significant changes in both of these attitudes were found among exposed panel respondents as well.

Individuals reporting having been influenced in one particular way were likely to report other influences as well. The extent of influence seemed to depend more on how much attention was paid to the ads, rather than how many times they had been seen or heard. Moreover, people who said they had been made more fearful of crime by the ads were likelier to report having been influenced in other ways as well. Less conclusive was evidence for campaign-stimulated changes in degree of concern about crime and sense of individual responsibility to help prevent it: Although about half of the exposed national sample respondents reported having gained more positive attitudes from the campaign on both dimensions, no significant differences were found within the panel sample.

On the most salient criterion of campaign success—behavioral change—the McGruff campaign appears to have had a noteworthy impact. Nearly a fourth of the exposed national sample said they had taken preventive actions as a result of having seen or heard the ads;

mentioned in particular were improving household security and cooperating with neighbors in prevention efforts, the two main themes of the McGruff PSAs.

Increased prevention activity was even more impressive in the panel sample. Prior to the campaign, the panel interviewees were asked about the extent to which they carried out 25 specific prevention actions. Of these activities, 7 were subsequently given particular emphasis in the McGruff PSAs, including locking doors, leaving on lights, and various neighborhood cooperative efforts. Panel members were then asked again about the same 25 activities when reinterviewed two years after the initiation of the campaign. Panelists exposed to the ads registered statistically significant gains over those who were not exposed in 6 of the 7 activities recommended in the PSAs. There were no such increases in the 18 nonrecommended actions.

Although the campaign had notable effects on the population as a whole, some types of people were more influenced than others. For example, campaign influences appeared to be associated with the opportunities people had for carrying out the actions recommended in the PSAs. Women and more affluent persons tended to show greater gains in "neighborhood cooperative" prevention activities. Lower-income persons increased in such activities as "reporting suspicious incidents to the police." Men showed increases in somewhat more individualistic behaviors, such as "acquiring a dog for security purposes." Finally, the campaign had greater impact on the behaviors than on the attitudes of citizens who saw themselves as more at risk from crime, although the opposite was true for those seeing themselves as less at risk.

In conclusion, the campaign appears to have had a wide range of effects across an even wider range of people, depending upon their personal characteristics, their individual circumstances, and their perceived vulnerability to crime.

Recommendations for Subsequent Campaigns

Based upon this research effort, as well as previous ones, several key issues arise that need to be taken into account in the planning of subsequent crime prevention campaign efforts, including those based upon McGruff. These include the following: (a) the salience of crime as an issue on the public agenda; (b) the necessity of community-based campaign efforts; (c) the perplexing role of fear arousal in campaign effectiveness; (d) the role of formative research; (e) the problem of audience targeting; and (f) the potential for neglect of the elderly as an audience.

The Salience of Crime as an Issue

The campaign began during a period when crime as an issue was decidedly high on the public agenda. Virtually every public opinion poll that measured importance of issues in the early 1980s found crime listed in the top three, and it often was the most important issue. Within weeks of each other in 1981, the three major national newsmagazines all had cover stories on the crime issue, such as "The Curse of Violent Crime" (1981) and "The People's War Against Crime" (1981). Newspapers and television newscasts devoted substantial amounts of continued emphasis to crime news (see Graber, 1980). Thus, the McGruff campaign was acting in an environment of already existing public interest and concern about the problem, and presumably a high level of willingness to listen to ideas regarding what to do about the problem.

This is not to say that the campaign was simply reinforcing citizen orientations that already existed: The wide-ranging influences of the campaign per se seem quite clear. Rather, it does imply that the first three phases of the campaign benefited from a climate of opinion that probably made it more likely that the campaign would have an impact. The opening phases of the campaign did not have to cope with public apathy toward the central issue being addressed.

Many, and perhaps most, information campaigns, of course, do not have such an advantage, and there is no guarantee that crime prevention campaigns will have it in subsequent years. In fact, the normal cycle of such public issues is one of peaks and valleys, and the state of the economy and unemployment may have edged out crime as the critical issues facing the country after 1981. On the other hand, it can be assumed that crime will always be with us, and that citizen concern over it is unlikely to drop soon to a trivial level.

However, subsequent prevention campaign efforts should not simply assume that because the early phases of McGruff made notable strides, future efforts will as well. Indeed, campaign designers might well want to consider strategies that will either keep crime and prevention high on the public agenda or increase the visibility of the issue should it be drastically reduced on that agenda.

In a sense, the challenge for campaign planners is much the same as that encountered when a highly successful product finds itself competing with newer products; marketing strategies have to be developed to keep the public from tiring of old ones or simply wanting to experiment with the new. Brand loyalty becomes a central issue. Those people who have improved in their crime prevention activities have to be reminded to keep doing what they have been doing regardless of various changes in the social climate.

The Necessity for Community-Based Efforts

Although underinvestigated in this study, the import of supplementing the national media campaign with strong local community-based input cannot be overemphasized. This is particularly necessary if the campaign is to have long-term impact once the initial novelty wears off. Studies of campaigns from Star and Hughes (1950) to Maccoby and Solomon (1981) have consistently demonstrated the strong power of interpersonal and community-level communication in information dissemination and persuasion efforts. Although the media campaign appears to have brought about significant effects on its own, there is every reason to suspect that, as Maccoby and Solomon empirically demonstrated, the effects would be substantially heightened with the placement of community action programs.

Such programs serve several purposes. For one, they reinforce the national campaign and provide it with greater visibility. This is particularly true if local broadcast and print media are encouraged to run more of the McGruff ads as a result of local concern. For another, local efforts give an important local "angle" to the campaign, letting citizens know that crime prevention is, indeed, a concern in "River City" as well as nationally. Concurrently, as is already apparently happening, the campaign serves as a focal point for various local agencies, groups, and interested citizens. The simple use of the logo provides an image of familiarity, and probably a certain degree of status conferral as well. The logo is "recognized" as a symbol that has gained a certain degree of legitimacy through its use in national media. Moreover, the McGruff character is quite well liked, leading to positive dispositions toward the campaign as well.

The main function of grass-roots support for the campaign, however, should be to facilitate face-to-face interaction with and among citizens on the issue of crime prevention. Without the element of personal contact, a great deal of the potential impact of community involvement will be lost. Local programs should attempt to maximize opportunities for crime prevention professionals to meet with citizens in groups or individually, and also stimulate greater discussion among citizens themselves about crime prevention.

I would also strongly advocate that local prevention professionals emphasize *instruction* in their meetings with citizens, as opposed to simply trying to motivate or persuade citizens to become more involved. Focus should be upon specifically how steps advocated in the general campaign could be applied by individuals within the community or neighborhood. For example, a neighborhood of apartment complexes is unlikely to have the same response pattern to neighborhood watch programs as is one of single, detached dwellings. Many useful and specific considerations concerning community-level prevention practices are found in Lavrakas (1980) and Podolefsky and Dubow (1981).

However, the main argument to be made here is that the most effective and efficient "targeting" of crime prevention information to specific subgroups of citizens is likely to be through narrow community-level channels, not the mass media. Moreover, the greater the role of interpersonal communication in those efforts, the greater the chance of meaningful impact.

Fear Arousal and Campaign Effectiveness

Although the McGruff campaign was quite cautious in terms of any deliberate use of fear-provoking themes, crime is a subject that is bound to raise anxiety among at least some citizens, as the findings presented here indicate. Subsequent campaign efforts doubtless will encounter the same problem. As we have found, however, the arousal of some minimal level of fear may not be wholly counterproductive, as long as the fear is justified by the reality of the situation being dealt with.

In a more practical vein, the findings do not necessarily contradict the view that information campaigns dealing with such loaded topics as crime prevention would do well to soft-pedal fear appeals in the design of messages. However, it is important to note that the reasoning should not necessarily be that low increased fear among audience members will be detrimental to the campaign goals. Fear arousal to a limited degree may well enhance the persuasive impact of a message. But, if the topic is such that one can assume that target audiences are already anxious over it, many individuals may become more fearful simply by having the topic brought to their attention. Such arousal can work to stimulate more effective persuasive changes, assuming that the message provides adequate information and argumentation to serve as a basis for them. On the other hand, for topics for which previous fear is unlikely to exist among audience members, it may at times be beneficial to introduce fear appeals within the message, assuming that they are legitimate and reasonably restrained. More extensive research is clearly needed in this area.

The findings more specifically suggest that the messages used here triggered more in the way of what McGuire (1973) has referred to as the *drive* component of fear as opposed to the *cue* component. The stimulation of the drive component of fear increases the likelihood of activity to reduce that fear, that is, attitudinal or behavioral change. On the other hand, if a message arouses fear by cuing undesirable consequences (such as being criminally assaulted) in the mind of the receiver, the message stands more of a chance of being unattended to or refuted without resulting in persuasion. The likely explanation here is that although the PSAs were quite bereft of specific fear-arousing cues, for many individuals the topic of crime in general aroused fear, resulting in a drive to reduce it. Had the PSAs included more in the way of particular information about how people are victimized, or the consequences of victimization, those cues may well have triggered fear in ways that would have interfered with the persuasive impact of the message.

It is likely also that the emphasis of the PSAs on offering concrete actions that citizens could reasonably take to protect themselves increased the persuasive force of fear arousal. As Leventhal (1970) has indicated, fear appeals seem more likely to succeed when specific and preferably immediate means of reducing the arousal are presented as well, and subsequent campaigns would do well to note that.

Given the range of fear arousal that occurred among audiences exposed to the low-fear McGruff ads, it seems clear that in instances in which fear as a message response is either likely or sought, extensive precampaign research among target audiences is very necessary.

The Role of Formative Research

It is hoped that the use described here of the panel survey design as an evaluative tool will serve as a "plug" for formative, precampaign evaluative research efforts. Our research was more to define and explain effects, but it should be clear that if the first stage of panel interviews had taken place prior to the design of the first phase of the campaign, things might have been learned about audience dispositions regarding crime and prevention that would have helped generate even more substantial effects. Precampaign research efforts—at the national or community levels—become even more important when specific kinds of target audiences are being delineated.

The Problem of Audience Targeting

Targeting is a very useful concept in campaign planning, but with a reliance upon public service advertisements a great deal of the rationale and work goes for naught. Even if PSAs are aimed at, say, women in higher crime areas, it becomes highly inefficient to produce the ads and then "throw them to the winds" in the media, hoping that some might just happen to show up on television programs or in publications with a respectable reach among that audience. This is not to say that it should not be done failing other alternatives, but just that it is quite wasteful of communication resources. Although this is a recommendation beyond the scope of this chapter, there seems to be a great deal of value in having representatives of the broadcast and print industries get together with those concerned with public service advertising (such as the Advertising Council) to attempt to work out a system through which PSAs would have a better chance of being placed in times and slots more appropriate to their intended audiences. Perhaps a standard method of coding PSAs by audience type could be devised, or a plan worked out for some "paid" PSAs to be run in more appropriate slots, but at rates much lower than regular commercial rates.

As the situation is at this time, however, targeting seems to be more in the bailiwick of campaign strategies within individual communities. In instances in which targeting is appropriate and possible, I recommend following the general conceptual strategy of seeking to build greater levels of prevention competence among citizens. Previous to implementing the campaign, research should establish the makeup of target groups in terms of (a) their awareness of crime prevention techniques; (b) their attitudes toward citizen-initiated prevention activities, that is, how effective they are and how responsible citizens ought to be; (c) how capable they feel about acting on their own; (d) how concerned or interested they are in protecting themselves and others from crime; and (e) the extent to which they have already taken prevention-related actions. Once an existing level of competence in terms of these factors can be identified, appropriate messages can be designed to attempt to stimulate change effects as warranted.

The Elderly:
A Potentially Neglected Audience

This evaluation suggests that the campaign made less of an impression upon one group with particularly strong concerns about crime: the elderly. Why that happened remains unclear, but one can speculate on a few possible reasons. For one, many of those aged 65 and over may not be as attuned to advertising in general, and television advertising in particular, including PSAs. Some may have felt less pulled to the dog character than, say, later generations weaned on movie and television cartoons. (However, elderly persons who were exposed to the PSAs were about as supportive of the format as were younger individuals.) In some instances, diminished ability to remember or recall the stimulus may have been a factor as well. One element that would be unlikely to turn off older audiences is the story content of the PSAs. The situations in the television ads could not be seen as age biasing in any obvious sense, and, in fact, the central character in "Mimi Marth" should have appealed to the elderly.

Be that as it may, what can be done to direct a stronger appeal toward older citizens, particularly those who see themselves as more vulnerable? One suspects that, for some of the above reasons and others, the mass media may be less effective in reaching the elderly than younger cohorts. Rather, local community and neighborhood campaigns focusing specifically on the problems of the elderly would seem to be far more effective.

CONCLUDING NOTE

In conclusion, the time may well be at hand for strategists involved with campaigns to formulate specific goals more elaborately as to what kinds of changes are desired in citizen crime prevention efforts, and to what extent. This seems particularly practical at the community level. One of the rather obvious difficulties in this study's evaluation process has been deciding at what points the campaign was succeeding or falling short, the simple reason for that being that no criteria for success or failure have been established by those responsible for the campaign. Nor could such criteria have been established: We have already alluded to the lack of baseline research on the efficacy of public information campaigns overall, not to mention crime prevention campaigns. Given the data provided in this report, however, it may now be quite appropriate for the campaign strategists to work with prevention and communications researchers to try to determine, for example, what citizen participation rates within communities are "optimal" for actual crime reduction. Or to determine what percentages of citizens involved in, say, neighborhood watch programs are effective for minimal reductions in household burglaries. Given such data, prevention campaigns could then be even more specifically directed at communities or neighborhoods with demonstrable shortcomings either in citizen participation or in crime rates. The task is not easy, because such variables as police protection and environmental factors enter in. Nonetheless, the effectiveness and efficiency with which prevention information campaigns can be disseminated are highly dependent upon having such baselines.

REFERENCES

Atkin, C. K. (1979). Research evidence on mass mediated health communication campaigns. In D. Nimmo (Ed.), *Communication yearbook 3.* New Brunswick, NJ: Transaction.

The curse of violent crime. (1981, March 23). *Time.*

Douglas, D. F., Westley, B. H., & Chaffee, S. H. (1970). An information campaign that changed community attitudes. *Journalism Quarterly, 47,* 479-487.

Graber, D. B. (1980). *Crime news and the public.* New York: Praeger.

Hanneman, G. J., & McEwen, W. J. (1973). Televised drug abuse appeals: A content analysis. *Journalism Quarterly, 50,* 329-333.

Lavrakas, P. (1980). *Factors related to citizen involvement in personal, household and neighborhood anti-crime measures.* Report submitted to the U.S. Department of Justice.

Leventhal, H. (1970). Findings and theory in the study of fear communication. In L. Berkowitz (Ed.), *Advances in experimental social psychology* (Vol. 5). New York: Academic Press.

Maccoby, N., & Solomon, D. (1981). The Stanford community studies in health promotion. In R. Rice & W. Paisley (Eds.), *Public communication campaigns.* Beverly Hills, CA: Sage.

McAlister, A., Puska, P., Koskela, K., Pallonen, U., & Maccoby, N. (1980). Mass Communication and community organization for public health education. *American Psychologist, 35,* 375-379.

McGuire, W. J. (1973). Persuasion, resistance and attitude change. In I. de Sola Pool et al. (Eds.), *Handbook of communication.* Chicago: Rand McNally.

Mendelsohn, H. (1973). Some reasons why information campaigns can succeed. *Public Opinion Quarterly, 37,* 50-61.

O'Keefe, G. J. (1985). "Taking a bite out of crime": The impact of a public information campaign. *Communication Research, 12,* 147-178.

O'Keefe, G. J., & Mendelsohn, H. (1984). *"Taking a bite out of crime": The impact of
a mass media crime prevention campaign.* Washington, DC: National Institute of
Justice.

O'Keefe, G. J., Mendelsohn, H., & Liu, J. (1980). *The audiences for public service
advertising.* Paper presented at the annual conference of the Association for Education in Journalism, Boston.

O'Keefe, M. T. (1971). The anti-smoking commercials: A study of television's impact
on behavior. *Public Opinion Quarterly, 35,* 248-257.

The people's war against crime. (1981, July 13). *U.S. News & World Report.*

Podolefsky, A., & Dubow, F. (1981). *Strategies for community crime prevention, collective responses to crime in urban America.* Springfield, IL: Charles C Thomas.

Rice, R. E., & Paisley, W. J. (Eds.). (1981). *Public communication campaigns.* Beverly
Hills, CA: Sage.

Salcedo, R. N., Read, H., Evans, J. F., & Kong, A. E. (1974). A successful information campaign on pesticides. *Journalism Quarterly, 51,* 91-95.

Schmeling, D. G., & Wotring, C. E. (1976). Agenda-setting effects of drug abuse public
service ads. *Journalism Quarterly, 53,* 743-746.

Schmeling, D. G., & Wotring, C. E. (1980). Making anti-drug-abuse advertising work.
Journal of Advertising Research, 20, 33-37.

Skogan, W. G., & Maxfield, M. E. (1981). *Coping with crime: Individual and neighborhood reactions.* Beverly Hills, CA: Sage.

Star, S., & Hughes, H. (1950). A report on an educational campaign: The Cincinnati
plan for the United Nations. *American Journal of Sociology, 55,* 389-400.

Chapter 13

EVALUATING POLICE-COMMUNITY ANTICRIME NEWSLETTERS
The Evanston, Houston, and Newark Field Studies

P A U L J. L A V R A K A S

This chapter reviews the findings from three evaluations of a new crime prevention strategy, the police-community anticrime newsletter. In 1981, the *ALERT* newsletter was developed jointly by the Evanston, Illinois, Police Department and its Residential Crime Prevention Committee (Lavrakas, Rosenbaum, & Kaminski, 1983). In 1983, the Houston Police Department developed the *Community Policing Exchange* newsletter and the Newark Police Department developed the *ACT 1* newsletter in conjunction with the Fear Reduction Project, funded by the National Institute of Justice (NIJ) and implemented by the two departments with the assistance of the Police Foundation (Pate, Lavrakas, Wycoff, Skogan, & Sherman, 1985).

These were not the first anticrime newsletters disseminated by local police departments; for example, law enforcement agencies in Montgomery County, Maryland, and Laguna Beach, California, were regularly distributing anticrime information in a newsletter format to their citizenry prior to 1981. But, as explained in this chapter, the initial distribution in Evanston, Houston, and Newark was done in a limited and controlled fashion that allowed for scientific assessments of the respective impact of the three newsletters.

HISTORICAL AND THEORETICAL PERSPECTIVES

Since the early 1970s, more and more criminal justice policymakers, practitioners, and scholars have been discussing the importance of an "involved citizenry" in the effort to prevent, and thus reduce, crime (Lavrakas, 1985). This community-focused approach to crime prevention emphasizes the cooperation that is necessary between the police and the citizenry to "coproduce" public safety (Percy, 1979). Yet after more than a decade of research and evaluation of community crime prevention programs, it is now known that citizens' involvement in anticrime activities is neither easy to initiate nor, once initiated, easy to maintain. Experience has shown that it does not suffice merely to disseminate the general message that citizens must become the "eyes and ears" of the police, and then expect the public to act accordingly (Lavrakas et al., 1983). Instead, most citizens appear to need more specific information to be fully motivated and effective in their efforts to prevent crime, especially those crimes that occur in their own neighborhoods (see Tyler, 1984; Tyler & Lavrakas, 1985).

What types of information might be used by citizens in their decisions to become involved in anticrime activities? First, citizens need to understand the range of anticrime responses available to them, and need to believe in the efficacy of these measures (see Becker, 1974; Lavrakas et al., 1981; Mendelsohn & O'Keefe, 1981). Second, citizens need to know something about the nature and magnitude of their own local crime problems before they can be expected to react in an appropriate manner (see Lavrakas et al., 1983; Lavrakas & Bennett, 1985).

The dissemination of information about crime and anticrime measures is controversial. Given that public policy for the past fifteen years has advocated the importance of vigilance on the part of the citizenry, the notion of *vigilantism* is clearly not an endorsed or desirable outcome of this policy. Although striving to avoid the failure of citizens to act appropriately, as in the case of the 38 witnesses to the Genovese tragedy, we also want to avoid reinforcing the apparent overreaction of a Bernhard Goetz (see Safire, 1985). Thus, it is important that we study closely the dynamics that underlie citizens' reactions to crime.

Furstenberg (1971) was the first to distinguish between two primarily independent *affective* reactions to crime. He found that a person's *fear of crime* was related to anxiety over his or her own vulnerability of becoming a crime victim, and *concern about crime* was related to a person's opinion of the magnitude and severity of crime in a given locale. Furthermore, these affective dimensions have been found to be related to separate *behavioral* responses (Lavrakas et al., 1981): Although *fear* seems most often to lead a person to restrict or limit his or her own behavior, *concern* appears related to the decisions to deploy anticrime measures in the home and to engage in neighborhood-based anticrime strategies.

In reviewing the literature dealing with risk-related media effects, and applying those general findings to the case of crime, Tyler (1984) has suggested three basic reasons traditional media efforts may produce little impact on citizens' crime prevention behaviors (see also Lavrakas & Lewis, 1980). First, citizens may find most mass media reports of crime to be uninformative; that is, in overreporting infrequently occurring sensationalistic criminal incidents, most news stories are of little utility to the average citizen. Furthermore, most mass media crime reporting tells the average citizen little about the level of crime in those particular areas that he or she lives and works. Second, mass media reports of crime may be ignored because they provide little direct or indirect information about effective behaviors for avoiding or preventing criminal victimization. Tyler (1984, p. 34) suggests that "perhaps individuals must both perceive a risk *and* see how to lessen that risk before they will be influenced." Third, the impact of traditional crime prevention messages may be restricted by the limited effect they produce, as hypothesized by the "fear appeal" approach to persuasion (see Leventhal, 1970).

Thus, a synthesis of past findings in this area suggests at least two major policy implications. First, anticrime messages must be relevant and informative to a particular citizen before he or she is likely to act on their content. Second, some level of arousal may be necessary before citizens will perceive the need to act, but arousal in the form of *fear* may have a less desirable effect than arousal in the form of *concern*.

These observations can serve as the basis for developing an anticrime police-community newsletter; one with the purposes of informing citizens about the range of preventive responses that are endorsed by law enforcement officials and of providing citizens with information that is likely to motivate them toward action. Informing citizens about the range of recommended anticrime responses is relatively straightforward, but deciding how to create "positive arousal" is another matter.

In order to test this reasoning, field experiments were conducted in which the effects of three anticrime newsletters developed and disseminated by three police departments, were investigated. In each of these three communities two versions of the newsletter were tested. One version contained information about citizen involvement in crime prevention activities, and the second version supplemented these anticrime messages with specific information about local crime rates. To my knowledge, these were the first occasions in which information about local crime rates was disseminated in a controlled, and thus testable, fashion.

Providing the public with information about local crime is a controversial issue. Historically, there have been many reasons that detailed crime information rarely has been released by public officials on a regular basis. For example, fighting crime has long been viewed as the exclusive province of law enforcement officials. Second, it is important to restrict full access to this type of information in order to protect the privacy of victims and safeguard ongoing investigations. Finally, and probably the most important reason, many local officials hold untested assumptions about the negative effects that releasing such information may have on their citizenry. Thus, the three field tests reported in this chapter also served as the first controlled evaluation of the impact of releasing detailed local crime information to citizens.

STUDY 1: EVANSTON

Development of the Newsletter

In 1981, the Evanston Police Department, in collaboration with a consortium of local community organizations (the Residential Crime Prevention Committee), developed and distributed an experimental newsletter to Evanston residents that contained specific information about crime prevention techniques and, in some instances, also contained specific information about neighborhood crime. Figure 13.1 shows a sample of a recent issue of the newsletter that was distributed in one area in Evanston (the last page of the issue shown in Figure 13.1 contains crime statistics for two areas in eastern Evanston).

In developing the form and content of *ALERT,* the planning committee tried to choose a layout that was visually attractive and, at the same time, addressed the specific crime prevention needs of residents. The design objective was to have a clear, concise, appealing format that was easy to read. The newsletter is now printed on 17″ × 11″ heavy stock paper, soft beige in color with black ink, and is folded as a four-page booklet.

Regarding content, the intent was to provide crime prevention information of a "how-to" nature, and to reinforce these concepts

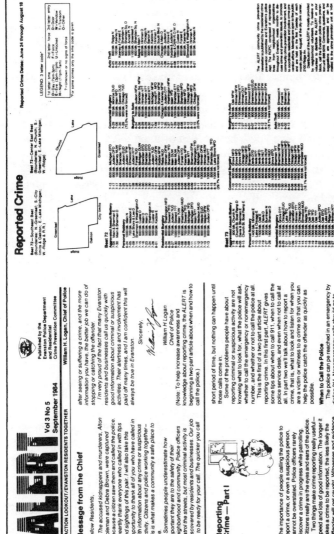

Figure 13.1 Sample of *ALERT*

through actual examples of success in Evanston. These articles are written by members of the department's Crime Prevention Unit and by select members of the Residential Crime Prevention Committee. In the "test" versions of *ALERT* that included local crime statistics, the statistics were prefaced with a fairly detailed explanation of why these statistics were being disseminated. This explanation concluded as follows:

> The purpose of providing this type of information to you as a resident, is to give you a better idea of what's happening in your neighborhood. We hope this will allow you to become more actively involved in looking out for each other's well-being. Remember, "by themselves, the police can only react to crime: they need an involved citizenry to prevent it!" (Lavrakas et al., 1983, p. 467)

As shown in Figure 13.1, the page that contained the crime statistics was different depending on in which of six areas one lived in the city. For example, if a resident lived in northwest Evanston, the last page of the newsletter he or she received contained the listings of recently reported index crimes (excluding theft) for the police patrol beat that covered the northwest section of the city. Each crime listed was identified by type, date of occurrence, and approximate address of occurrence (for example, the 300 block of Main St.).

Methodology

During the field test of *ALERT,* 1,500 issues of the version with crime statistics and 1,500 issues of the version without statistics were disseminated to residents in six different areas of the city. All recipients in three of the areas received one type of newsletter, and all recipients in the other three areas received the second type. After the dissemination of three monthly issues, a random sample of 96 heads of households who received the version with statistics and 73 heads of households who received the version without statistics were interviewed via telephone. At the same time, a random citywide sample of 322 residents who did not receive either version of the newsletter was interviewed via telephone as part of another ongoing research project. This provided a quasi-experimental test of the impact of the newsletter. It was quasi-experimental due to the fact that the two versions of *ALERT* were not distributed randomly throughout the city. Rather, households in three areas of the city received the version with crime

statistics and those in three other areas received the version without
statistics. Within areas, local community organizations disseminated
the newsletters in the neighborhoods they represented. All persons interviewed were asked standardized questions about their exposure to
and assessment of *ALERT,* their concern about and fear of crime,
their crime prevention attitudes and the anticrime measures they
deployed, and their demographic characteristics.

Results

Comparing the responses from the three different groups who were
interviewed, the evaluation determined that although residents'
perceptions about the magnitude and severity of crime in their
neighborhoods were greater ($p < .05$) for those who received the
newsletter (regardless of version), their own fear of crime was not
significantly greater than that of residents who were not exposed to
ALERT. These results supported the reasoning that the newsletter,
especially the version with crime statistics, served an "information-
transmission" function without an accompanied "fear-arousal" effect (Lavrakas et al., 1983). The findings also indicated that residents
who received the newsletter (especially those who received the version
with crime statistics) were more likely to report taking a variety of proactive anticrime measures and to hold more positive attitudes toward
citizens' responsibilities for coproducing neighborhood safety than
were those who had not received the newsletter.

Furthermore, those persons who received the version of *ALERT*
with crime statistics rated the newsletter as significantly ($p < .01$)
more interesting and more informative than those who received the
version without the crime listings. In addition, of all persons who
received the newsletter, better than nine in ten wanted to coninue to
receive it, and a similar proportion stated that the listing of crime
statistics should continue.

Although the results of this quasi-experimental evaluation were
quite positive, Lavrakas et al. (1983) caution that the generalizability
of the findings to other communities and to other "types" of anticrime newsletters is unknown. They acknowledge that the absolute
amount of crime experienced by a community may interact with the
"treatment," for example, the residents in high crime communities
may well be scared by the listing of local crime statistics. Furthermore,
with *ALERT* an explicit effort was made not only to raise concern
about crime, but also to provide readers with clear and detailed sug-

gestions about what to do with their concerns. Had *ALERT* been composed of a different information mix, or disseminated in a demographically different community, it is uncertain what effects would have been observed. Finally, it is worth noting that based on the results of this quasi-experimental test, and on the very positive anecdotal feedback received by the department, *ALERT* (including local crime statistics) has now been disseminated every other month in Evanston neighborhoods for the past three years.

STUDY 2: HOUSTON

Development of the Newsletter

In 1983, in conjunction with the NIJ-funded Fear Reduction Project, conducted by the Police Foundation, the Houston Fear Reduction Task Force began planning to test an anticrime behavior newsletter by reviewing several examples of police-generated neighborhood newsletters from around the country. Ultimately the Evanston *ALERT* was chosen as the principal model to follow, and consultation was initiated with those who produced that newsletter. (See Pate et al., 1985, for a detailed explanation of the Houston newsletter field experiment.)

The Houston newsletter, *Community Policing Exchange,* was planned to contain a mix of general and neighborhood news items. The general items were aimed at giving the reader a sense that there were anticrime measures that could be employed to increase personal, household, and neighborhood safety. Among the general items was a regular column, "Community Comments," written by Houston's Chief of Police. (See Figure 13.2 for a sample of the *Community Policing Exchange* layout and content.) Included among neighborhood-specific news items was information about local police officers and "good news" stories about crimes that had been prevented or solved because of the efforts of police and citizens in the area. Unlike in Evanston, however, time did not allow for the participation of area residents in writing articles for the newsletter.

In addition to the standard content of the newsletter, one version contained a one-page insert showing a line drawing of the area's boundaries, a listing of index offenses that had occurred in the previous month, the date of each crime, the location of each crime (by street and block number), and the time of occurrence. Figure 13.2 also displays an example of this insert.

Community Policing Exchange

PUBLISHED BY THE HOUSTON POLICE OFFICERS SERVING YOUR NEIGHBORHOOD

Vol. 1, No. 2   DECEMBER

Urgent calls handled first

It is 11:00 p.m., and all appears calm in Houston. Sam Smith, a retired plumber, arrives home after vacation to find a van in front of his family. Upon arriving home, the family discovers that their home has been burglarized. Meanwhile, in another section of the city, a storeowner is being held up by an armed assailant.

Within seconds of one another, the calls are received by the Department's Dispatch Division at 222-3131. Both individuals are victims of crime. Which of the two victims does the police department respond to first?

This type of circumstance is not uncommon for a police department the size of Houston's. Your police department serves an area covering over 565 square miles and receives about 4,500 calls for service daily. While all requests for service are given immediate police attention, some calls have priority over others based on the "urgency" of the call.

Under response prioritization, requests for police services are categorized into three designated levels.

● CODE 1 Responses. An officer will proceed to a call, but the assignment involves no emergency to the situation. Delay will not deteriorate because of delayed police action. Examples of CODE 1 assignments are parking

violations, speeding cars, and abandoned vehicles.

● CODE 2 Responses. An officer will proceed directly to the call, giving it immediate response and could deteriorate if prompt police action is not initiated. Examples of CODE 2 assignments are traffic accidents, criminals in custody, and report calls.

● CODE 3 Responses. An officer will proceed to the call using red lights and siren, as the situation is an emergency that poses a threat to human life. Which of the two examples are a felony crime in progress, or an immediate threat to life, is imminent.

Going back to our example of Mr. Smith and the local store owner, who both requested police service at almost the same time: we can now determine, of the two, whose situation requires the priority response.

Since the local store owner's situation is a felony crime in progress - CODE 3 - this would be the priority call. Failure of the police to respond immediately could result in the situation deteriorating and becoming life threatening. Whereas, in Mr. Smith's case - CODE 2 - the crime has already occurred, and a police officer is needed to take a report.

The Houston Police Department responds to every citizen call for service, but we do so using common sense. We want to keep citizens informed of our services and how we operate as a department, so that we can continue to serve this exciting and responsive city.

Community Comments

Lee P. Brown, Chief of Police

On behalf of the Houston Police Department, I would like to thank you for your continued support in helping us to make our city a safer city. Also, all the members of the Houston Police Department especially your neighborhood beat officers, would like to extend to you and your family warm wishes for the Holiday Season and a sincere hope for prosperity in the New Year.

Holiday joys & fears

The holiday season always brings with it an increase in home burglaries and thefts, and this year will be no exception. The display of gifts, coupled with the probability of an empty home while families are shopping or visiting with friends, provides more temptation than most burglars can resist.

If you are planning to be away from home during the holidays - for a short or extended time - keep these safety precautions in mind:

● Keep all doors and windows locked, including the garage.

● Keep gifts out of view from windows or entryways.

● Leave on a light or two or invest in a timer to automatically turn lights on and off.

● Don't let daily deliveries accumulate. Ask a neighbor to collect the newspaper or milk bottles.

REPORTED CRIME

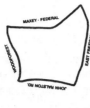

This attachment to your copy of Police Community Exchange is an attempt to provide you with information about crime in your neighborhood. It tells you the number and types of crime that were reported from your area to the Houston Police Department during a recent two (2) month period. The purpose of providing this type of information to you, as a resident,

is to give you a better idea of what's happening in your neighborhood. We hope this will provide you and your neighbors with the information needed to take specific crime prevention measures. Remember, "by themselves, the police can only react to crime; they need an involved citizenry to prevent it."

DISTRICT - BEAT 10C30
Northeast Houston
Boundaries: N-Woodforest   S-East Fwy.
E-Maxey-Federal   W-John Ralston Rd.)

LEGEND
hundred block = blk
6:00 a.m. to 2:59 p.m. (D)
3:00 p.m. to 10:59 p.m. (E)
11:00 p.m. to 5:59 a.m. (N)

COMMERCIAL BURGLARY
9/9	900 blk Maxey	(D)
10/11	11000 blk E. Fwy	(D)

BURGLARY MOTOR VEHICLE
9/9	11000 blk E. Fwy	(E)
9/16	600 blk Maxey	(E)
10/1	800 blk Autumn Wood	(D)
10/18	11000 blk Dawn Wood	(D)
10/25	11000 blk E. Fwy	(D)

THEFT
9/1	1200 blk Fleming	(N)
9/9	11000 blk E. Fwy	(D)
9/11	11000 blk Fleming	(D)
9/14	12000 blk Maxey	(D)
9/16	1000 blk Dawn Wood	(D)
9/21	11000 blk E. Fwy	(E)
9/22	800 blk Autumn Wood	(D)
9/22	11000 blk Dawn Wood	(D)
10/1	11000 blk Fleming	(E)
10/11	11000 blk E. Fwy	(E)
10/12	800 blk Maxey	(N)
10/28	11000 blk Fleming	(D)

BURGLARY RESIDENCE
9/19	11000 blk E. Fwy	(D)
9/20	12000 blk Fleming	(N)
9/29	900 blk Center Wood	(N)
10/30	12000 blk Fleming	(D)

AGGRAVATED ROBBERY
9/2	900 blk Maxey	(D)
9/3	1000 blk Center Wood	(N)
9/17	12000 blk Fleming	(D)
9/17	500 blk Ken Wood	(D)
10/11	1000 blk Federal	(D)
10/11	800 blk Maxey	(E)
10/14	1000 blk Federal	(D)

ASSAULT
9/4	500 blk Wood Vista	(E)
10/4	12000 blk Fleming	(N)
10/3	12000 blk Maxey	(D)
10/6	800 blk Autumn Wood	(N)
10/13	12000 blk Fleming	(N)
10/13	12000 blk Fleming	(N)
10/15	12000 blk Fleming	(N)
10/15	12000 blk Fleming	(E)

AUTO THEFT
9/1	11000 blk E. Fwy	(N)
9/5	700 blk Coolwood	(N)
9/11	900 blk Center Wood	(N)
10/3	600 blk Maxey Rd.	(D)

Figure 13.2 Sample of *Community Policing Exchange*

277

Methodology

Within the Houston target neighborhood, randomly selected households were assigned randomly to one of three experimental conditions. The two treatment conditions were represented by each version of the newsletter, with households in these conditions scheduled to be mailed five monthly issues of the newsletter. The random subsample of households that was not mailed the newsletter constituted the control group. Thus, the evaluation design was a "true experiment" (see Campbell & Stanley, 1966).

To provide a more robust test of the effects of the newsletter, two separate analytical strategies were employed. For one, a *panel sample* in each of the three experimental conditions was interviewed before and after the distribution of the newsletter, which was produced for five months (November 1983 through March 1984). In the second, a *posttest only* design, random samples in each of the three experimental conditions were interviewed only after the five months of distribution of *Community Policing Exchange.*

These two analytical strategies were chosen because they complemented each other's methodological weaknesses. A panel design has the greater internal validity and statistical conclusion validity (see Cook & Campbell, 1976) because the effects of extraneous variables not associated with the treatment can be minimized by gathering data on the same group of people at two points in time. That is, pretest differences among respondents can be controlled through the use of pretest scores as covariates. However, a posttest only design has greater external validity (Cook & Campbell, 1976) because the generalizability of the panel is hampered by *panel attrition,* that is, the loss of a nonrandom portion of the original random panel sample, due primarily to residents who moved in the intervening period between the Time 1 and Time 2 data collection stages. Finally, a posttest only design avoids the reactivity that might result from respondents being interviewed at the pretest stage.

The Houston panel sample was randomly selected from a pool of 767 households in the target area at which an interview had been completed at Time 1 (July-August 1983). A working sample of 249 of these households was then randomly assigned among the three experimental conditions. The posttest only sample was randomly selected from those households that had not been interviewed at Time 1. A working sample of 411 of these households was randomly assigned among the three experimental conditions.

Time 2 interviews for the three panel and the three posttest only conditions were conducted in March and April of 1984. A total of 127 of the 249 respondents chosen for the panel were reinterviewed (51%). Panel attrition was due mostly to Time 1 respondents having moved, and was correlated with being younger, having lived in the neighborhood for fewer than 10 years, and being white. It is important to note that there was no "differential attrition" across the three experimental conditions, that is, attrition was unrelated to the treatment.

Of the 411 addresses sampled for the posttest only groups, over one-third were found to be vacant (unoccupied). In all, 189 interviews were completed with posttest only households. For both the panel and posttest only samples, one adult per household was randomly selected using the standardized Kish procedure, and interviews were conducted in person.

A carefully developed and extensively revised questionnaire (including several pilot tests) was employed to gather data. Multi-item scales were used to provide reliable measures of such constructs as fear of crime, concern about crime, crime prevention dispositions, and assessment of the newsletters. Analysis of covariance was performed using Time 2 outcome measures as dependent variables, experimental condition as the independent variable, and sex, age, race, and education as covariates. In the panel analyses, Time 1 (pretest) scores for the outcome measures were also used as covariates.

Results

Exposure to Treatment. In both the panel sample and the posttest only sample, about two-thirds of those living in households that were scheduled to receive (via U.S. mail) the version with the crime statistics insert reported that they were aware of *Community Policing Exchange.* This compared to approximately one-half of those in households that ostensibly received the version without the crime statistics insert, and one-tenth of those living in households that did not receive a newsletter.

Using aided recall (that is, the interviewer showed the respondent the latest issue of the newsletter), about six in ten of those living in households scheduled to receive five monthly issues with the insert reported that they were aware of at least one issue being received at their home. A slightly smaller percentage of those living at addresses ostensibly receiving the other version indicated they were aware of receiving at least one issue. About one in ten of those living in households that were not to receive any newsletters said they had been mailed at least one issue. On the average, respondents in the two treatment conditions indicated receiving two to three issues of the newsletter, with those living in households that were scheduled to be mailed the version with the insert reporting a somewhat higher average number of issues received than those in households mailed the newsletter without the insert. (In both the panel and posttest only samples, all measures of exposure were correlated positively with the educational attainment of respondents.)

Fear of Crime. There were no significant differences among groups in either the panel sample or posttest only sample regarding respondents' perceived vulnerability to personal crime victimization in the target area. Regarding one's vulnerability to property crime victimization in the target area, the panel sample group that was scheduled to receive the newsletter with the crime statistics insert were significantly (albeit only "slightly") more fearful than the other two groups ($p <$ .05). As shown in Table 13.1, this finding was not replicated in the posttest only sample.

Respondents who recalled viewing at least one issue of *Community Policing Exchange* were asked if it had affected the extent to which they worried about becoming crime victims. As shown in Table 13.1, panel sample respondents who lived in households that ostensibly received the newsletter with the crime statistics insert indicated they had become slightly more worried, and panel sample respondents who lived in households scheduled to receive the newsletter without the insert indicated they were slightly less worried; this latter difference was statistically significant ($p <$ .05). These findings were not replicated in the posttest only sample, in which both groups indicated that the extent to which they worried was basically unchanged.

Concern about Crime. No significant differences were found in residents' perceptions about the magnitude of personal crime victimization in the Houston target area: On average, all three groups in both the panel and posttest only samples indicated they regarded this type of victimization as a rather minor problem. Similarly, as shown in Table 13.1, there were no significant differences among groups in concern about property crime in the target area.

Those who had viewed one or more issues of the newsletter with the insert that had been mailed to their homes were also asked if the insert had changed their beliefs about the magnitude of crime in the target area. Both the panel and posttest only samples indicated that they now thought there was significantly more (albeit only "slightly" more)

TABLE 13.1   Houston Panel Sample and Posttest Only Sample: Wave 2 Adjusted Means

Outcome Measure	Panel Sample			Posttest Only Sample		
	No Newsletter	Newsletter without Stats	Newsletter with Stats	No Newsletter	Newsletter without Stats	Newsletter with Stats
Fear of personal victimization	1.53	1.55	1.52	1.52	1.55	1.62
n	42	41	43	69	58	61
Fear of property victimization	2.16	2.12	2.29	1.99	2.14	2.24
n	42	41	43	69	58	61
Change in worry due to newsletter	NA	1.64	2.27	NA	1.90	1.90
n		20	23		20	28
Concern for personal crime problems	1.42	1.49	1.38	1.40	1.43	1.39
n	41	40	41	69	58	61
Concern for property crime problems	2.04	2.07	1.99	1.87	1.89	2.01
n	42	41	43	69	58	61

NOTE: In fear of personal victimization scale, higher scores represent more fear. In fear of property victimization scale, 3 = very worried, 2 = somewhat worried, 1 = not at all worried. In change in worry due to newsletter item, 3 = more worried, 2 = no difference, 1 = less worried. In concern for personal crime problems scale, 3 = big problem, 2 = some problem, 1 = no problem. In concern for property crime problems scale, 3 = big problem, 2 = some problem, 1 = no problem. In all analyses, adjusted means were produced by using gender, age, education, and race as covariates. In the panel analysis, Wave 1 measures for each outcome measure were also used as covariates.

crime than they had thought existed prior to exposure to the insert ($p < .05$).

A number of other items were asked regarding beliefs about changes in local crime rates. None of the observed differences among groups in either the panel sample or the posttest only sample proved to be statistically significant. Nor were there any marginally significant trends in these results.

Anticrime Dispositions. A number of multi-item scales were used to assess respondents' attitudes and proclivities toward engaging in various citizen crime prevention measures. These included attributed responsibility for crime prevention, perceived efficacy of personal protection measures, perceived efficacy of property protection measure, use of personal protective measures, and use of household anticrime measures. In none of these comparisons were there any significant differences among the three groups in either the panel sample or the posttest only sample.

Those who reported looking at one or more issues of the newsletter were also asked questions about the effect of the newsletter on their anticrime dispositions. There was no significant relationship between which version had been mailed to the respondents' homes and whether or not they reported taking any of the anticrime advice in the newsletters. But when asked if their confidence in avoiding victimization had been affected by exposure to the newsletter, each of the groups in both samples indicated that they now felt significanty more confident ($p < .05$).

STUDY 3: NEWARK

Development of the Newsletter

In 1983, the Newark Fear Reduction Task Force, in conjunction with the NIJ-funded Fear Reduction Project, decided to test the effects of an anticrime newsletter. As in Houston, the Evanston *ALERT* was chosen as the principal model to follow, and consultation was initiated with those in Evanston who produced that newsletter. (See Pate et al., 1985, for a detailed explanation of the Newark newsletter field experiment.)

The Newark newsletter, *ACT 1* (based on the acronym "Attack Crime Together"), was planned to contain a news mix similar to that of the Houston newsletter. Among the general items was a regular column, "From the Desk of the Police Commissioner." (See Figure 13.3

for a sample of the *ACT 1* layout and content.) As with Houston, included among neighborhood-specific news items was information about local police officers and "good news" stories about crimes that were prevented or solved because of the efforts of police and citizens in the area. Although citizen involvement in the production of the newsletter was considered, time did not allow for this suggestion to be implemented. As shown in Figure 13.3, one version of *ACT 1* contained a one-page insert showing a map of the Newark target area and a listing of index offenses that had occurred in the previous month by day of occurrence and approximate location.

Methodology

The same analytical strategy that was employed in Houston was used in Newark. This included testing two versions of the newsletter, using an untreated control group, and using both a panel sample and a posttest only sample. As in the Houston field experiment, households were randomly assigned to conditions. Six issues of *ACT 1* were produced (October 1983 through March 1984), and were ostensibly received (via U.S. mail) by all households in the two treatment conditions.

The Newark panel sample was randomly selected from a pool of 543 households at which interviews had been completed at Time 1 (July-August 1983). A working sample of 198 of these households was then randomly assigned among each of the three experimental conditions. As in Houston, the Newark posttest only sample was randomly selected from those households that had not been interviewed at Time 1. A working sample of 303 of these households was randomly assigned among the three experimental conditions.

A total of 117 of the 198 respondents chosen for the panel were successfully reinterviewed (59%). Panel attrition was due mostly to Time 1 respondents having moved, and was associated with being younger, having lived in the neighborhood for fewer than five years, and being male. As in Houston, there was no differential attrition among the experimental conditions.

Of the 303 addresses sampled for the posttest only groups, nearly 15% were found to be vacant (unoccupied), and another 10% refused to be interviewed. In all, 181 interviews were completed at posttest only households. Respondents were selected using the standardized Kish procedure and interviews were conducted in person, using the same questionnaire as in Houston.

ACT 1

Published by the
NEWARK Police Department
and Neighborhood Residents

ATTACK CRIME TOGETHER VOL. 1, NO. 8 MAY 1984 Hubert Williams, Police Director

"From the Desk of the Police Director"

Since we have kept recorded statistics on crime in America, the young have dominated the crime/offense category. The proliferation of youth in our society, resulting from the baby boom, has had a dramatic impact on American cities, the crime rate, and our direction in the respect for authority. Graffiti, debris-strewn lots, broken bottles and windows all attest to the absence of discipline and respect for the rights of others of this young generation.

Crime results as much from our system of values as it does from the existence of an opportunity to commit an offense. If our moral principles tell us it is wrong to steal, even if we think that we can get away with it, we will not steal. Thus, a public safety network is inadequate if it does not have an active, viable community with a strong, morale prerogative acting in concert with the law enforcement authority. American institutions must provide direction in this regard. The church, the home, and the schools are critical components of the public safety equation. If we are to truly upgrade the cities and enhance the quality of life for all of us, then we must pull

together these fundamental components of our society.

As Police Director, I recognize the acute need for discipline in all areas of our life. But I hasten to add that in too many instances children are abused by excessive adult authority. If a child is subjected to harsh discipline in the home, that child could bear scars of resentment for the rest of his or her life. Many a criminal has been produced by overly strict parents who used a hard-nosed, mechanical approach to child bearing. Early family training begins in the home where personalities are developed that will determine what type of society our nation will have tomorrow. The home is the first training school in love and in behavior and parents serve as the first teachers for the inspirational education of youth. In the home, the child learns that others beside him/herself have rights which he/she must respect. Here the foundation is laid for instilling in the child those values which will cause him/her own affairs but also share in the responsibility for the affairs of others.

Our direct responsibility as a parent is to reinforce the child's good behavior with love and praise, while discouraging criminal behavior by teaching and offering better alternatives and by providing discipline when necessary. The most important contribution by a parent, however, is a good example. So join with me toward achieving that abiding way by giving, loving, and helping to preserve our future - our children.

Report Rape to
SAGA IMMEDIATELY
CALL
733-RAPE

HOMEOWNER TIPS

Your Home: As Safe as You Think?

Traditionally, most of us have regarded our home as a castle, a refuge and a place safe from the intrusions of crime in the streets. But your home may not be as safe as you think. Residential burglary is a real and present danger.

You may not recognize the typical burglar. He's often one of the neighborhood kids, a young male who usually lives within a mile or two of his targets, but not always. He is usually an opportunist - and an amateur - but that doesn't mean he can't find his way into your home.

He selects homes he can enter quickly and quietly, and exit with a minimum risk of detection. And he can find those homes easily.

SECURITY SURVEYS...

CRIMINALS KNOW THE BEST WAYS TO ENTER YOUR HOME AND POLICE CAN SHOW YOU THE BEST WAY TO KEEP THEM OUT.

We are working hard for you: call right now at the Newark Police Crime Prevention Bureau. Dial 733-6101

KNOW YOUR NUMBERS

To all Newark residents who have followed in our effort to study crime in your area, we would like to extend our thanks. As in the past, we present you with data reflective of your neighborhood. Listed herein is the crime, type, date, and location of occurrence.

Since our last issue, for the same length of time, major crime has decreased by nearly 3%. It is our sincere wish that this participation on the part of neighborhood residents will continue to increase. Let us continue to work as a team . . . and succeed!:

AGGRAVATED ASSAULT

4/12 Lehigh Ave., between Hunterdon/Elizabeth

BURGLARY (Resid.)

3/29 Porter Ave., btn Porter Pl./Elizabeth Ave.

Time Period: March 16 - April 15

BURGLARY (Resid.) Con't.

4/2 Mapes Ave., btn Hunterdon/Elizabeth
4/2 Mapes Ave., btn Hunterdon/Elizabeth
4/9 Mapes Ave., btn Osborne/Bergen
4/8 Mapes Ave., btn Osborne/Bergen

ROBBERY

3/18 Cor. Elizabeth/Lyons
3/26 Cor. Bergen/Lyons

THEFT OF AUTO

3/20 Cor. Lehigh/Osborne T.
3/22 Lehigh Ave., btn Parkview/Bergen
3/30 Lehigh Ave., btn Osborne/Parkview
4/5 Elizabeth Ave., btn Lehigh/Stengel
4/8 Cor. Bergen/Lehigh
4/14 Cor. Lehigh/Osborne

THEFT (Pers.)

3/22 Cor. Lehigh/Osborne

THEFT (Pers.) Con't.

3/24 Cor. Elizabeth/Mapes Ave.
3/26 Cor. Bergen/Lyons
4/9 Lehigh, btn Bergen/Hunderton

TOTAL INCIDENTS: 18

Figure 13.3 Sample of *ACT 1*

Results

Exposure to Treatment. In the Newark panel sample, 59% of those living in households that ostensibly received the version with the crime statistics insert reported that they were aware of *ACT 1*. This compared to only 40% of those in households that received the version without the crime statistics insert, and 16% of those living in households that were not mailed newsletters. In the Newark posttest only sample, about four in ten respondents in households that ostensibly received the newsletter (regardless of version) recalled seeing it, as did one-fifth of those in households that ostensibly were not mailed any newsletters.

With the aided recall technique, 59% of those in the panel sample who lived in households that had been scheduled to receive the six monthly issues with the insert reported that they were aware of at least one issue being received at their homes. A considerably smaller proportion, 36%, of those in the panel sample living at addresses ostensibly receiving the other version indicated they were aware of receiving at least one issue. About one in ten of those living in households that were ostensibly *not* mailed any newsletters said they had been mailed at least one issue. In the posttest only sample, a little more than one-third (35%) of those living in households that were scheduled to be mailed the newsletter (regardless of version) reported that they had received at least one copy, as did one in ten of those who lived in households that were ostensibly not mailed any newsletters.

On the average, respondents in the two treatment conditions indicated receiving one to two issues of the newsletter, with those in the panel sample (but not the posttest only sample) living in households that were scheduled to be mailed the version with the insert reporting a somewhat higher average number of issues received than those in households purportedly mailed the newsletter without the insert. (As in Houston, in both the panel and posttest only samples, all measures of exposure correlated positively with the educational background of respondents.)

Fear of Crime. As shown in Table 13.2, there were no significant differences among groups in either of the two samples regarding respondents' perceived vulnerability to personal crime or property crime victimization in the Newark target area. Also, when asked if the newsletter had affected the extent to which they worried about becoming crime victims, there were no differences between those who lived in households ostensibly mailed the version with the crime statistics insert and those who were not mailed the insert.

Concern about Crime. As also shown in Table 13.2, no significant differences were found in residents' perceptions of the magnitude of personal crime victimization or the magnitude of property crime victimization in the target area. Those who indicated that they received and looked at at least one newsletter also were asked if *ACT I* had changed their beliefs about the magnitude of crime in the target area. Neither group indicated any significant change after their exposure to the newsletter. As in Houston, a number of other items were asked regarding respondents' beliefs about changes in local crime rates. None of the observed differences among groups in either the panel sample or the posttest only sample was statistically significant.

Anticrime Dispositions. The same set of items was asked of Newark respondents as was asked of those in Houston regarding their attitudes toward and proclivities to employ crime prevention measures. In general, no statistically significant differences were found among the three groups in either the panel sample or the posttest only sample. The exception was the finding that those in the panel sample that lived in households that were not mailed newsletters reported taking significantly more household-based anticrime measures than those who received either version of the newsletter. This "surprising" result was not replicated in the Newark posttest only sample.

Finally, as in Houston, those who had been mailed a newsletter and had looked at it (regardless of version) reported that they now felt significantly more confident ($p < .05$) in knowing what to do to avoid criminal victimization since their exposure to *ACT 1.*

DISCUSSION

Highlights of the findings of three field tests of the "police-community anticrime newsletter" concept have been presented above. In each of the cities, results indicated that residents were overwhelmingly positive in their assessments of the newsletters, especially the versions that included crime statistics. Not only was exposure greater to the version with crime statistics, but it was rated as significantly more interesting and more informative. Yet, in contrast to the nearly ideal findings of impact in the Evanston quasi-experiment, the Houston and Newark experiments showed no consistent effects on fear, concern, or anticrime dispositions.

There are several perspectives from which to view these null findings. First, there may have been differences in the strength of the treatment that accounted for the differences in the findings in Evan-

TABLE 13.2 Newark Panel Sample and Posttest Only Sample: Wave 2 Adjusted Means

	Panel Sample			Posttest Only Sample		
Outcome Measure	No Newsletter	Newsletter without Stats	Newsletter with Stats	No Newsletter	Newsletter without Stats	Newsletter with Stats
Fear of personal victimization	2.01	1.74	1.86	1.89	1.85	1.93
n	39	42	32	56	65	57
Fear of property victimization	2.13	2.09	2.14	2.27	2.15	2.28
n	39	41	31	56	65	57
Change in worry due to newsletter	NA	1.85	1.91	NA	1.97	1.91
n		20	20		29	24
Concern for personal crime problems	1.77	1.62	1.86	1.74	1.76	1.79
n	38	42	31	55	65	57
Concern for property crime problems	2.07	2.02	2.17	2.18	2.02	2.02
n	38	41	32	56	65	57

NOTE: In fear of personal victimization scale, higher scores represent more fear. In fear of property victimization scale, higher scores represent more fear. In change in worry due to newsletter item, 3 = more worried, 2 = no difference, 1 = less worried. In concern for personal crime problems scale, 3 = big problem, 2 = some problem, 1 = no problem. In concern for property crime problems scale, 3 = big problem, 2 = some problem, 1 = no problem. In all analyses, adjusted means were produced by using gender, age, and education as covariates. In the panel analysis, Wave 1 measures for each outcome measure were also used as covariates.

ston versus Houston and Newark. In Evanston, only a few of those living in households that ostensibly received three monthly issues of *ALERT* were unaware of it when queried via telephone by interviewers. In contrast, and even with aided recall and in-person interviewing, a sizable proportion of those interviewed in Houston and Newark reported no exposure, even though each respondent lived in a household that ostensibly had been mailed five to six issues. This may be due to differences in the method of respondent selection, newsletter dissemination, and/or the demographics of the respective communities.

In Evanston, those interviewed in the quasi-experimental test of *ALERT* were either male or female heads of household. In Houston and Newark, respondents were any randomly selected adult within the household. Granted, the majority of those interviewed in Houston and Newark were probably heads of their respective households, but there were many other adults (for example, adult children and older parents) who may well have never been shown the newsletters by the "resident" (that is, the head of the household) to whom they were addressed.

If this is a valid explanation for the lower levels of reported exposure in Houston and Newark, then a clear implication for future evaluative efforts would be to make certain that newsletters are personally addressed to those persons from whom data will be gathered later. From the standpoint of policy, addressing the newsletter to an individual rather than "occupant" or "resident" personalizes the message. Furthermore, it is likely that heads of households are the best recipients for these newsletters, because they often have the greatest vested interest in the safety and security of their neighborhoods and can, if they choose, make a conscious effort to share crime prevention information learned via the newsletter with the rest of the members of their families.

Another methodological difference between the Evanston treatment and that employed in Houston and Newark was the mode of disseminating the newsletters. In Evanston, during the three-month quasi-experimental testing phase newsletters were, in most cases, hand delivered to residents by local community groups. In Houston and Newark, the U.S. mail was chosen as the most feasible system to maintain the random assignment of households to experimental conditions. It is possible that mail addressed to a "resident" is not as reliably delivered in lower-income neighborhoods, such as those chosen as the target communities in Houston and Newark, compared to upper-middle-income communities such as Evanston. It is also possible that an anticrime newsletter receives more credibility when it is disseminated by community groups rather than when it comes directly from the police, especially in lower-income neighborhoods, which often harbor above-average suspicion of police. Additionally, *ALERT* was coauthored by the police and community group representatives, which also may have helped to signal residents that this was "their" newsletter.

Another possible explanation for the inconsistent findings among the three evaluations may lie in the demographic nature of the target populations, specifically in educational differences. In Evanston, nearly all the adults surveyed (regardless of race) had graduated from high school, the majority had graduated from college, and about one in four had a master's degree. This is an extraordinarily well-educated population. In contrast, in the Houston target area, one-fourth had not graduated from high school, and only one in ten had a college degree. Similarly, in the Newark target area, over one-third were not high school graduates, and less than one in ten had a college degree.

It is possible that the effects in the Evanston quasi-experiment may be partially explained by the high levels of education among those who received *ALERT*. The use of information conveyed via the print medium (for example, a newsletter) is correlated with the educational level of consumers (Bogart, 1981). That is, the more educated a person, the more likely that person is to consume information via books and newspapers. If educational level served as a filter that determined who was exposed to the newsletters in Houston and Newark, and with what effect, then one would expect a treatment by covariate interaction (see Skogan, 1985). As mentioned earlier, exposure to the newsletters was significantly correlated with residents' educational background in both Houston and Newark. Furthermore, post hoc analyses of the Houston and Newark data showed a few instances in which newsletter effects were present among those with more than a high school education, although not present or in the opposite direction for those with lower levels of education. None of these results, however, was of sufficient magnitude or consistency to merit publication. Suffice it to say that persons involved in the future dissemination of and research on police-community anticrime newsletters would be well advised to consider the educational levels of the population being exposed and sampled.

In conclusion, these three field tests suggest that such newsletters merit consideration elsewhere as one strategy in the arsenal in the fight against crime. There is no evidence that disseminating crime prevention information and crime statistics has any sizable negative effects on the citizenry, at least none as measured by these evaluations. At the same time, there is some evidence that such newsletters may have positive effects in reinforcing citizen coproduction of community safety. In all three cities, those who received the newsletters were overwhelmingly enthusiastic about continuing the dissemination of this type of information, including the inclusion of crime statistics. Although this should not be viewed as a blanket endorsement of the police-community anticrime newsletter concept in all communities, it should at least be given careful consideration by local law enforcement authorities and community groups.

From the standpoint of research and evaluation there is much more that needs to be known about the long-term effects of exposure to such newsletters. Is citizens' initial enthusiasm for such newsletters transitory? Do such newsletters have the potential to contribute directly to increased precautionary actions on the part of the public, or are they, at best, only a supplementary strategy that may be indirectly effective when used with some other less passive strategy? Are there communities in which such newsletters are not only not helpful, but may even be damaging? These and other questions about the effectiveness of police-community anticrime newsletters must await more rigorous testing.

REFERENCES

Becker, M. H. (1974). The health belief model and personal behavior. *Health Education Monographs, 2,* 326-352.

Bogart, L. (1981). *Press and public.* Hillsdale, NJ: Erlbaum.

Campbell, D. T., & Stanley, J. (1966). *Experimental and quasi-experimental designs for research.* Chicago: Rand McNally.

Cook, T. D., & Campbell, D. T. (1976). *Quasi-experimentation: Design and analysis issues for field settings.* Chicago: Rand McNally.

Furstenberg, F. F. (1971). Public reaction to crime in the streets. *American Scholar, 40,* 601-610.

Lavrakas, P. J. (1985). Citizen self-help and neighborhood crime prevention. In L. Curtis (Ed.), *American violence and public policy.* New Haven, CT: Yale University Press.

Lavrakas, P. J., & Bennett, S. F. (1985). *The bubble-up approach to community anticrime programming.* Paper presented at the annual meeting of the American Psychological Association, Los Angeles.

Lavrakas, P. J., & Lewis, D. A. (1980). Conceptualizing and measuring citizen crime prevention behaviors. *Journal of Research in Crime and Delinquency, 17,* 254-272.

Lavrakas, P. J., Rosenbaum, D. P., & Kaminski, F. (1983). Transmitting information about crime and crime prevention to citizens. *Journal of Police Science and Administration, 11,* 463-473.

Lavrakas, P. J., Skogan, W. G., Normoyle, J., Herz, E. J., Salem, G., & Lewis, D. A. (1981). *Factors related to citizen involvement in personal, household, and neighborhood anti-crime measures.* Washington, DC: Government Printing Office.

Leventhal, H. (1970). Findings and theory in the study of fear communications. In L. Berkowitz (Ed.), *Advances in experimental social psychology* (Vol. 5, pp. 119-186). New York: Academic Press.

Mendelsohn, H., & O'Keefe, G. (1981). *Public communications and the prevention of crime.* Denver: University of Denver, Center for Mass Communications.

Pate, A. M., Lavrakas, P. J., Wycoff, M. A., Skogan, W. G., & Sherman, L. W. (1985). *Neighborhood police newsletters: Technical report.* Washington, DC: Police Foundation.

Percy, S. L. (1979). Citizen co-production of community safety. In R. Baker & F. Meyer (Eds.), *Evaluating alternative law enforcement policies.* Lexington, MA: D. C. Heath.

Safire, W. (1985, April 8). Genovese to Goetz. *New York Times,* p. 17.

Skogan, W. G. (1985). The ill effects of treatment-covariate interactions. Manuscript submitted for publication.

Tyler, T. R. (1984). Assessing the risk of victimization: The integration of personal victimization experience and socially transmitted information. *Journal of Social Issues, 40,* 27-38.

Tyler, T., & Lavrakas, P. J. (1985). Mass media effects: Distinguishing the importance of personal and societal level effects. In S. Krauss & R. Perloff (Eds.), *Mass media and political thought: An information-processing approach.* Beverly Hills, CA: Sage.

VI

SUMMARY AND CRITIQUE

Chapter 14

COMMUNITY CRIME PREVENTION
A Synthesis of Eleven Evaluations

R O B E R T K. Y I N

ARE WE CLOSER TO
PREVENTING CRIME IN URBAN AREAS?

Although national attention to crime in the cities has waned since the 1970s, urban communities must still deal daily with crime prevention and crime problems. Thus, any new information about effectively combating crime can still be considered welcome news.

Can such news be drawn from the preceding chapters? Each chapter has evaluated a public attempt, mainly supported by federal funds, to prevent community crime. On the surface, the evaluation results are positive and encouraging—in most cases, the targeted crime was reduced and the perceptions of citizens were changed in a desirable direction. Furthermore, the evaluations used sound research methods and were done by experienced research investigators, giving credence to the results. If eleven careful evaluations point to generally positive outcomes, can other communities now be encouraged to replicate the interventions, and are we thereby closer to preventing crime in urban areas?

The purpose of the following synthesis is to examine the eleven evaluations more closely and to determine whether or not there are such general lessons for further action. The synthesis is organized according to a series of questions that must be answered before further action can be considered.

(1) Were the interventions unique?
(2) Were the results really favorable?
(3) Were the efforts targeted toward the highest crime areas?
(4) Are the reports representative?

(5) What lessons are to be learned about crime prevention?

(6) Where do we go from here?

In other words, to the extent that the interventions were unique, or the results really unfavorable in some manner, or the interventions not targeted to high-crime areas, or the reports unrepresentative of conditions elsewhere in the country, the lessons from these interventions might have limited implications for future action. Conversely, a positive reading would lead to greater promise for crime prevention in other urban communities.

As a preview, the aggregate answers across the eleven interventions do yield an overall pattern, which is that *we do in fact know more about crime prevention as a result of these eleven experiences, but we may still not be able to do much about it.* This possibly paradoxical conclusion is discussed further in the final portion of this chapter.

WERE THE INTERVENTIONS UNIQUE?

The first barrier to be surmounted is to determine whether or not the eleven interventions were unique. Thus, the presence of (a) special technologies, (b) distinctive historical circumstances, or (c) the availability of unusual resources might reduce the possibility of replicating the results in other communities. As an aid in examining this proposition, Table 14.1 summarizes the general activities that were attempted in each intervention, along with the authors of the evaluation, the site and calendar period of the interventions, and the type of crime addressed by the intervention.

A perusal of this table indicates the true variety of the efforts, as well as the general conclusion that the interventions were *not* unique. Small and large cities in all regions of the country were covered, including one national campaign in which "McGruff," the crime dog, appeared in numerous public service announcements and pamphlets. Other interventions were directed at reducing crime vulnerability through improvements in street lighting, reducing automobile traffic through neighborhoods, increasing foot patrols, or encouraging individual households or businesses to take precautions against burglary and robbery. Many of the interventions also included efforts to organize citizens on a formal basis—by block watching, increasing knowledge about crime prevention tactics, or improving coordination with the local police. Overall, the interventions covered five different strategies:

(1) changes in *environmental design,* largely following the tenets of Oscar Newman and "Crime Prevention Through Environmental Design" (CPTED), including improvements in street lighting and changes in traffic patterns;

(2) changes in the *deployment of local police* officers, mainly emphasizing decentralized tactics and foot patrols, and including specific attempts to increase the contacts between police and citizens;

(3) initiation and support for *community organizations,* including organizations of residents and of neighborhood proprietors;

(4) attempts to increase *public awareness and education* about crime and crime prevention, through media campaigns and through the distribution of community newsletters; and

(5) *individual participation in crime prevention efforts,* such as in the engraving of personal property, the conduct of security surveys, and block watching.

Some of these interventions involved high costs and sustained efforts. In one redesign of the physical environment, for instance, $9.5 million was made available from state highway funds, just for the portion of the intervention concerned with changing the pattern of streets. Likewise, the mass media campaign for McGruff, the crime dog, involved $100 million in donated broadcast time and the printing of nearly 2 million pamphlets for dissemination. Finally, in three cases (the Hartford Project, the Portland Project, and the Newark Foot Patrol), the intervention spanned a period of more than six years.

However, the high costs were not beyond those normally incurred in servicing cities and neighborhoods. Many of the same actions could be undertaken elsewhere, by communities across the United States. Simply put, the interventions were not exotic and can be repeated in other locations.

WERE THE RESULTS REALLY FAVORABLE?

Another barrier to further action would be created to the extent that the outcomes from these interventions, upon closer examination, were not genuinely positive. This possibility was explored by summarizing the eleven evaluations and their outcomes, shown in Table 14.2.

The table indicates the types of outcomes that were measured, the general direction of the results, and whether or not statistical techniques were used to analyze the data. A perusal of the table (discussed

TABLE 14.1 Summary of Eleven Evaluation Studies (by type of intervention)

Study Author(s)	Intervention Sites and Period	Type of Crime Addressed	Description of Intervention
Fowler & Mangione (Chapter 5)	Hartford, Connecticut 1973-1979	residential	*Hartford Project:* physical redesign, police redeployment, and community organizing
Lavrakas (Chapter 13)	Evanston, Illinois, 1981 Houston, Texas, 1983 Newark, New Jersey, 1983	residential	*Crime Newsletters:* distribution of community newsletters in target neighborhoods
Lavrakas & Kushmuk (Chapter 10)	Portland, Oregon 1974-1980	commercial	*Portland Project:* physical redesign, police assistance, and business organizing
Lindsay & McGillis (Chapter 3)	Seattle, Washington 1974-1975	residential	*Seattle Community Crime Prevention Program:* block watch, security inspections, and property engraving
O'Keefe (Chapter 12)	Nationwide campaign, 1979	residential	*McGruff National Media Campaign:* information used in mass media and in pamphlets
Pate (Chapter 7)	Newark, New Jersey 1973-1979	residential	*Newark Foot Patrol:* foot patrols from 4 p.m. to midnight
Rosenbaum, et al. (Chapter 6)	Chicago, Illinois 1983-1984	residential	*Urban Crime Prevention Program:* block watches and related neighborhood meetings
Schneider (Chapter 4)	Portland, Oregon 1973-1974	residential	*Portland Anti-Burglary Program:* street lighting, property engraving, and community education
Tien & Cahn (Chapter 11)	Denver, Colorado, 1981 Long Beach, California, 1981 St. Louis, Missouri, 1981	commercial	*Commercial Security Field Test:* security surveys undertaken by business proprietors
Trojanowicz (Chapter 8)	Flint, Michigan 1979-1982	residential	*Neighborhood Foot Patrol:* foot patrol and community organizing
Wycoff & Skogan (Chapter 9)	Houston, Texas 1983-1984	residential	*Storefront Police Office:* location of storefront office, staffed by police, in local neighborhood

297

further below) suggests that the findings from the eleven evaluations were indeed positive, and that they were robust and credible methodologically. Thus, the results were favorable, and this facet of the interventions also should not be considered a barrier to further attempts to replicate the interventions in other communities.

The positive nature of the results can be inferred from Table 14.2 in the following manner: Crime reduction actually occurred in six of the eight interventions for which such reduction was a goal or was relevant to the intervention—the interventions reported by Fowler and Mangione, Lavrakas and Kushmak, Lindsay and McGillis, Schneider, Tien and Cahn, and Trojanowicz. Crime reduction occurred at one of the four sites of a seventh intervention (Rosenbaum et al.), but this positive effect was negated by the fact that significant crime increases occurred in two of the other sites. In the eighth case (Pate), no change, in either direction, was found. Although the remaining three interventions (Lavrakas; O'Keefe; Wycoff & Skogan) did not have crime reduction as a goal, the desired outcomes tended to occur in a positive direction, with the possible exception of the Lavrakas study, in which such outcomes occurred only at one of the three sites in the study. Overall, therefore, the interventions did succeed.

Methodologically, the results also stand up to closer scrutiny. First, each study examined at least two different types of outcomes, typically covering both the incidence of crime and the perceptions held by key participants. Where possible, the incidence of crime was measured through victimization surveys and not just crime incidents reported to the police, thereby avoiding one of the major pitfalls in previous assessments of crime prevention. Such a rich focus on outcomes, based on the analysis of available data and the collection of new survey information, was in most cases complemented by thoughtful research designs and rigorous methods, as a reading of the eleven chapters will indicate.

Second, in virtually every case the data were analyzed with statistical techniques. Not shown by the table is the fact that nearly all eleven chapters were based on much more extensive, detailed reports issued previously by the authors (see each chapter for the appropriate references). Thus, any potential shortcomings in the data reported in these eleven chapters are likely to have been addressed in these more detailed reports.

Third, and also not shown in the table, the authors of the eleven studies were genuinely concerned with the problems of developing an appropriate evaluation design. The ultimate approaches reflected truly potent designs, given the state of the art. In some cases, the designs

TABLE 14.2 Outcomes of Eleven Evaluation Studies

Study Author(s)	Types of Outcomes Examined	Nature of Outcomes	Analytic Criteria Used to Test Outcomes
Fowler & Mangione (Chapter 5)	informal social control; burglary and robbery victimization rates; fear of crime	crime reduction when whole intervention in place	statistical significance
Lavrakas (Chapter 13)	awareness of newsletter; perceived crime problem; fear of crime	positive changes at one of three sites	statistical significance
Lavrakas & Kushmuk (Chapter 10)	reported burglaries; fear of crime; quality of life	burglary reduction	statistical significance
Lindsay & McGillis (Chapter 3)	burglary victimization rate	burglary reduction	statistical significance
O'Keefe (Chapter 12)	awareness of announcements; reported learning; reported preventive actions	reported learning and actions increase	data in supplemental report
Pate (Chapter 7)	reported crime victimization rates; perceived crime, safety, and satisfaction with police	no crime reduction changed perceptions	statistical significance
Rosenbaum et al. (Chapter 6)	victimization rates; perceived crime; fear of crime; perceived efficacy; social disorder; physical deterioration	crime reduction at only one of four sites; increases at others	statistical significance
Schneider (Chapter 4)	Reported burglaries; victimization rates	burglary reduction	statistical significance
Tien & Cahn (Chapter 11)	burglary victimization rates; fear of crime	burglary reduction at one of three sites	statistical significance
Trojanowicz (Chapter 8)	reported crime; satisfaction with police	crime reduction increase in satisfaction	descriptive data only
Wycoff & Skogan (Chapter 9)	fear of crime; perceived crime, safety, and satisfaction with police	fear reduction improved perceptions	statistical significance

actually approximated "true experiments," with random assignments made to treatment conditions (for example, Lavrakas). In other cases, compromises had to be made between generally acceptable quasi-experimental designs and the limitations imposed by the real-life constraints of the interventions, but these compromises appeared more than acceptable. For example, Lavrakas and Kushmuk developed a "theory-based evaluation" design for their study, because they had no opportunity to collect either a broad range of pretest data or data from a comparison group. Such a theory-based approach, in fact, follows a recommended "pattern-matching" procedure under such circumstances (Campbell, 1975)—a procedure that has come to be recognized as a variant of the nonequivalent dependent variables design in Cook and Campbell (1979) as applied to single-case studies (Yin, 1984).

In summary, the results from the eleven interventions were favorable and the methodologies used in the evaluation solid. Alone, this facet of the interventions would therefore lead to the encouragement of future attempts to replicate the interventions in other communities.

WERE THE EFFORTS TARGETED TO THOSE IN THE HIGHEST-CRIME AREAS?

The highest rates of community crime in American cities have been concentrated in neighborhoods with the highest proportion of minority and low-income residents. The presumed priority for any further crime prevention efforts would therefore be these kinds of neighborhoods. As a result, a third logical barrier is the extent to which the eleven interventions might not have been "targeted" on the highest-crime neighborhoods in any given city. On this dimension, the eleven evaluations do not provide sufficient information (this information was generally absent from the fuller reports upon which the chapters were based, as well).

Table 14.3 shows the extent to which each intervention focused on a small geographic area. The table indicates that nine of the interventions indeed were small-area interventions, but only two of the evaluations provide a narrative description of the social characteristics of the pertinent area (Fowler & Mangione; Lavrakas & Kushmuk). Moreover, none of the evaluations presents empirical data—covering demography or crime rates—indicating whether the target areas were those with the highest crime rates or with the highest proportion of low-income or minority residents in the target city.

TABLE 14.3   Identity of Small Geographic Areas in
             Eleven Evaluation Studies

Study Author(s)	Description of Geographic Focus
Fowler & Mangione (Chapter 5)	North Asylum Hill area in Hartford, Connecticut
Lavrakas (Chapter 13)	Unspecified neighborhoods or small areas in three cities (Evanston, Illinois; Houston, Texas; and Newark, New Jersey)
Lavrakas & Kushmuk (Chapter 10)	A 3.5-mile long urban arterial commercial strip, located in the northeast section of Portland, Oregon.
Lindsay & McGillis (Chapter 3)	Unspecified sites in Seattle, Washington, deliberately avoiding census tract with highest crime rates.
O'Keefe (Chapter 12)	No geographic parameters relevant
Pate (Chapter 7)	Unspecified small geographical areas in Newark, New Jersey.
Rosenbaum et al. (Chapter 6)	Four unspecified neighborhoods in Chicago, with none predominantly black.
Schneider (Chapter 4)	Citywide program with focused efforts in several high-crime areas in Portland, Oregon.
Tien & Cahn (Chapter 11)	430 commercial establishments located in 10 unspecified commercial areas, throughout three cities (Denver, Colorado; St. Louis, Missouri; and Long Beach, California).
Trojanowicz (Chapter 8)	14 unspecified neighborhoods in Flint, Michigan, comprising 20% of the population of Flint, with definition of neighborhoods expanded during the program.
Wycoff & Skogan (Chapter 9)	Unspecified small area in Houston, Texas

The evaluation studies might have addressed this problem another way, but this second alternative also was not exploited. Because most of the evaluations involved surveys of individuals—either residents or proprietors—the data analysis might have included stratifications by race or by income. Such analysis might then have (a) revealed the incidence of such population groups in the interview sample, and (b) explored the possibility of differential results and effects for different population groups. This type of analysis would have been relevant even for the two interventions with a nationwide or citywide focus (O'Keefe; Schneider), as respondents to a nationwide campaign or participants in a citywide antiburglary program might still include people of different racial and income characteristics. Overall, however, this type of analysis was ignored by all but one of the evaluations. The single evaluation for which it was done, in fact, found that, despite the generally positive outcomes of the intervention, a racial polarization had occurred in terms of complaints of police harassment and excessive use of force, on the part of the black residents (Lavrakas & Kushmuk).

The absence of the needed data, either about the characteristics of the small areas or about the characteristics of the participants and respondents to survey questions, leads one to suspect that the eleven interventions did not, in reality, focus on those neighborhoods with the worst crime problems. (This suspicion was corroborated by an informal polling of the evaluation authors, conducted by the editor of this book.) In other words, although the interventions did deal with crime-ridden neighborhoods and ones with substantial minority populations, the highest-crime neighborhoods were *not* covered, and, in some cases, were deliberately avoided. This observation may be explained in part by knowledge of the priorities of the major federal funding agency at the time—the Law Enforcement Assistance Administration (an agency within the U.S. Department of Justice). By the mid-1970s, numerous federal efforts already had been undertaken in minority and low-income neighborhoods—those having the worst crime rates. Such efforts had typically required too high a commitment of funds, with little corresponding evidence of success. The new efforts, some of which became the subjects of the eleven evaluations, were therefore directed at areas that still had significant levels of crime or proportions of minority residents—but in which more modest interventions might make a difference.

Although such a sense of priorities was justifiable from a resource allocation (and a bureaucratic) perspective, the result is that the lessons from the eleven interventions probably do not address the needs of those neighborhoods with the worst crime problems— predominantly neighborhoods with the highest proportions of minority or low-income residents. Furthermore, the unique history of blacks in American cities, and especially of the relationship between black residents and the criminal justice system, precludes any extrapolation of the results from the eleven interventions to these types of neighborhoods.

ARE THE REPORTS REPRESENTATIVE?

Another dimension of concern is the representativeness of the eleven evaluations. Are they a peculiar group, and might they reflect a bias in the selection of the interventions to be evaluated? In other words, if one were doing a comprehensive review of all crime prevention evaluations, would the same picture emerge?

This issue is difficult to address without doing a comprehensive review of all crime prevention evaluations and taking into consideration the nature of the various evaluations. My experience indicates (see Yin, 1977, 1979) that the eleven evaluations are probably not representative of the results from crime prevention evaluations more broadly. For instance, the results of many other efforts sponsored by the U.S. Department of Justice—such as the Citizen Anti-Crime Program (CAC) and the Comprehensive Community Crime Prevention Program (CCPP)—have been far less positive. In part, this was because the interventions were not designed with as much care or based on adequate theory. The results also may have been discouraging due to sloppy research designs and other methodological flaws. However, a counterpoint is the fact that the eleven evaluations, though not necessarily representative of other evaluations in crime prevention, probably do reflect the much smaller group of studies in which sound interventions and robust evaluation methods were used. To this extent, greater confidence can be placed in their usefulness for guiding future policy actions.

WHAT LESSONS ARE TO BE LEARNED ABOUT CRIME PREVENTION?

Even if the eleven interventions were judged positively by the preceding four questions, a final question has to do with the nature of the lessons about crime prevention. Possibly, such lessons might produce an unpalatable array of recommended steps, either politically or ethically, and no further extension of the results would be considered practical. For example, one way of reducing crime is to bar all windows in a neighborhood. However, this would not be viewed as an acceptable policy, from either an aesthetic or a social point of view.

The lessons were certainly not unpalatable in any sense. For instance, the successful interventions did not rely on extreme methods of target hardening—thereby producing a potentially antisocial effect or a threat to our basic sense of community. Nor was crime prevention attained at the cost of any invasions of privacy or threats to citizens' rights. In fact, many of the interventions were extremely palatable and reflect steps that every ordinary citizen might be encouraged to take, if concerned with preventing crime.

The lessons do, however, present a potentially complex picture that is worth further examination and that gives important clues about what might (or might not) be done about crime prevention in the future. These lessons point to the desirability of joint police-citizen initiatives in successful community crime prevention efforts. The rationale is as follows.

Likely Ineffectiveness of Crime Prevention Steps, Taken Singly. The first finding is that no single crime prevention step—redeploying police alone, publishing a newsletter alone, or doing a security survey alone—may be effective. This can be discerned from a dichotomous pattern of outcomes in Table 14.2 in the following manner: Five evaluations had the most unambiguously positive outcomes in terms of actual crime reduction (Fowler & Mangione; Lavrakas & Kushmuk; Lindsay & McGillis; Schneider; Trojanowicz). All of these evaluations also covered interventions with complex crime prevention measures—for example, in which both community and police changes, often of a varied nature, were installed.

Of the remaining six evaluations, three had positive outcomes but did not involve crime reduction as a goal (Lavrakas; O'Keefe; Wycoff & Skogan), a fourth showed crime reduction but at only one of three test sites (Tien & Cahn), and a fifth showed no positive changes even though crime reduction was a goal (Pate). The sixth and last had positive outcomes at one site, but significantly negative outcomes at two other sites (Rosenbaum et al.). Importantly, all six of these evaluations covered rather singular crime prevention activities—the dissemination of a community newsletter (Lavrakas), a public media campaign (O'Keefe), a storefront office for neighborhood police (Wycoff & Skogan), a security survey (Tien & Cahn), the use of foot patrols (Pate), or block watching and related neighborhood activities but with no concerted police involvement (Rosenbaum et al).

Thus, a general conclusion from this dichotomous arraying of the evaluations is that the interventions that showed the strongest crime reduction outcomes were those that involved a more complex array of activities.

Possible Importance of Improving Resident-Police Relationships. A further finding has to do with the possible nature of these more complex interventions. Did they have a general pattern, or was any collection of crime prevention activities sufficient? On this point, a general observation is that the desirable activities appeared to involve actions by both residents and the local police. This pattern could be found in all five of the interventions in which the crime reduction outcomes were the most positive.

The first intervention, the Hartford Project (Fowler & Mangione), involved three types of activities:

(1)   extensive physical redesign to change vehicular traffic patterns and to improve the visual boundaries of the neighborhood
(2)   a decentralized police team assigned permanently to the area
(3)   the formation of a community organization—the Police Advisory Committee—that represented the major community groups and conducted many different crime prevention activites.

The implementation of these activities, as one might suspect, was uneven, as different agencies and resources were involved. In particular, during the latter stages of the intervention (1977-1979), there was "a significant erosion of the police team component of the program [due to cutbacks to the police budget]." At the same time, the outcomes also varied, with the burglary victimization rates decreasing between 1973 and 1977 and then actually increasing between 1977 and 1979. As a result, the authors suggest that both the residential and police efforts might have been important to the positive outcomes, summarized as follows: "One could surmise that what the residents were doing was helpful to fear levels, but that the police component was essential to affecting crime rates."

This combination also was important in the Portland Project (Lavrakas & Kushmuk), the second intervention that had strongly positive crime reduction outcomes. The evaluators attributed much of the positive outcomes to the fact that there was both increased help and attention by the police and the formation of an active business group. Similarly, citizen leaders and the police worked together in a number of ways—including the selection of sites—in the third intervention, the Seattle Community Crime Prevention Program (Lindsay & McGillis). For this program, the evaluators noted the importance of police-citizen collaboration in the following way: "The police and CCPP staff were fully aware that it was not an exercise in courtesy and public relations, but rather an expert consultation."

The evaluators of the fourth intervention, the Portland Anti-Burglary Program (Schneider), called attention to the degree to which the police and residents implemented the program on a neighborhood rather than a simple household basis: "The Crime Prevention Bureau specifically sought to increase not only the protection of individual households, but the protection of the entire neighborhood." One upshot was that emphasis was placed not just on protecting individual properties (for example, through increased use of alarms and locks, as well as through a property-engraving procedure), but also on door-to-door canvassing, the sponsorship of neighborhood meetings, and communication about crime prevention procedures. In all of these activities, residents had to develop a positive relationship with the police.

Finally, the fifth intervention also had the same attribute, even though the intervention was primarily carried out by the police department (the installation of foot patrols in Flint, Michigan). Trojanowicz's evaluation called attention to the fact that this intervention was in the planning stage for a year, with the goal being to draw citizen attention and cooperation to the project. As the author notes: "When, therefore, the program actually began, it had wide support among the citizens, who felt that it was, in a real sense, 'their program.'" A possibly important contrast may be made between this situation and the foot patrols in Newark, New Jersey, as reported by Pate (and one of the six interventions for which crime reduction either did not occur or occurred more ambiguously): The Newark effort appears not to have involved resident groups in any formal or informal way.

Even one of the other interventions, the crime newsletters, suggests the same pattern. Lavrakas's evaluation did not deal with crime reduction as an outcome, but had positive changes (in perceptions about the crime problem and in fear of crime) at one of three sites. The distinctive attribute of the intervention at this site (Evanston, Illinois) was that the newsletter was (a) initiated by the police in collaboration with a consortium of local community organizations, (b) hand delivered by local community groups, and (c) coauthored by the police and community group representatives, which also may have helped to signal residents that this was 'their' newsletter." At the two other sites (Houston, Texas, and Newark, New Jersey)—in which no positive outcomes were found—the newsletters followed the design of the Evanston newsletter, but were published by the police departments with no participation by the residents.

In summary, the results do yield a general pattern, and the major lesson about crime prevention may be the following: *Successful crime prevention efforts require joint activities by the residents and police, and the presumed improvement of relationships between these groups.* Although the specific activities may vary from the redeployment of police to the target hardening of individual properties, the collaborative ventures are what seem to be critical.

WHERE DO WE GO FROM HERE?

This analysis of the eleven interventions may be summarized in the following manner.

(1) We Know More About How to Prevent Community Crime. The evaluations and their largely positive outcomes do point to the fact that crime can be prevented, under a variety of circumstances. Changes in physical design, in the deployment of police officers, and in the activities of neighborhood groups all are possible interventions that communities can undertake in the future. The variety of specific activities can emulate those taken in the cities covered by the eleven interventions, and citizens can feel confident that positive outcomes will ensue.

(2) The Successful Efforts Are Likely to Involve Citizen and Police Relationships. Independent of the variety of activities, the most successful efforts among the eleven interventions contained a similar pattern: Citizens and police either collaborated directly or were both involved in the intervention. Where the intervention was a simple activity, conducted by one party but not the other, crime reduction was not likely to occur.

(3) The Evaluations Were Not Targeted to the Highest-Crime Neighborhoods. Although no direct evidence was provided, the eleven interventions appeared not to have concentrated on those minority-dominated, low-income neighborhoods where community crime is the most prevalent. To this extent the interventions do not provide direct lessons regarding what might be done in the future, in these kinds of neighborhoods, to prevent crime.

(4) Those Communities with the Highest Levels of Crime Also May Be Those in Which Resident-Police Relations Are Difficult to Improve. Although the interventions did not directly focus on the highest-crime neighborhoods, one might be tempted to extrapolate the major lessons about crime prevention from the eleven interventions, and suggest that joint resident-police efforts also be tried in such neighborhoods.

Such an attempt would be suspect for the following reason: Given the peculiar history of racial and ethnic relationships in American cities (for example, see Yin, 1973), and especially the social and cultural distance between black residents and city police, such joint efforts might be particularly difficult to mount. To reduce or eliminate such social distance, much might be required in terms of *time* (possibly decades), *money* (possibly tens of millions of dollars), *patience* (possibly over several political administrations, at national and local levels), and *fortune* (the facilitative effect of largely uncontrollable, external events)—which may be, retrospectively, why federal criminal justice agencies have been less willing to attempt to initiate action in these neighborhoods.

(5) Though We Know More About Preventing Crime, We May Not Be Able to Do Much About It. To the extent that the neighborhoods in greatest need cannot be served in the immediate future, the incidence of crime is not likely to be reduced significantly as a result of community crime prevention efforts. In effect, the elimination of the social distance between urban police and minority residents in these high-crime neighborhoods calls for a cultural and social change, and is not likely to be induced simply by the design and implementation of any single public program. Thus, the ultimate prevention of crime in urban communities may be beyond the means of what can be "done" within the current reality of public policy.

REFERENCES

Campbell, D. T. (1975). "Degrees of freedom" and the case study. *Comparative Political Studies, 8,* 178-193.

Cook, T. D., & Campbell, D. T. (1979). *Quasi-experimentation: Design and analysis issues for field settings.* Chicago: Rand McNally.

Yin, R. K. (Ed.). (1973). *Race, creed, color, or national origin: A reader on racial and ethnic identities in American society.* Itasca, IL: Peacock.

Yin, R. K. (1977). *Evaluating citizen crime prevention programs.* Santa Monica, CA: Rand Corporation.

Yin, R. K. (1979). What is citizen crime prevention? In *How well does it work? Review of criminal justice evaluation.* Washington, DC: National Institute of Law Enforcement and Criminal Justice.

Yin, R. K. (1984). *Case study research: Design and methods.* Beverly Hills, CA: Sage.

INDEX

ABOUT THE CONTRIBUTORS

Michael F. Cahn is Vice President for Operations of Public Systems Evaluation, Inc., Cambridge, Massachusetts, and has a master's degree in electrical engineering from the Massachusetts Institute of Technology. His criminal justice-related research interests include police field operations; urban emergency service (police, fire, and ambulance) command, control, and communications systems; and commercial and residential premise security. He has directed numerous federally funded research projects and has been a consultant to many public and private organizations, including the American Bar Association and IBM.

Floyd J. Fowler, Jr., is a Senior Research Fellow at the Center for Survey Research at the University of Massachusetts—Boston. He was Director of the Center from 1971 to 1982. He received his Ph.D. in social psychology from the University of Michigan in 1966. His research activities and interests have been focused largely on methodology and applications of survey research to public policy. He has taught survey research methods at the Harvard School of Public Health and elsewhere. His publications include a recent textbook on survey research methods.

Jane A. Grant is an Assistant Professor of Public and Environmental Affairs at Indiana University-Purdue University at Fort Wayne. She received her Ph.D. in sociology in 1981 from the University of California, Berkeley, and served as the Director of Field Research for the Ford Foundation-funded evaluation of community crime prevention in Chicago during 1982-1984. Her research has focused on the role of citizen participation in policy, in areas such as health planning, the environment, and community crime prevention.

James W. Kushmuk received his B.S. in psychology from the University of Illinois in 1973 and his M.S. in psychology from Portland State University in 1975, and is currently a doctoral student in psychology at the Claremont Graduate School in Claremont, California. While conducting the Portland CPTED reevaluation in 1980, he worked as a program coordinator and staff assistant to the City of Portland's Public Safety Commissioner. He has also worked as a Research Associate for Portland State University, as an Evaluation Specialist for the Portland Public Schools, and as a private consultant.

Paul J. Lavrakas is Associate Professor of Journalism and Urban Affairs at Northwestern University, Evanston, Illinois, and Director of the Northwestern Survey

Laboratory. During the past eleven years, he has been involved in most major research and evaluation projects funded by the federal government on community crime prevention. He is currently the principal investigator on the national evaluation of the Eisenhower Foundation Neighborhood Program. He has a Ph.D. in applied social psychology from Loyola University of Chicago, and has published widely on citizen crime prevention and fear of crime.

Dan A. Lewis is an Assistant Professor of Education and Urban Affairs at Northwestern University. He has spent the last 10 years studying the issues of crime prevention and fear of crime. He has written extensively on these topics in academic journals and is also the editor of *Reactions to Crime* (Sage Publications, 1981). His new book, *Fear of Crime: Incivility and the Production of a Social Problem,* was published in November 1985 by Transaction Books.

Betsy Lindsay's career in crime prevention started in 1973 with the Seattle Community Crime Prevention Program, where she held several positions including Program Director. In 1980, she moved to Washington, D.C., and worked on a technical assistance contract for LEAA and ACTION's Urban Crime Prevention Program. Since 1982, she has been the director of the national Neighborhood Anti-Crime Self-Help Program administered by the Eisenhower Foundation. This program focuses on planning, implementing, evaluating, and sustaining innovative community-based crime prevention programs in 10 high-crime, low-income, minority communities. In 1973 she received a B.A. in sociology from the University of Washington; she received a master's degree in planning and administration in 1978.

Arthur J. Lurigio is a social psychologist and Research Associate at Northwestern University's Center for Urban Affairs and Policy Research, and is the Director of Research and Evaluation at the Cook County Adult Probation Department (Chicago). He received his Ph.D. from Loyola University in 1984. His current research interests are in the areas of social cognition, the psychology of criminal victimization, and the identification and treatment of dangerous and mentally disordered offenders.

Thomas W. Mangione is the Director and Senior Research Fellow at the Center for Survey Research at the University of Massachusetts—Boston. He received his Ph.D. in psychology from the University of Michigan in 1973. His research activities have focused on evaluations of drunk driving law changes, gambling enforcement, and neighborhood crime prevention programs. He has taught survey research methods at the Boston University School of Public Health and the Harvard School of Public Health.

Daniel McGillis is the Deputy Director of Harvard Law School's Center for Criminal Justice. He has conducted research on a number of criminal justice topics, including alternative dispute resolution, victim compensation, and violent crime. He recently coauthored a book entitled *Dangerous Offenders* (Harvard University Press, 1985). He has testified before House and Senate Committees on criminal justice policy and has conducted comparative criminal justice research in a number of countries, including the People's Republic of China. He is currently working on a project with the U.S. Secret Service dealing with strategies for assessing threats to the president.

Garrett J. O'Keefe is Professor of Technical Journalism at Colorado State University. His research interests include social and political uses and effects of mass media and, in particular, the impact of informational and persuasive campaigns. In addition, he has written on the effects of media on political behavior and public opinion regarding crime and the role of communication in socialization processes.

Antony M. Pate has been a member of the evaluation staff of the Police Foundation since 1972. He has been involved in the Foundation's research on preventive patrol, response time, apprehension techniques, peer review panels, police stress, foot patrol, community crime prevention, and, most recently, fear reduction. He received a bachelor's degree in political science from the University of Texas at Austin and is a doctoral candidate at the University of Wisconsin—Madison.

Dennis P. Rosenbaum is jointly appointed in the Departments of Psychology and Urban Affairs at Northwestern University. He received his Ph.D. in social psychology from Loyola University of Chicago in 1980. He has served as principal investigator on large-scale evaluations of crime control programs for the National Institute of Justice and the Ford Foundation. His research interests and publications have focused on citizen and police reactions to crime, fear of crime, the prevention of employee theft and shoplifting, and the causes of juvenile delinquency. He is also interested in knowledge utilization in the public policy arena and methodological advances in evaluation research.

Anne L. Schneider is Associate Professor of Political Science at Oklahoma State University and the Director of Research for the College of Arts and Sciences. Her research in criminal justice has included victimization surveys and the effectiveness of community crime prevention programs, as well as evaluations of victim-witness programs. In juvenile justice, she has undertaken research on the effectiveness of restitution programs, the use of sentencing guidelines, and the impact of the federal deinstitutionalization movement.

Wesley G. Skogan is Professor of Political Science and Research Faculty for the Center for Urban Affairs and Policy Research at Northwestern University. His research focuses on victimization and fear of crime. He is the author of *Coping with Crime, Issues in the Measurement of Victimization,* and other books and monographs in the field.

James M. Tien is currently Associate Professor of Computer and Systems Engineering at Rensselaer Polytechnic Institute, Troy, New York, and the Executive Vice President of Public Systems Evaluation, Inc., Cambridge, Massachusetts. He holds a doctorate degree in systems engineering and operations research from the Massachusetts Institute of Technology. His areas of research interest include the development of computer and systems engineering techniques and the application of these techniques to public sector problems. He has also been an employee of the Bell Telephone Laboratories and the Rand Corporation, and has authored numerous reports and papers.

Robert C. Trojanowicz is Professor and Director of the School of Criminal Justice at Michigan State University, East Lansing. He holds a B.S. in police administration, an M.S.W. in social work, and a Ph.D. in social science, all from Michigan State University. He has had experience in various police and social agencies. He is the author of several textbooks and has contributed numerous articles to management and criminal justice journals.

Mary Ann Wycoff joined the Police Foundation in 1972 and since then has directed research on organizational change, the crime-effectiveness of police, the police role, and police supervision. She is completing her Ph.D. dissertation in sociology at the University of Wisconsin—Madison. Her areas of interest include socialization, supervision, organizational change, service delivery, and the measurement of attitudes and performance.

Robert K. Yin is Chairman of the Board of COSMOS Corporation, having served as its first President from 1980 to 1985. He conducts research on a variety of topics at COSMOS, including the evaluation of neighborhood programs initiated by the Ford Foundation and the MacArthur Foundation; economic development and high-technology firms; and the use of office automation and other advanced technologies (for example, robotics and artificial intelligence) by organizations. He has degrees from Harvard College (B.A.) and the Massachusetts Institute of Technology (Ph.D.), worked for eight years at the Rand Corpooration, and has published numerous books and articles, including *Case Study Research: Design and Methods* (Sage Publications, 1984). COSMOS Corporation is a social science research and consulting firm located in Washington, D.C.